ICI
The Company that
Changed our Lives

ICI

The Company that Changed our Lives

SECOND EDITION

Carol Kennedy

P·C·P

Paul Chapman
Publishing Ltd

Paul Chapman Publishing Ltd
144 Liverpool Road
London
N1 1LA

British Library Cataloguing in Publication Data

Kennedy, Carol
  ICI: Company That Changed Our Lives. –
  2 Rev. ed
  I. Title
  338.766

  ISBN 1-85396-160-4 (paperback)
  ISBN 1-85396-161-2 (hardback)

Typeset by Inforum, Rowlands Castle, Hants
Printed and bound by Cromwell Press Ltd, Broughton Gifford, Wiltshire

A B C D E F G H   9 8 7 6 5 4 3

CONTENTS

To all the scientists, past and present, whose achievements are celebrated in these pages as milestones in a great industrial odyssey.

PREFACE TO THE SECOND EDITION

When I began work on revising and updating this book, which was first published to mark the diamond jubilee of ICI in 1986, the company was in the process of radically restructuring itself to meet changing global conditions in the chemical industry – changes that had intensified since 1990 under the shadow of international recession. As I talked to ICI's top management about this process of evolution and redirection, I had no idea – and I doubt if any of them did – that we would soon be at an historic point of departure for Britain's biggest manufacturing company.

As this new edition is published, we cannot know how successful the bold decision will be to contemplate splitting ICI, itself the product of a great merger in 1926, into two separately quoted companies, to be known as ICI and Zeneca. But the connecting thread of the book remains as strong as in 1986: the skein of innovation which has come out of this great corporation over the decades, and which will henceforth come out of two companies instead of one.

As I wrote in the original Acknowledgments, I did not set out to write another history of ICI: that, at any rate up to 1952, had been definitively accomplished by the company's official historian, the late Dr W. J. Reader. His two monumentally authoritative volumes, gleaming here and there with half-buried nuggets of scientific brilliance, inspired me to explore the stories behind a dozen or so of the great inventions and discoveries that had come out of ICI's laboratories since the 1930s – discoveries that, in a very real sense, have changed the way we live and work.

I wanted to talk, wherever possible, to the men who made these breakthroughs, and to convey to a wider public something of what it felt like to be in at the birth of experiments that shaped the future; to understand, also, something of the mysterious nature of invention itself and how its processes are developed into marketable assets. Japan's MITI organization has surveyed all the world's significant inventions since the Second World War and identified over half of them as originating in the United Kingdom; yet it is a truism that Britain, time and

ix

again, lets the fruits of inventiveness slip away through lack of shrewd development and marketing.

My original acknowledgments of gratitude stand, notably to Sir John Harvey-Jones, chairman of ICI from 1982 to 1987, and all those in the Public Affairs Department and the divisions who gave willing help in tracking down the stories and the scientists behind the company's great innovations. Not least, I owe a great debt to the inventors and discoverers themselves, who gave unstintingly of time and often of hospitality, as well as the loan of books and scientific papers. Two, alas, have died since 1986 – Sir Michael Perrin, CBE, and Dr Frank Rose, CBE, FRS – but to them and all the following I remain deeply grateful: the late Sir Peter Allen; Dr William Boon, FRS; Dr Charles Suckling, FRS; Professor Sir James Black, FRCP, FRS; Professor Derek Birchall, FRS; Dr D Garnet Davey, OBE; Dr Ron Coffee; Dr Peter King; Jeff Thorp; Ron Feasey; John Rigg; Reg Hurd; R. R. Melhuish; and Dr Brian Newbould.

In preparing this new edition my thanks also go to the ICI chairman, Sir Denys Henderson, and senior members of his board including Ronnie Hampel, Chris Hampson, Dr Peter Doyle, and Dr David Barnes. At Runcorn, John Beckitt made time in an incredibly packed schedule to expound one of the first breakthrough products of the environmental age, the HFA substitute for ozone-destroying CFCs. The press office of ICI under Martin Adeney has been ever helpful and moved at speed to help meet deadlines which, as the company wrestled with its future shape, at times seemed to be in constant flux.

As I noted in the original Acknowledgments, scientific achievement is usually a matter of teamwork, and if I have failed to give credit to any unsung members of those teams, I have to plead again the pressure of deadlines in order, this time, to bring the book out for the genesis of the new companies.

This is very much an individual lay person's view of ICI's scientific achievements and is in no way an official company publication. It is also primarily concerned with discoveries rather than the ways in which they are developed and brought to the marketplace, which would have furnished material for a whole new book.

Scientists might have preferred a more learned treatment, but as a non-scientist, yet someone fascinated by the nature of invention and discovery, my aim was to interest other non-scientists in what I felt to be one of the great industrial and scientific sagas of the century. As the saga embarks on its historic new chapter, I hope also that it may inspire the feeling that industry – certainly when it produces life-changing achievements like these – is a worthwhile and exciting way to spend a working life.

Carol Kennedy
February 1993

INTRODUCTION

'How can the world be changed? It's changed in the laboratory, not in the marketplace.' Professor Derek Birchall, FRS, senior research associate at Imperial Chemical Industries and one of Britain's leading industrial scientists, is off riding a favourite hobbyhorse, arguing that the great leaps in discovery have come from being 'science-driven, curiosity-driven' rather than being targeted on some product the world is deemed to want. He is fond of quoting a story about Michael Faraday, the father of electrical engineering. 'When Faraday built a dynamo, someone said to him, "What's the use of electricity?" And his answer was, "What's the use of a new-born child?"' If you ask the market what it wants and then invent it, he maintains, what you get is merely 'a little bit of change', an improvement to something that already exists – because people can't want something that they don't know about. 'Alexander Graham Bell didn't do a market survey and ask, do you want a telephone? People would have said, what's a telephone? Bell just went ahead and did it. Nobody said we must have polythene . . . the big discoveries you can't predict.'

In the ICI of today, which consciously pursues a policy of being business-driven and 'inventing into the marketplace', in the phrase of its high-profile, former chairman, Sir John Harvey-Jones, this strikes a distinctly iconoclastic note. But throughout its sixty-seven years of corporate life, ICI has been a company of individualists. It is hard to find anything resembling 'corporate man' in Britain's biggest industrial corporation, though it retains a powerful sense of corporate ethos; towns have been built around its activities and, like any large organization, it has its hierarchies and twinges of institutional arthritis.

No one better embodies this individuality than Derek Birchall, an impishly humorous man in his early sixties with a shock of wayward white hair, who plainly enjoys playing up to the image of the absent-minded professor, the oddball inventor. The second time we met, over lunch at ICI's Mond Division in Runcorn, he looked down at his feet with some surprise: he was wearing odd shoes, one with a toecap and one without.

1

Birchall is an original, a Fellow of the Royal Society who left school at fourteen and educated himself by evening courses at Wigan and Manchester Polytechnics while working in a laboratory washing test-tubes by day. He registered his first patent at the age of nineteen – a sealing mechanism for oil tanks – and has lost count of the number since. He has been responsible for several major ICI inventions of recent years, notably Saffil, an inorganic fibre that can do many of the things asbestos does without its toxicity; Monnex, a revolutionary powdered alkaline compound for extinguishing fires; and macro-defect-free cement, whose absence of air holes gives it such tensile strength that it can even be bent into a spring.

In his cluttered office at Mond, its steel filing cabinets stuffed to bursting with papers ('I'm a Victorian, I use a pen, not a word processor'), Birchall enjoys a unique position in ICI as a kind of licensed intellectual gadfly, along with running his research team and travelling extensively to lecture abroad. 'One of my jobs', he explained, 'is to look at a vision of what the world will be and get ICI interested. The world is not going to be the same, and it won't be driven by the market – there's nobody out there to ask.'

One of the key characteristics of ICI, as I discovered when I came to study its workings for a magazine profile in 1984, is that it *is* interested in how the world will be. Its individualism and quiet fostering of scientific brilliance, inherited from its remarkable corporate ancestry, have combined to make this a strong thread running through its sixty-seven-year history, though the thread, inevitably, has sometimes become knotted or tangled by a wrong management decision here, a failure of vision there. Opportunities to innovate have occasionally, as in any 'institutional' group of people working together, been missed or delayed. But the interest in tomorrow, whether guided by market considerations or 'curiosity-driven' at the laboratory bench, has over those sixty-seven years produced a notable crop of inventions and discoveries that have effectively changed the way we live and work.

Innovation is, one might suppose, the life-blood of a science-based company like ICI. But it is not a term that is easy to define. People understand it in different ways. It is more than invention or discovery; more than the development of an invention or discovery, yet combining elements of all three. Charles Suckling, the discoverer of a world-beating anaesthetic for ICI, wrote a paper on the subject with two colleagues in which they identified the innovative process as 'the time when the perceived qualities of a new material and the perception of a need are brought together'. Innovation, they suggested, was larger than discovery ('the finding or uncovering of new knowledge') or invention ('the discovery which is perceived to possess utility'). To them the central question to be answered was: 'Why do some firms or individuals see opportunities or threats which do not impinge on the consciousness of others?'

There are some who see the mysterious process of invention itself as the model of innovation. An influential book published in 1958 by John Jewkes, David Sawers and Richard Stillerman and called *The Sources of Invention* took this approach, seeing it as a linear progression from original idea through to commercial development, at the mercy of chance, timing and the state of existing technology. 'Invention is the stage at which the scent is first picked up, development the stage at which the hunt is in full cry. All the money in the world could not have produced nylon or the jet engine or crease-resisting fabrics or the cyclotron in 1900 . . .' Those first steps on the path, Jewkes and his co-authors argued, could be taken as easily by small firms as by large ones – indeed, owed everything to determined individuals with original minds, and could be easily curbed or snuffed out by the bureaucratic procedures of large corporations.

Suckling and his fellow scientists, M. C. McCarthy of ICI and F. R. Bradbury, a professor of industrial science, rejected this model in favour of one which emphasizes the 'screening' of new knowledge with a view to its practical application, and in which the large corporation has a far more positive role to play. In this view, innovation is 'a process in which a new technique, product or manufacturing process, may be translated from an idea to a complete achievement'. Research targets may change, they point out: among ICI's great chemical innovations, the bipyridyl herbicide known today as paraquat was at first dismissed because the research team was looking for a selective weedkiller. It was only the perception and dogged persistence of one man, rightly now recognized as the architect of its discovery, who looked at its properties through the other end of the telescope, as it were, and saw that it would revolutionize man's historic ideas of ploughing. Other companies have experienced similar changes of target through a lucky accident, like Bayer of Germany, one of whose chemists was experimenting in the 1920s with a dyestuff for furs when he noticed that a streptococcyl infection among the rats being patch-tested with the dye was clearing up. Thus was born the first sulphonamide drug.

In ICI's first great invention, the chance creation of a new polymer called polyethylene in a laboratory accident (theoretically still regarded as impossible today in the circumstances in which it happened), the research target did not so much change as remain undiscovered itself for a long time. Five years elapsed between Fawcett and Gibson discovering their strange waxy compound in a 'science-driven' experiment in 1933 to see what happened to certain gases reacting under high pressure, and an expert on electrical cables suggesting that it might make a substitute for gutta-percha as an insulating material. Another decade or so passed, by which time polythene insulation had given Britain a decisive wartime advantage in radar, before the German Karl Ziegler took polythene to a stage where it found its true world-changing role as a material for moulding into cheap, cheerful and convenient household wares.

In this book, I have highlighted a dozen or so inventions and discoveries, from plastics like polythene and Perspex to pharmaceutical breakthroughs like the anti-malarial Paludrine, and the beta-blocker heart drugs, all of which seem to me to have changed the world we live in from that of sixty or seventy years ago. Some were the kind of quantum leap, like polyethylene, which Professor Birchall says you can't predict or target through market research. Some were goal-driven by the exigencies of war, like Paludrine, or were the result of targeted research like Fluothane, which took anaesthetics out of the age of chloroform and ether and is now used in hospital operations worldwide.

Still others, like paraquat and the beta-blockers, were the result of an obsessive drive by one man with the ability to make an imaginative leap beyond the perceptions of others working along similar lines. Another, Terylene, the first polyester, was invented by two men in a small printing company in a Manchester back street, succeeding against the odds where the massed scientific resources of du Pont and I G Farben had failed: the company lacked the means to develop it and it was fostered by ICI to its true, gigantic potential. Electrodyn, the brainchild of a lone inventor working in a neglected field, was also brought to ICI's doors in search of development funds: it took the research manager at Jealott's Hill, where the company's plant protection research is done, just two minutes to realize that here was an invention of truly revolutionary scope.

Several, like polythene and its various offspring, Terylene, fast-colour dyes, polyurethane foam and solid emulsion paints, contributed greatly to the profound social revolution wrought in Western industrialized countries by plastic housewares, self-service shopping (impossible without plastic film to keep food fresh on the supermarket shelf), low-priced fridges and freezers small enough to fit into modern flats, and the whole burgeoning do-it-yourself culture of the last forty years. One, sadly, missed its moment in history; the single-cell protein designed to fill a 'protein gap' in the world that never materialized. But even here, the technology involved may yet change our lives in one way or another.

All have fascinated me by the ways they emerged from or were developed by individuals within one mammoth industrial corporation. Other companies, of course, have had their world-shaking inventions, notably du Pont with nylon, in which the company talent-hunted a brilliant young Harvard chemist, Wallace Carothers, to find a new business product. But as Imperial Chemical Industries ('imperial in aspect and imperial in name', its first chairman grandly told the Board of Trade in 1926) reached its diamond jubilee at the end of 1986, it seemed a fitting moment to examine the roots of some of the household-name products it has cultivated within its eventful history; to meet, where possible, the men who helped to change the world at the laboratory bench, and to understand from them a little of what invention and discovery feel like at the moment of conception.

They were all very different, the distinguished scientists and chemists to whom I talked in the mid-1980s. The trail ran from Derbyshire to Devon; from the Hampstead terrace home, chiming with clocks, of Sir Michael Perrin, the last surviving patentee of polythene and a man with a key role in Britain's wartime atomic work, to the cramped and cluttered office in ICI's Pharmaceuticals Division in Cheshire where Dr Frank Rose, CBE, FRS, the discoverer of Paludrine, still worked on research projects. (Perrin and Rose both died in 1988.) Rose could recall the beginnings of ICI's drugs business in 1936, in heavily polluted Blackley, near Manchester, where 'you couldn't open a window for the smuts'.

But they all shared one striking characteristic – a vitality, enthusiasm and delight in communication which I have found typical of scientists who have achieved great things. They also, perhaps, shared something else: the prepared mind that sees what others miss. Dr William Boon, FRS, the scientist who enabled the discovery of paraquat to be made, and Dr Garnet Davey, who nursed James Black's discovery of the beta-blocker, Inderal, say discoveries are often the result of 'the right mind, the alert mind, being in the right place at the right time'. Davey adds: 'I once read a definition of luck as taking your opportunities, and only pretty good people take their opportunities.' Boon reflects: 'It's astonishing how many major inventions are traceable to one, perhaps two, people seeing the significance of an unusual and unexpected result'. He cites the example of Fawcett and Gibson, the polythene pioneers, trying to react benzaldehyde with ethylene. 'They got something that looked like paraffin wax, instead of a nice pure crystalline product. I believe that 999 chemists out of a thousand would have made a rude remark and thrown it in the bin. Then you have Leo Baekeland, who made an industry out of Bakelite – again something most chemists at that time (1906) would have thrown away.'

This, maintains Boon, is 'the true nature of invention . . . identifying the potential and the commercial possibilities from an unexpected result'. Jewkes in *The Sources of Invention* would agree: 'Chance and accident seem often to have played an important part in discovery, but so, too, has brilliant and disciplined thinking and a persistence amounting almost to obsession.'

The brilliant and disciplined thinkers who have contributed these recognized landmarks among ICI's 33,000 patented inventions over the last sixty-seven years are all, without exception, modest and unassuming men. Sir James Black disclaims with some impatience the suggestion that he is due any special regard because Inderal has saved hundreds of thousands of lives and enabled even more hundreds of thousands of people to lead normal lives: the fact that so many suffer from heart ailments or hypertension, he feels, should not make people believe there is something special about his scientific achievements. The science would have been just as good if it had treated some rarely encountered disease and been far less commercially successful as a result.

None are rich men, though if ICI had operated a royalty system like some foreign companies, several would now be multi-millionaires. The question of a royalty arrangement was once put to a referendum in ICI and the vote was against it: the general feeling in the company now is that it would be an unfair principle because so many people can be involved in a ground-breaking discovery, not least those who, like a research director, can kill or nurture an idea, and those in the long chain of development and marketing who finally bring the product to the customer.

In the endlessly fascinating story of human innovation, indeed, it is often the developer of an idea rather than its progenitor who reaps the fame and fortune: we talk today of the Diesel engine, not the Ackroyd-Stuart, although it was the Bletchley iron-founder Herbert Ackroyd-Stuart who first designed an ignition-less engine in 1890 to run on heavy fuel, and for lack of capital left it to Rudolf Diesel to take the final steps in development seven years later.

None of the inventors in this book is a household name; neither are any of the developers – where they are even known. In a company you dedicate your scientific talents to the corporate good; but many fascinating stories lie behind the familiar ICI logo, soon to be two, not least the story of the company itself, formed sixty-seven years ago out of four British businesses, engaged in alkali manufacture, explosives and dyestuffs, against the backdrop of a fierce international race for command of the world's chemical markets.

It is with these companies that the story begins. Two of them in particular, founded by men who combined in extraordinary measure scientific genius, business acumen and a northern European, nonconformist regard for the rights of the individuals who worked for them, left their stamp on ICI from its beginnings in the nationalistic business world of nearly seventy years ago.

1

THE RACE FOR
CHEMICAL SUPREMACY

New York in September 1926 was a place full of promise, where anything seemed possible. Despite the collapse of the land speculation boom in Florida, where hurricanes devastated miles of property in mid-September, Wall Street quickly steadied. By the new year an unprecedented bull market would be roaring ahead. The speakeasies were full and the Broadway theatres were preparing for the new season's openings, among them George and Ira Gershwin's *Oh, Kay!* with England's Gertrude Lawrence in the lead.

Elsewhere on the entertainment scene, new inventions were in the air. That summer, Warner Brothers had introduced their talking-picture process, the Vitaphone, at the Warner Theatre in New York. The feature film, *Don Juan*, starring John Barrymore, was in fact a silent to which a synchronized musical accompaniment by the New York Philharmonic had been added. The opening on 6 August was a portentous affair: Will H. Hays, President of the Motion Picture Producers and Distributors of America, made an introductory speech from the screen; opera singers contributed a live performance backed by the Metropolitan Opera Chorus, and violin recitals were given by Mischa Elman and Ephrem Zimbalist. The film industry was not fully convinced of the technological revolution, however, until a year later when Warners unleashed *The Jazz Singer* in October 1927, with Broadway's biggest star, Al Jolson, ad-libbing the screen's first spoken words.

Something else was happening in New York in late September 1926. In hotel rooms, in panelled officers and over restaurant tables, urgent talks were taking place between the leaders of the chemical industries of Great Britain, Germany and the United States. They were engaged in a game of moves and counter-moves which would ultimately determine the control of vast and lucrative markets around the world. The four principal players, three of whom disembarked from transatlantic liners in the last week of the month, were Sir Alfred Mond of Brunner, Mond, Britain's leading alkali manufacturer; Orlando F. Weber of Allied Chemical and Dye Corporation, America's top-ranking chemical group alongside du Pont; Sir Harry McGowan of Nobel Industries

Ltd, the powerful British arm of the international explosives business founded by Alfred Nobel, the inventor of dynamite; and Carl Bosch, head of IG Farbenindustrie, the formidable combine which in barely a year since its formation was threatening to give Germany supremacy in the world's chemical markets.

'The IG', as it was known in the industry, was itself the culmination of a long process of centralization in Germany's chemical businesses, a process which had been watched with mounting apprehension by the other leading manufacturing countries. It had begun in 1904 with mergers among the German dyestuffs companies, already world leaders in their field, and progressed to the formation in 1916, in the middle of the Great War, of a 'little IG' – IG Teerfarbenfabriken – which brought in the heavy chemical manufacturers. When in 1925 the German explosives companies joined in to form IG Farben, the threat of a virtual German monopoly made it imperative for the British and the Americans to take action, either by seeking an alliance with the IG or by forming defensive pacts against it. In New York that autumn, no one engaged in the talks was certain who would end up with whom.

Before the First World War

The war had accelerated chemical technology in all three countries, but in none was it so powerfully organized and harnessed to research as in Germany, whose science-based system of education gave the industry a well-established tradition of innovation. Carl Bosch of BASF (Badische Anilin-und Soda-Fabrik), a leading member company of the IG along with Hoechst, Bayer and Agfa, was no mean inventor himself. His discovery in 1908, with Professor Fritz Haber of Karlsruhe, of synthesizing ammonia by 'fixing' the nitrogen in the atmosphere was ranked as one of the greatest steps forward in the history of heavy chemicals (so called because of the bulk tonnages in which they are sold, unlike 'fine' chemicals such as dyes and pharmaceuticals). The Haber-Bosch process went into production in 1913 and so vital was synthetic ammonia to the manufacture of military explosives that a British government report after the war described it as 'the key to Germany's war production of explosives'. Without it, some believe, Germany might have had to capitulate in 1916.

In dyestuffs, an area in which Germany had led the world in 1914, producing 88 per cent of all synthetic dyes on the market, the country had not only by 1926 recovered its prewar markets (with surprisingly little loss of goodwill) but had also leaped ahead in connected fields like pharmaceuticals and photographic supplies. Before the war, German dyestuffs chemists were already exploring other allied technologies – in plastics, varnishes, cellulose fibres, insecticides, pigments, perfumes and phenolformaldehyde resins similar to the formula which the Belgian-

American Leo Baekeland had discovered in 1907 and patented as 'Bakelite'. Bayer had produced a synthetic rubber as early as 1912. The Germans were also far advanced in work on the technological grail which every industrialized country sought in the 1920s, before the discovery of the vast Middle East oil reserves – the process of extracting oil from coal by hydrogenation. Altogether, the world of 1926 was a far more competitive and aggressive one for the chemical industry than the cosy pre-1914 cartel in which two large European groupings, each with a strong British component, agreed to share out their international markets in blithe defiance of all accepted free-trade principles of the time.

From 1870 to 1914, in a world before plastics, petrochemicals or the rise of pharmaceuticals, chemical production had been chiefly a matter of the heavy bulk products required for industrial processes – the alkali products of soda ash, chlorine, sulphuric acid and bleach, and the industrial explosives essential for mining and the construction of roads and railways. In the 1870s Britain had the world's largest heavy chemical industry, centred on Merseyside, which was close to the Cheshire salt deposits for making soda ash and chlorine, to supplies of limestone and coal and to the busy port of Liverpool. The leading company was Brunner, Mond, founded in 1873 by John Tomlinson Brunner, a Merseyside businessman of Swiss extraction, and Ludwig Mond, a brilliant German chemist who saw that the future for soda-ash production lay in the Belgian Solvay process. This not only produced a purer and more economical ash than the older Leblanc manufacturing process, but also did it with far less industrial pollution. Soda ash was a key raw material for such industries as glass, paper, soap and textiles, and its consumption served as an indicator of national industrial growth.

Within twenty years of licensing the Solvay process in 1873, Brunner, Mond had built up the world's biggest alkali manufacturing business. It was a member of the Solvay Group of associated companies, which by the 1880s stretched throughout Europe as far as Russia. The group had a German company (Deutsche Solvay Werke) and an American company (Solvay Process Co. of Syracuse, NY) and its founder, Ernest Solvay, dreamed of administering from his Brussels base a multinational alliance 'so intimate', as he explained on the silver jubilee of Solvay et Cie in 1888, 'that it will yield the advantages of a universal company without its inconveniences and difficulties'.

Through Solvay's comfortable market-sharing arrangements, the group's Continental partners controlled the European markets including Germany, a source of lucrative custom until the Germans raised high tariff walls in the 1880s and began to develop their own alkali industry. Brunner, Mond had Britain and the US export trade, while in the vast markets of the British Empire, some areas were shared by both, with Brunner, Mond setting the prices. When the American Solvay company's operations started to bite into its American trade, Brunner,

Mond simply negotiated a share of Solvay Process Co.'s profits in return for agreeing to withdraw from the US export market.

Although the Solvay process produced better soda ash, the Leblanc makers – Tennants of Glasgow was one of the biggest – managed to survive by their ability to produce chlorine as a by-product, something even the brilliant Ludwig Mond had not succeeded in mastering from the Solvay technique. A by-product in turn of chlorine was bleaching powder, extensively used in the textile industry and again a product Mond had failed to recover from the Solvay system. In 1891 the British Leblanc companies amalgamated under the presidency of Sir Charles Tennant, a leading industrialist of the day and socially one of the best connected: he was the father of Margot Tennant, who married H.H. Asquith, the Liberal politician and later prime minister. The United Alkali Company, as the new combine was named, was capitalized at more than £8 million and was the largest chemical business in the world at the time, with forty-eight factories. For a while it appeared a serious threat to Brunner, Mond and the Solvay Group, though it proved fatally unable to recognize advances in technology such as electrolysis in the production of chlorine, and its power soon faded. Brunner, Mond by contrast was quick to take on the electrolysis process invented in the 1890s by an American, Hamilton Y. Castner, and an Austrian, Carl Kellner. The Castner-Kellner process became a pillar of Brunner, Mond's strength in the 1920s and one of ICI's plants at Runcorn still commemorates the name.

The chemical industry in the last third of the nineteenth century had been largely shaped by two great areas of innovation – Solvay's ammonia-soda revolution and the string of brilliant inventions in explosives by the Swede, Alfred Nobel. The international network of companies that grew out of Nobel's innovations, starting with the first safe detonator for nitroglycerin, matched that of Solvay in the alkali business. How Nobel and his contemporary Ludwig Mond between them revolutionized much of nineteenth-century industry will be told in detail in Chapter 2; their legacy of inventive research applied to business problems was to contribute substantially to the ethos of Imperial Chemical Industries, the giant that would emerge in 1926 from the flurry of New York talks. Like the Solvay Group, Nobel companies stretched throughout Europe and also operated in America. They were strong in France, Germany and Italy but nowhere stronger than in Britain, where Nobel had founded his industrial empire in 1871 with the British Dynamite Company in Glasgow. (Sir Charles Tennant was one of his backers.) The British company, whose title soon changed to Nobel's Explosives Ltd, was by 1886 linked to four Nobel companies in Germany under a holding company – a novel principle at the time – called the Nobel-Dynamite Trust Company Ltd, and this powerful combine endured until the First World War.

Nobel's companies had led the world in blasting explosives for industrial use; first dynamite, his own invention, which was safer and easier to handle than nitroglycerin, and later on 'blasting gelatin', sold under several trade names including gelignite. In the late 1880s Nobel's invention of ballistite, a smokeless powder whose formula was the subject of the famous cordite lawsuit of the 1890s, gave the group a dominating position in military explosives at a time when weapons were becoming more sophisticated and requiring cleaner, more efficient propellants than old-fashioned gunpowder. Both the British and German Nobel companies worked closely with the great arms manufacturers, Vickers, Armstrong Whitworths and Krupps, apparently unaware, despite the intensifying arms race, that their products would soon be fuelling a world war centred on their own countries. (The leaders of the international explosives industry were so much taken by surprise by the events of late summer 1914 that in June, shortly before Archduke Franz Ferdinand was assassinated at Sarajevo, a conference of British, German and American explosives manufacturers met in London to work out new market-sharing agreements. The Nobel-Dynamite Trust Co. was not finally disbanded until January 1915.)

For both the explosives makers and the alkali producers, the cosy market-sharing arrangements of the years before 1914 rested on a broad acceptance by all parties that the British Empire should remain a British trading preserve, with the right of British companies at least to fix prices if not to have sole entry into the market. Even the Americans, du Pont included, were ready to accept this provided the British firms looked strong enough to enforce the arrangement. Brunner, Mond and Nobel could both convince the world on that score.

Where Britain was undeniably weak was in dyestuffs, an area in which Germany reigned supreme. This was ironic, since it had been a British chemist, W. H. Perkin, who first succeeded in 1856 in synthesizing a natural dye, the colour mauve, which he extracted from aniline. In 1869, Perkin synthesized alizarine, the red colouring matter of the madder plant, from experiments with anthracene. Both aniline and anthracene were by-products of coal, which Britain had in rich abundance. It looked as though Britain might establish a world lead in the new aniline dye industry. But three German chemists were working along the same lines and although Perkin's company was the first to market synthetic alizarine, no substantial British company was formed until the 1880s, after Perkin's patents had run out and the Germans with their well-organized laboratory research programmes were in virtual control of the market.

The British Alizarine Company, based in Silvertown in London's East End, was reasonably successful within its own speciality, but its German competitors broadened their range of dyestuffs, consolidated into powerful mergers and sold at competitive rates. The textile manufacturers of Yorkshire and Lancashire went for the best prices and were not disposed to support the growth of a British dyestuffs industry if they could buy cheaper supplies in Germany. In August 1914 this led to the bizarre situation in which Britain, which imported seventy-five per cent of its dyestuffs requirements from Germany, found itself unable to supply enough khaki dyes for Kitchener's armies. A crash programme to gear up home production was directed by Lord Moulton, a seventy-year-old Law Lord brought out of retirement to weld together British Dyes Ltd from a number of leading dyestuffs firms. It was, in effect, to be a prototype of nationalization; the first significant involvement of a British government in the running of a private enterprise. But it never achieved its intended size and for most of the war remained simply a nationalization of one family business, Read, Holliday of Huddersfield. The shortfall of khaki dyes was made up, not by the new State company but by Levinstein Ltd, another family firm based in Blackley, Manchester. Levinstein, whose owners were of German Jewish origin and had profited from the innovative skills of German chemists before the war, estimated that by the end of March 1915 it had rushed out enough 'Thionol' khaki dye to supply uniforms for nine million soldiers.

Levinstein and British Alizarine and a dozen or so lesser dyestuffs manufacturers remained outside the net of British Dyes Ltd. It wasn't until the war was well over, in the summer of 1919, that they joined in a larger combine known as the British Dyestuffs Corporation.

The First World War

From the start of the war, however, it was evident that the building of a consolidated domestic dyestuffs industry was going to be undermined by the more urgent need for munitions. The compounds of dyestuffs technology shared considerable common ground with those used in military explosives. Coal-tar, for example, as well as forming the basis of aniline and anthracene dyes, gave derivatives for making TNT and lyddite. Lord Moulton, brought in by Asquith's government to centralize the dyestuffs industry and make it an effective replacement for German imports, soon found himself under pressure to divert coal-tar supplies to munitions; particularly toluene, which was used in making TNT. Moulton had been a distinguished scientist and Fellow of the Royal Society as well as a lawyer, and he had acted for Nobel in the cordite patent case of 1892–5 against the government chemists Frederick Abel and James Dewar. As the demand for high-explosive shells rose insatiably, it became clear to Moulton that even by giving the munitions makers top priority for toluene, not enough TNT could be made. There was, however, an alternative which would provide a satisfactory explosive when combined with TNT. This was amatol, which could be made with as little as twenty per cent TNT to eighty per cent ammonium nitrate.

Moulton encountered stiff opposition from the chiefs of staff, who wanted nothing less than pure TNT and argued that amatol was more difficult to detonate. Nevertheless, the Law Lord defeated the generals and asked Brunner, Mond to take over large-scale production of ammonium nitrate, which could be manufactured by a process similar to that for ammonium soda. In two years, from 1915 to 1917 in plants based in Cheshire and Swindon, they pushed up production from 4,764 tons to nearly 92,000 tons, and supplied virtually all Britain's requirements of ammonium nitrate during the war.

Brunner, Mond were also heavily involved in two other areas of high-explosives work, the purification of TNT and the manufacture of synthetic phenol for making lyddite, the form of explosive still favoured by the Royal Navy and the French Army. In January 1917 there was a major tragedy at a factory in Silvertown where the purification work on TNT was going on. A fire triggered a devastating explosion which destroyed the works and the surrounding houses and killed sixty-nine people including sixteen of Brunner, Mond's employees.

Both Brunner, Mond and Nobel's emerged considerably stronger from the war, having grown by acquisition and mergers respectively. Brunner, Mond shrewdly invested in the future of electro-chemistry by taking a twenty-five-per-cent stake in the new Castner-Kellner company at Runcorn, and at the end of the war Nobel's merged about two dozen explosives firms under its leadership in a new combine called Explosives Trades Ltd, capitalized at £18 million. It was registered in the month of the Armistice and in September 1920 was renamed Nobel Industries Ltd. The other leading dyestuffs companies had at last come together with British Dyes Ltd to form the British Dyestuffs Corporation. This left Britain's chemical industry in four major groupings: two of them strong (Nobel's and Brunner, Mond, the latter capitalized at just over £13 million) and two relatively weak (Dyestuffs Corporation, valued at £9.8 million, and United Alkali Co., with assets of around £7 million).

Thanks to a piece of daring opportunism in the flush of Allied victory, Brunner, Mond was now also in possession of Germany's key Haber-Bosch process for synthesizing ammonia, a technology which, as ICI's official historian W. J. Reader put it, 'amounted to the formation of an entirely new industry [and] was Brunner, Mond's most important technical contribution to ICI'. The search for a method of 'fixing' nitrogen from the air had been going on since the late 1890s, mainly in order to increase the supply of fertilizers and therefore of crops for food production. In 1898 Sir William Crooke had pointed out that since eighty per cent of the atmosphere was composed of nitrogen, roughly twenty million tons of it were sitting above every square mile of the earth's surface. Nitrogen otherwise came from ammonia – in the nineteenth century chiefly a product of gasworks coke ovens – or from sodium nitrate, which occurred in its greatest deposits in Chile. Much Chilean ore had been sent to the bottom of the sea on its way to Britain in the Great War. Haber and Bosch were aided in designing their process by Krupps, the armaments firm, whose advanced technology gave the two chemists the ability to work with large volumes of gas at 600°C under extremely high pressures.

The Spoils of War

On the day after the Armistice, with most of London still roaring drunk and rioting joyfully in the streets, a young Army major named Francis Freeth, who had been a chemist with Brunner, Mond before the war, called on Lord Moulton in his office and urged him to send a chemical mission to join the British Army as it advanced through Germany towards the Rhine. The object, in Freeth's words, was 'to pinch everything they've got'. Specifically, he had in mind the BASF plant near Oppau on the Rhine where the Haber-Bosch process had been in production since 1913. Raiding Oppau's secrets as part of the spoils of war seemed to Freeth a much more satisfactory method than painstakingly trying to unravel the German patents. (BASF's British patents were taken over anyway in the aftermath of war.)

Moulton demurred, though not with great conviction. Others in Whitehall supported Freeth's idea and in April 1919 a group of five British chemists duly moved into Oppau, then occupied by French troops. The BASF management protested to the French commanding officer that if he let the British in, they would shut down the plant and throw 10,000 people out of work. The British party was accordingly asked merely to observe the works, not to take measurements or draw plans. As they moved through the BASF plant, they found blacked-out dials on the machinery and great gaps where stairs and ladders had been removed between floors. The British scientists had to rely on memory, making up sketches and reports as quickly as they could after leaving. On the way home to England, their luggage was stolen from a locked and guarded railway wagon. One member of the party, however, had prudently kept his notes with him in a kitbag, and from these a report was put together, which enabled Brunner, Mond to work out how the system could be constructed. Thirteen rough drawings formed the basis of the plant; they were drawn in such haste and enthusiasm by one of the Oppau party, Captain A. H. Cowap, that Brunner, Mond's office manager had to stand by him sharpening coloured pencils as quickly as he broke them in his eagerness to get the details down.

With Brunner, Mond now capable of developing a British nitrogen industry, the Ministry of Munitions arranged for the purchase of 266 acres of farm land near Billingham on the Tees, near Middlesbrough, to build a plant for the production of 60,000 tons a year of ammonium nitrate by the Haber-Bosch method. By a stroke of pure good fortune, the site turned out to be on top of a thick bed of anhydrite, a form of calcium sulphate, from which could be made ammonium sulphate, the basic ingredient of fertilizers. Billingham was to be the biggest single working asset brought to the ICI combine, though one that turned into a millstone when the nitrogen market collapsed in the 1930s.

The Battle with Lever Brothers

As the 1920s opened, Brunner, Mond was riding high on the anticipation of vast imperial markets for ammonium sulphate, a commodity that all developing agricultural countries needed. It had also, it thought, come to the end in 1919 of a long and acrimonious battle with Lever Brothers, fought through the courts in the last two years of the war.

Lever was probably at this time the world's biggest soap manufacturer. Its chairman, Sir William Lever (later Viscount Leverhulme) had virtually invented the modern soap industry by packaging and brand-marketing what had previously been a dull bulk commodity of un-wrapped bars. Lever had also pioneered the concept of the industrial garden city at his Port Sunlight works in Cheshire. The firm was by far Brunner, Mond's biggest customer for soda ash, and the chemical company had been alarmed in the 1890s to find Lever Brothers setting up their own alkali works to make caustic soda, a defensive reaction to the creation of the United Alkali Company and fears of consequent price rises. In 1907, when it was negotiating a new alkali contract with Lever Brothers, Brunner, Mond inserted a clause barring the soap company from engaging in the alkali market outside its own manufacturing requirements. But it made no reciprocal undertaking to keep out of the soap business. When, in 1911, Levers bought a quantity of salt-bearing land in Cheshire, with the obvious intention of expanding its alkali manufacture at some future date, Brunner, Mond promptly reacted by buying two of the biggest soap companies after Levers – Joseph Crosfield and Sons and William Gossage and Sons, collectively known in the business as 'Crossages'.

Thus began an eight-year wrangle which was partly resolved before the outbreak of war by an agreement guaranteeing Levers a share in the profits of 'Crossages'. Then in 1916 an agreement between Levers and 'Crossages' to found a third company along with Price's Candle Co. of Battersea triggered off a lawsuit when Levers discovered it would be very much a junior partner in the venture. The litigation, in which Sir William Lever took a personal part, ended with his company agreeing to buy out the two Brunners' soap subsidiaries for £4 million – £1 million more than Levers considered a fair market price. A new alkali contract was signed on the same day. It had all, as the presiding judge made clear from his somewhat jaundiced summing up, been an unnecessary way for two experienced firms to conduct their business.

The saga was not yet over, however. In 1924, Lever Brothers resorted to the law against Brunner, Mond again, this time with a more substantial cause for grievance. The 1919 agreement had bound the soap company to take all the alkali it required for its own operations and those of its associated companies at home and abroad from Brunner, Mond. The price set was seventy-five per cent higher than in the previous contract, and in return Brunner, Mond undertook not to sell alkali more cheaply to any other soap maker. In fact they did so, through a series of bungled contractual involvements, chiefly with the Co-operative Wholesaler's Society (CWS). Levers got to hear about it through an obscure Australian subsidiary of theirs. Lord Leverhulme was furious. By this time his old antagonist Sir John Brunner had long been succeeded as chairman by his third son Roscoe Brunner, and Sir John had died shortly after the signing of the 1919 agreement.

Leverhulme took things to a personal level, asking Roscoe Brunner whether any other soap maker was getting a lower price than Levers. Brunner at first indignantly denied it, then a few days later wrote a naive admission about CWS to Hulme Lever, Lord Leverhulme's son, pleading weakly that Brunner, Mond had not been able to persuade CWS to alter the terms of their pre-1919 purchase agreement. In June 1924, Lever Brothers sued Brunner, Mond for fraudulent misrepresentation and breach of the 1919 contract, claiming damages of £1 million. The trial was set for 9 November 1925, but Brunner's lawyers advised them that they had no real defence and should settle out of court, otherwise the publicity would badly damage the company's reputation, especially among the bright young scientists it hoped to recruit from the universities. Brunner, Mond agreed and Lever Brothers got their £1 million, upon which cynical observers commented that they had at least got their change out of the price they had been forced to pay for 'Crossages' in 1919. Roscoe Brunner resigned on grounds of ill health and was succeeded as chairman by Sir Alfred Mond, second son of the firm's other founder, Ludwig Mond.

Sir Alfred Mond and 'Rationalization'

Sir Alfred Mond was a man of far greater stature than Roscoe Brunner. He was fifty-seven, had trained as a lawyer and after a short period of reluctant involvement in the family business as a young man had devoted himself to his real love, politics, becoming successively Liberal MP for Chester, Swansea and Carmarthen, which he still represented in Parliament. He had been First Commissioner of Works in Lloyd George's wartime administration and Minister of Health in 1921–2, and had returned to the board of Brunner, Mond in 1923 after the fall of the coalition government. Despite his early resistance towards making Brunner, Mond his career, Alfred was a natural businessman, with a particular flair for long-term strategy. He believed that the future lay with bigger business units like the IG in Germany, all part of his philosophy of 'rationalization'. He was the first to apply the term to business organization and in 1929 Nuttall's *Standard Dictionary* asked him for his definition and published it: 'The application of scientific organization to industry, by the unification of the processes of production and distribution with the object of approximating supply to demand.'

Across the Atlantic, the philosophy of 'bigger is better' was already well established in the chemical industry. Orlando F. Weber, an aggressive financier known as the 'Fire Chief' from his reputation for sacking people, had put together Allied Chemical and Dye Corporation in 1920 from five companies making everything from alkali to dyes and including the Solvay Process Co., formerly of the Solvay Group, as well as General Chemical Co., which already had a synthetic ammonia process developed independently of Haber-Bosch. In February 1920, Weber proudly told Belgium's Solvay et Cie and Britain's Brunner, Mond that his new combine would be 'as complete, if not more complete and more wealthy than the IG' (at that time the smaller IG formed in 1916). Allied came to the market at the end of 1920 valued at $282.7 million, the equivalent then of £77.2 million – bigger indeed than the Germans and far bigger than all the British companies combined. Brunner, Mond had a holding worth about £1.5 million in Allied through its interest in the Solvay Process Co. but its own alkali business, big though it was in the imperial markets, now looked at risk if the Americans chose to launch a price war. Weber had no patience with the cosy European cartel system and made it clear early in 1926 that he wanted Allied to have a bigger share of export markets.

As Sir Alfred Mond moved into the chairman's seat at Brunner, Mond, the company was realizing its difficulties in competing with the large German and American combines, particularly in applying scientific developments to industry on a large enough scale. The cost of the synthetic ammonia and nitrate plant at Billingham, coming on top of the costly Lever lawsuit, forced them to raise their share capital from £500,000 to £3 million and to seek government backing for a public issue of debentures, £2 million at five per cent repayable in twenty years. Only two thirds of the issue was taken up by the public. From that moment in 1925 Sir Alfred Mond began actively seeking potential merger partners.

His first inclination was to look to IG Farben. As the son of a gifted inventor – he had been present in his father's laboratory when Ludwig Mond and an assistant discovered nickel carbonyl, the basis of a whole new industry for Brunner, Mond – Alfred Mond admired the IG's technical brilliance and was particularly interested in their work on extracting oil from coal. His interest stemmed from more than the business possibilities, though it was then generally thought that the world's reserves of oil would run out in the mid-1950s. As a Liberal MP for a Welsh constituency, he thought the process might save the coal-mining industry in the depressed Welsh valleys he knew. The bitter coal strike of 1926 which developed into, and long outlived, the nine-day General Strike in May added strength to this conviction.

Nobel Industries and du Pont

The twenty-week coal strike, which demoralized the industry for years and was to damage industrial relations for two generations, severely hurt Nobel Industries, which had emerged from the war strong and freshly consolidated with the bulk of Britain's other explosives manufacturers. Imperial markets had seemed limitless to them as they had to Brunner, Mond. In 1920 Sir Harry McGowan, the rough-hewn Glaswegian who had risen from clerk to chairman of the company, told shareholders: 'Commerce *is* the Empire. Never before has Britain had a chance of developing as it has today.'

Nobel had strong transatlantic links with Allied's great rival, du Pont de Nemours of Delaware. These had been cemented during the war when Nobel worked in technical harness with du Pont in a plant near Bristol producing nitrocellulose propellant. McGowan was a personal friend of Irenee du Pont, the American company's president, and du Pont saw Nobel as a useful ally against the Germans. As early as 1920, McGowan told his shareholders that he believed the best opportunity for Nobel's expansion on a really big scale lay in the motor industry. Automobile production in the United States had more than doubled in the years between 1914 and 1919 and would quadruple between 1919 and 1925. By 1922, McGowan saw that the car in America was 'as essential in the economic development of the United States as are railways'. Nobel technology was suited to certain manufactures connected with the motor business – for example, leathercloth for upholstery (Rexine was the trademark of a Nobel subsidiary, the British Leather Cloth Manufacturing Co.) and cellulose finishes. In the early 1920s, sixty per cent of Nobel's business lay outside the explosives which had been its heart. It was even considering going into car components through one of its metal-working companies, Kynochs of Birmingham, which had been saved from bankruptcy in the mid-1920s by acquiring the patents to manufacture the first zip, the American-invented 'Lightning' fastener. Affirming its faith in the future of the automobile, Nobels invested heavily in General Motors, in which du Pont held twenty-five per cent of the equity.

Du Pont would be a natural ally for Nobel in any new Anglo-American grouping. But du Pont also had agreements with British Dyestuffs for exchanging technical information and a common policy against German competition. In the event it was to be the dyestuffs industry, the catalyst of the original German chemical growth in the 1900s, that would prove the key in the British moves in 1926 to counteract IG Farben's expansion.

Germany in the mid-1920s still held the whip hand in dyestuffs. In 1923 the home sales manager of British Dyestuffs, A. W. Scott, predicted gloomily: 'In 1931 we can hope to be technically and practically as efficient as the German manufacturers are today, but to keep pace with their development in the same period would require a further ten to twenty years.' There was a web of agreements linking British, American and German dye companies, but British Dyestuffs needed some closer alliance with the new IG Farben if it was to keep pace with technological developments and survive. In return it could offer the IG entry into the British markets which had been closed to German manufacturers since wartime import restrictions.

By now the British government was taking an interest in saving the national dyestuffs industry it had been responsible for attempting to consolidate. In late January of 1926 Sir Harry McGowan had lunch with Reginald McKenna, chairman of the Midland Bank. McKenna had been chancellor of the exchequer in Asquith's war cabinet and still maintained close links with government. He suggested to McGowan that it would be acceptable in the highest circles of government if a coalition of British chemical companies were to rescue British Dyestuffs. As a first step, McKenna suggested, Nobel Industries should take it over. McGowan replied that BDC was not their 'line of country'. Why not, he countered, think more ambitiously in terms of 'a British IG' – a combination of, say, Nobel Industries, Brunner, Mond and British Dyestuffs, perhaps bringing in United Alkali as well? This would provide a mighty counter-balance to the German combine. Something of the kind would have to happen, McGowan was convinced, or in ten years' time, he estimated, 'Great Britain would be a second-class power in Heavy Chemicals'.

McKenna agreed – so enthusiastically that he wanted to take the plan straightaway to the prime minister, Stanley Baldwin. But as McGowan recalled twenty years later, 'I said no, it was purely a personal opinion which I had not submitted to my board, and that in any case I was leaving for South Africa in a few weeks'. The proposal hung fire, but McGowan was convinced that the choice for his company lay either in a British IG or in some sort of alliance with the Germans 'so that we could work with them in a friendly way in certain parts of the world'.

A British Combine

As time passed and the options were argued back and forth within the company, opinion came down heavily in favour of a British chemical combine to challenge IG. For one thing, there was 'the Empire view' to be taken: 'Commerce *is* the Empire', McGowan had so confidently declared. For another, Nobel needed a supplier of nitrogen and solvents for its business in fertilizers and in nitrocellulose products for the car industry. After considering and discarding an approach to BASF, McGowan and his board were left with Brunner, Mond, the only British company with the chemical engineering required for both nitrogen products and solvents.

Mond, however, was looking to a German alliance, an arrangement by which his company could acquire IG's oil-from-coal technology in exchange for entry to the British dyestuffs market. Under restrictions imposed in the war this would normally remain closed to a German exporter for another five years. As a first step, Brunner, Mond needed to get control of British Dyestuffs Corporation, on whose board Sir Alfred Mond already sat, along with McGowan. In 1923 BDC had attempted its own deal with IG's smaller predecessor, to gain German technical knowledge in exchange for half BDC's net profits less £200,000 for each of the first five years, £150,000 a year thereafter. This had been vetoed by the British government and BDC's chairman, Sir William Alexander, resigned. The Board of Trade put in a new chairman, Lord Ashfield, and a government director, Alfred Mond. But three years had brought about a change in the government's thinking, at least to the extent that it no longer believed BDC could go it alone, and this view McKenna relayed to McGowan over their lunch. Indeed, as the ICI historian Dr Reader commented: 'In the face of IG, newly reconstructed with even greater power, could any British chemical company stand alone? Could Nobel Industries? Could Brunner, Mond? And if not, what allies should they seek?'

At this point Mond and McGowan met for the first time, in July 1926. Their personal chemistry worked almost at once. Both men looked like a cartoonist's dream of a powerful capitalist; heavy-featured, imposing of presence, fond of big cigars. McGowan has been described as looking like the model for a Victorian painting of 'Success'. He was the ultimate self-made man, expensively dressed, loving opulent accessories and tending towards a kind of heavy-handed mateyness with the workmen which went down well enough when he toured his factories. Mond was much more reserved and buttoned-up, an intellectual theorist where McGowan went straight to the business point. When he proposed to his wife, Violet Goetze, he had been unable to believe that he had any charm or attraction for women, and he was still conscious of the heavy German accent which even Cheltenham College and Cambridge had been unable to eradicate. 'He had desperately sought Englishness and Englishness had eluded him,' in Dr Reader's words. He wore tightly formal clothes, always with a wing collar, and his guttural accent was made more incomprehensible by his shy habit of tucking his chin down into his collar as he spoke.

His meeting with McGowan had been arranged to discuss McGowan's idea of a British IG; nothing conclusive came of it, though Mond suggested carrying on talks a little longer on an unofficial basis. He was still preoccupied with an oil-from-coal technology deal, and in early August 1926 went to Belgium to confer with the Solvays at their family estate near Brussels. Carl Bosch and two other high-ranking executives of IG Farben were also at the meeting, and put forward glittering forecasts of the turnover their oil-from-coal process could achieve – £50 million for the UK alone was their prediction. Everyone assumed the Americans would want to come in, although they had their own oil supplies. Notes taken at the meeting by a Brunner, Mond director recorded that the IG were willing to contemplate an arrangement (a) with Solvay, (b) with Brunner, Mond and (c) with du Pont and Allied Chemical for working the process in their respective territories. Brunner, Mond would form a 'British IG' with a holding company capitalized at a minimum of £20 million which would then proceed to acquire a controlling interest in British Dyestuffs and possibly also United Alkali. Nobel Industries might be too large to swallow, and should be worked with on a separate basis outside the combine. 'By these arrangements,' wrote Reader, 'Brunner, Mond and the rest were to gain the knowledge they sought from IG and IG was to be paid for it by very widespread participation in the associated businesses. The whole plan, perhaps, cannot be described as a German takeover bid for most of the world's chemical industry, but it came fairly close to one.'

To put the plan into action, three parties needed to give their consent: the British government, British Dyestuffs Corporation and Allied Chemical. Sir Alfred Mond despatched his son Henry to London to negotiate the first two, while he himself planned to cross the Atlantic to see Orlando Weber. IG Farben promised at Brussels to send representatives to New York at the same time.

Mond decided to combine his visit to New York with some business in Canada, and sailed on 21 August on the *Ile de France* with his wife Violet and sons Robert and Emile. The rest of the Brunner, Mond party, including the young Sir John Brunner, Roscoe's elder brother, left Liverpool on 11 September on the *Franconia*, reaching New York on the 20th. Mond joined them within a couple of days, as did a representative of Solvay et Cie. Carl Bosch of IG Farben sailed from

Germany on 15 September, hoping to get a binding agreement from Allied's Weber before the end of the month.

McGowan meanwhile had been on a business trip to Africa. He returned to London to find Lord Ashfield, chairman of British Dyestuffs, ready to give his approval to a Brunner, Mond takeover if his fellow directors agreed – including, of course, McGowan. The Nobel chairman could see the alternative 'British IG' taking shape without Nobel Industries, and linking up with IG and Allied if the New York talks went as planned. On 15 September he told his directors in a memorandum: 'It is perfectly clear that negotiations of a very important character are pending between Brunner, Mond and the IG people, and possibly also with the Allied Chemical Company of America, in which Brunner, Mond are financially interested. I have no doubt also that the representatives of the IG will be talking over matters with the du Pont people, and I feel it essential that I go to New York at once to make our position clear to these various people. Synthetic ammonia may be our lifeblood, and we cannot afford to be left outside of any possible combination of the companies I have just indicated . . . If we find that Brunner, Mond are using the proposed acquisition of the British Dyestuffs Corporation to further their own general interests with the Badische Company [IG] and that they are not now disposed to go on with the big financial merger in this country, then we know where we are, and we shall immediately get busy with the Badische Company, and make a deal with them accordingly.'

McGowan caught the next fast westbound liner, the Blue Riband holder *Mauretania*, leaving Southampton on 18 September and arriving in New York on 24 September. He arrived at a fortuitous moment. That very day, Alfred Mond and Solvay's representative, a Monsieur Janssen, met Orlando Weber in his office. Weber was in an aggressive mood and announced right away that he wanted to repudiate the three-way market-sharing agreement for alkali between Brunner's, Solvay and Allied. On Saturday, 25 September, a letter was drafted, presumably by Mond, offering the IG rights in future profits from oil from coal within the British Empire. The letter proposed a meeting on Monday, 27 September, to open formal negotiations. But McGowan intercepted proceedings. He and Mond met for lunch that Saturday, and over the lunch table McGowan argued strongly for a merger of the four leading British chemical companies, hinting that if Mond did not agree, Nobel Industries would turn its own attentions to linking up with the IG 'in a substantial fashion'.

Mond was persuaded. In the afternoon the proposal was agreed with his co-directors, the offer to IG was presumably torn up and on Sunday morning, 26 September, McGowan called at the Ambassador's Hotel where the Brunner, Mond party was staying. Years later he recalled that then, 'for all practical purposes, the merger was through'.

ICI is Formed at Sea

With Carl Bosch and the IG team left high and dry, Mond and McGowan together booked passage on the *Aquitania*, which was sailing for Southampton on 6 October. Several members of the Brunner, Mond party were also on board, and discussions went on day and night during the six-day voyage: Mond was at his intellectual best around one in the morning. It was decided that the new company was to acquire, by exchange of shareholdings, the capital of Brunner, Mond, Nobel Industries, United Alkali (which had not yet been consulted) and British Dyestuffs Corporation. Mond and McGowan drew up a preliminary list of directors and suggested a committee for deciding the earning capacity of each company over the years 1924, 1925 and 1926, so that an equitable basis for an exchange of shares could be worked out.

They thought about 900 people might be required to staff the head office of the new combine, and they sketched out the general shape of its departments, leaving the detailed organization until later. The 'Proposed Amalgamation' of the four companies, representing some 5,000 products and nearly £100 million in assets, was typed out on four sheets of Cunard Line writing paper. It opened with the suggestion that the combine be known by the name Mond and McGowan had chosen during the crossing – Imperial Chemical Industries Ltd. As prospective shareholders were told with the company prospectus, the name was deliberately chosen 'to lay emphasis upon the fact that the promotion of Imperial trading interests will command the special consideration and thought of those who will be responsible for directing this new Company'. The British Empire, shareholders were reminded, was 'the greatest single economic unit in the world', and it would be the avowed intention of the new combine 'without limiting its activities in foreign overseas markets, specially to extend the development and importance of the Chemical Industry throughout the Empire'.

The thorny question of who was to be chairman was settled amicably as the *Aquitania* ploughed her way towards Southampton. McGowan graciously ceded the title to Mond while he became deputy chairman and president of the board. For all practical purposes, however, they would run the company in tandem. All that remained, on landing, was to seek United Alkali's consent to the four-way marriage. UAC was not as eager as Mond and McGowan had expected, but eventually its chairman, Sir Max Muspratt, and his board were persuaded. On 21 October the four companies publicly announced their intention to merge.

Then began six weeks of intensive work, twelve hours a day in a small room overlooking Smith Square in Westminster, as the four chief executives fleshed out the bones of the 'Aquitania Agreement', as it

RMS Aquitania. The constitution of ICI, the 'Aquitania Agreement', was drawn up on a crossing from New York in October 1926 and typed out on 4 pages of ship's stationery.

became known (see Appendix). Imperial Chemical Industries was to have an initial authorized capital of £65 million – £31 million in £1 ordinary shares and the rest in cumulative preference shares and deferred shares. Shareholders in Brunner, Mond, Nobel and United Alkali were to receive three ICI shares for every two they held; those in British Dyestuffs were to have eight for twenty. On 7 December ICI was formally incorporated and by 1 January 1927 was ready for business.

There was one tragic postscript. Roscoe Brunner, the ex-chairman of Brunner, Mond, had never got over the Lever lawsuit and his part in the debacle that had cost his company £1 million. When his name was not announced among the fourteen directors elected from the member companies to the board of ICI, he and his wife felt it deeply. Ethel Brunner, who was a novelist, took it particularly hard and gave interviews to several newspapers fiercely defending her husband's part in the Lever affair. On 3 November 1926, thirteen days after the new company was announced, the Brunners were found dead in the bedroom of their daughter's house in London while she was away visiting Austria with her husband. Roscoe Brunner had first shot his wife and then shot himself.

2

GODFATHERS OF INVENTION

The new company was born with innovation in its blood. Alfred Nobel and Ludwig Mond, the founders of ICI's principal components, were two of the most remarkable scientific geniuses of nineteenth-century Europe, in whom prolifically inventive minds were matched with business ability of a rare degree. They were more or less contemporaries, born six years apart in Sweden and Germany, and their careers marched on broadly parallel lines during the 1860s and 1870s, years in which their discoveries and application of new principles to industry revolutionized the manufacture of explosives and heavy chemicals. In 1871 and 1873 respectively, both came to Britain to start businesses which made their fortunes and established the foundations of a powerful British chemical industry. Their early lives and circumstances were, however, quite different.

Alfred Nobel was born in 1833 in Stockholm, the son of Immanuel Nobel, a builder and mechanical engineer of an inventive turn of mind. He built floating bridges, made machine tools and was granted a patent in 1828 for 'Nobel's mechanical movement', a method of translating circular movement into a backwards and forwards effect, out of which developed a new type of clothes mangle. He founded Sweden's first rubber factory for the manufacture of elastic cloths and various surgical, military and industrial utensils, and invented an ingenious combination for military use of knapsack, mattress, life-saving vest and pontoon section. He also became deeply interested in the techniques of explosives, and unsuccessfully offered the military authorities in Sweden his invention of powder-charged explosive mines for destroying an attacking enemy 'at considerable distance both on land and at sea'. Near-bankruptcy drove him out of Sweden to work first in Finland and then in Russia, where he resumed his experiments with mines and won a monetary award from the Tsarist government with which he set himself up as part-owner of an engineering business. Among other things, it constructed the first central-heating pipes seen in Russia.

While in St Petersburg in 1855, and with his son Alfred working alongside him, Immanuel Nobel came across nitroglycerin, a violently

unstable compound obtained by letting water-free glycerin run down
into a cooled mixture of concentrated nitric acid and sulphuric acid.
Because of its unpredictable nature, and the difficulties of its manufacture and transport, nitroglycerin was not yet being put to any practical
use, but both Immanuel and Alfred Nobel were convinced that if a
controllable method of detonating could be found, it would prove a far
more effective explosive than the black gunpowder which had been
used for over 500 years.

In 1859 Immanuel Nobel returned to Sweden while Alfred continued to work and study as a chemist in St Petersburg. Both remained
convinced of the huge potential of nitroglycerin and each was working
separately on its possibilities as a blasting agent. In 1863 Alfred re-
joined his father and after more than fifty experiments in their
ramshackle wooden workshop in Helensborg, produced Nobel's Patent Detonator, an epoch-making invention which has been described
as the greatest advance in the science of explosives since the invention
of gunpowder. Ragnar Sohlman, who worked closely with Nobel in his
last years, said that, 'from a purely inventive point of view, and as
regards technical importance', Nobel's invention of the blasting cap
and initial ignition of explosives should be placed well ahead of his
subsequent invention of dynamite.

The detonator, patented in 1863, worked by containing the liquid
nitroglycerin in a metal cap or blocked-up borehole, into which a smaller
charge of gunpowder was inserted in a separate container and was fired
by a fuse. The 'blasting cap' which improved on it in 1865 was a container charged with detonating mercury – the 'initial ignition' principle
which gave rise to all later developments in the field of explosives. In a
history of research within the Nobel Division of ICI, published in 1955,
F. D. Miles remarked that 'the application of the percussion cap to the
initiation of a blasting explosive, made with a clear perception of the
nature of the detonating shock wave, is certainly the greatest discovery
ever made in both the principle and practice of explosives. On it the
whole of the modern practice of blasting has been built'.

A year after Alfred Nobel's first historic breakthrough in October
1863, tragedy struck the family business. On 3 September 1864, the
workshop at Helensborg was wiped out by an explosion which killed
five people, among them Alfred's younger brother Emil, aged twenty,
who had just graduated and was helping with the experiments on
nitroglycerin. Public fear of the new explosive, known as 'Nobel's
Patent Blasting Oil', made it difficult to find sites to build factories, and
the inventor was eventually driven to manufacture it aboard a covered
barge moored on a lake outside the Stockholm city boundaries. It was,
however, officially approved as an explosive by the Swedish State railways board, and was used for blasting railway tunnels in Stockholm.
Nobel's invention also made possible one of the great engineering feats

of the age, the driving of America's Central Pacific Railroad through the mountains of Sierra Nevada.

In 1864, Nobel found a wealthy backer in a Stockholm merchant named J. W. Smitt, who helped him set up a company to manufacture nitroglycerin at an isolated spot called Vintervinken. This plant continued to produce Nobel explosives and blasting powders from 1865 until 1915. Nobel acted as managing director, works engineer, correspondent, traveller, advertising manager and treasurer. He went on to patent his 'blasting oil' in England, Norway and Finland, and founded his first foreign company, Alfred Nobel and Co., in Hamburg in 1865, manufacturing in a remote valley at Krummel on the Elbe south of Hamburg. From here, nitroglycerin was despatched, packed in tin canisters and demijohns crated in wood, throughout Germany and to export destinations in Austria, North and South America and later Australia. Its first use in Britain was for blasting in slate quarries in North Wales, but it was expensive, ten times the price of ordinary blasting powder at 3s. 3d. a pound against fourpence halfpenny.

So many accidents occurred with the new substance that at one time it looked as though Nobel would have to stop manufacturing it altogether. In spite of setbacks, however, Nobel went to the United States in 1866 and against powerful opposition from the leading American gunpowder maker, du Pont de Nemours of Wilmington, Delaware, started up an American company called the United States Blasting Oil Co. When its planned share capital of $1 million failed to be subscribed, Nobel transferred his US patent rights to another company, the Giant Powder Co. of San Francisco. In 1868 the Atlantic Powder Co. was formed in New York to control most of Nobel's American activities.

General Henry du Pont, the head of Nobel's rival company, warned that it was only a matter of time before a man lost his life working with nitroglycerin, but the race was on to push the railroads west across the continent, and the new explosive soon dominated the market. After Nobel's death in 1896, the Atlantic Giant Powder Co. was incorporated in du Pont, which sixty years later acknowledged that its large development in explosives had been based on the nitroglycerin introduced into America by Nobel.

The accidents that plagued the industrial development of nitroglycerin included an explosion that destroyed Nobel's own works at Krummel in 1866, while he was in the States, and one in a ship in Caernarvon docks bringing a consignment to the Welsh slate quarries in 1869. It was imperative to find a means of making the volatile substance less dangerous without diminishing its explosive force. Nobel tried adding methyl alcohol to it and allowing it to be absorbed in porous, non-explosive substances such as paper, wood waste, brick dust, coal, dry clay and gypsum bars. The best medium turned out to be *kieselguhr* clay, which was extremely porous and had no chemical reactivity at all. This led directly to Nobel's great invention, dynamite. The historic compound was made up of three parts of nitroglycerin to one part calcined and sifted *kieselguhr*. The result was a solid, plastic explosive, easily handled and although twenty-five per cent less effective than nitroglycerin as a blasting agent, much safer in terms of sensitivity to shock and changes in temperature. It was also much easier to transport than a liquid explosive and could be formed into sticks to put into a bore-hole for blasting.

Nobel called his new substance 'Dynamite, or Nobel's safety blasting powder', after the Greek word *dynamis,* meaning power. It was patented in 1867 in England, Sweden and the United States, after a series of successful demonstrations in German mines. Among the great engineering works to which it was soon contributing were the blasting of the St Gotthard Tunnel in 1872–82, the clearing of underwater rocks in New York's East River in 1876 and 1885, the clearing of the Danube at the Iron Gates in 1890–6, and the cutting of the four-mile-long Corinth Canal in Greece in 1881–93. Production of dynamite rose from eleven tons in 1867 to 3,120 tons in 1874 and began the build-up of an international network of companies. The Nobels, father and son, were honoured in 1868 by the joint award of the Gold Medal of the Swedish Academy of Sciences.

Nobel was always irritated by stories which suggested that dynamite had been accidentally discovered when some nitroglycerin leaked out of a faulty canister into *kieselguhr* which was being used as a packing material. He said he had noticed the great bulkiness of the clay when dry, which indicated its porous qualities. 'Dynamite did not therefore come about by chance, but because from the outset I saw the disadvantage of a fluid explosive and set about finding a means of counteracting this drawback.'

Ludwig Mond's Discoveries

While Nobel was inventing his revolutionary explosives, the discoveries of Ludwig Mond were beginning to change industrial processes in a less spectacular but equally influential way. From his earliest work as a chemistry student, Mond was driven by the conviction that the wasteful process of nineteenth-century industry contained a huge potential for new products and businesses. It was this which led to the first of his scores of patents, filed in 1861 when he was twenty-two, for recovering sulphur from alkali waste, and ultimately to his perception that the future of the alkali industry lay with the Belgian Solvay process for producing soda ash. On this he was to found his British business in Cheshire with John Tomlinson Brunner, and eventually build it into the world's largest alkali manufacturer.

Unlike Alfred Nobel, Ludwig Mond was born (on 7 March 1839) into a non-scientific, comfortably off Jewish middle-class family of silk merchants in Cassel, in the grand duchy of Hesse in Germany. As a child, Ludwig showed an inquiring turn of mind, asking such questions as what became of the wool when a hole appeared in his stocking. He studied a wide range of scientific subjects at Cassel Polytechnic, which at that time had a reputation for science probably unmatched by any school in Europe. Robert Bunsen had taught there until 1852, when he went to the University of Heidelberg as professor of chemistry. From Cassel young Mond went to study chemistry at the University of Marburg and in 1856, having decided to make the chemical industry his career, moved to Heidelberg to study under Bunsen, who became a lifelong friend as well as mentor. Bunsen was then forty-five and celebrated for his work on the analysis of gases and the electrolysis of metals. His discoveries were a formative influence on modern organic chemistry and their many successful industrial applications included the use of waste gases to improve the economy and efficiency of blast furnaces. In 1859 he invented the process of spectral analysis which led him to discover two new elements, caesium and rubidium.

Bunsen directed Mond's studies along practical lines, encouraging him to experiment in such areas as improving the poor burning qualities of lignite, the local fuel, and the potential of peat for industrial

ICI's godfathers; Alfred Nobel (left) and Ludwig Mond. Nobel's Explosives and Brunner, Mond were the principal partners in the 1926 merger that became Imperial Chemical Industries.

purposes. His own successes in making waste products efficient may well have shaped Mond's thinking in this direction. The young chemist spent vacations with his aunt Johanna and uncle Adolf Lowenthal, who owned a galvanoplastic factory at Cologne (and whose daughter Frida, then a child of ten, he was to marry eight years later). On one visit he wrote home proudly that he had already earned his travelling expenses 'by utilizing by-products which have hitherto been thrown away in considerable quantities. The process is cheap and simple; the materials now recovered are zinc sulphate and nitric acid'.

Mond left Heidelberg in 1858 without taking his degree. He said that a chemical manufacturer did not need such formal qualifications (but there was also a question of some student debts) and that he would prefer a doctorate to be awarded for original work of his own. In later years he was to be showered with academic honours from around the world, including fellowship of the Royal Society in London. For a while after leaving university he worked in various chemical factories, including his uncle's in Cologne, and discovered a process for producing verdigris, then used as a pigment in the printing of textiles, as a by-product of acetic acid. In the early part of 1860 he was out of a job and spent six months at home, time which his mother Henrietta urged him to spend on improving his knowledge of foreign literature. She had always been concerned to broaden his cultural horizons and in his first year at Marburg offered to send him a French book or a novel by Sir Walter Scott. Shakespeare, however, she regarded as having to be 'sifted before he is acceptable to us Germans. He is often too blunt and too coarse, and deep though he looked into the human heart, his villains are too cruel and his female characters too fickle'.

In June 1860 Ludwig was offered the job which was to determine his life's work, in a Leblanc soda plant at Ringenkuhl, near Cassel. Soda was a key chemical in many industrial processes, particularly in soap, glassmaking, paper, as a bleaching agent in textiles and in a range of other manufactures from food to pottery. Demand for it was rising fast in all the industrializing countries, especially from the glassmakers, but the current method for its manufacture, which had been devised in the late 1780s by Nicolas Leblanc, surgeon to the Duke of Orleans, in response to a shortage of vegetable ash from Spain, was wasteful, expensive in fuel and a shocking pollutant of the landscape. The method of making soda from sea salt by evaporating the brine and mixing the crystals with sulphuric acid had long been known; Leblanc's discovery was to add finely ground limestone to the resulting sodium sulphate and roast the mixture in a furnace. Chemical reactions turned it to a heavy black ash from which soda was extracted by solution, leaving behind a black sludge consisting mainly of calcium sulphide.

The process had many disadvantages. Valuable sulphur, two fifths of the cost of the raw materials, was going to waste. The sludge disfigured the landscape with dumps that smelled of rotten eggs. Hydrochloric acid escaped up the factory chimneys to fall over the surrounding country, where it rotted the leaves on the trees, destroyed crops and corroded agricultural machinery and the stonework of buildings. In effect, the Leblanc process made one chemical at the cost of wasting two. But no chemist before Mond had succeeded in extracting sulphur from the sludge.

Mond spent only a few months at Ringenkuhl, but he continued with his experiments, some of them carried out in his uncle's house in Cologne, where his cousin Frida helped to keep away the mice and rats attracted by the smell of the alkali waste. By 1861 he had patented his discovery and the following year returned briefly to the Ringenkuhl works to put it into practice. He then moved to Holland to work in a new plant for the recovery of sulphur from iron pyrites but concluded that England, not Holland, offered the best opportunities. England was Europe's largest soda producer and had huge markets in its colonies. Mond was reasonably fluent in the language, thanks to his mother's insistence on a diet of English literature, though he continued to speak it with a heavy German accent until the end of his life. He had also once been told that in England, where few chemical-company owners were qualified chemists, he would be at an advantage.

In 1862, he arrived in London, where one of the first things he did was to visit the Great Exhibition of that year in the Cromwell Road. Afterwards he said he had never learned so much in such a short time. Among new products on display were brick-making kilns, vessels of acid-resisting material and Bryant and May's revolutionary safety matches. While in London, Mond took out a British patent on his sulphur recovery process and also on another intermediate process in the manufacture of soda, for the recovery of nitric and nitrous acid. He then went up to Manchester, noted for its small but hard-working and influential German business community, and here he met John Hutchinson, a leading Leblanc soda manufacturer, who gave him the chance to show what his sulphur recovery process could achieve. Mond was offered £300 a year if the firm could make £450 from his system. In England it wasn't as immediately profitable as on the Continent, because British manufacturers used Irish iron pyrites, cheaper than Sicilian, and wages in England were higher than on mainland Europe. Nevertheless, a month after arriving in England, Mond was working for Hutchinson at Widnes, one of the first and ugliest of the chemical towns along the Mersey.

Widnes was a natural location for alkali manufacture, being situated close to the Cheshire saltfields, supplies of coal and port facilities for the export trade. But already in 1862, the pollution from Leblanc's process provided graphic evidence that a better method had to be found. As Mond's biographer, J. M. Cohen, wrote: 'From the

Soda ash for glass, soap-making and other basic industries was the main business of Brunner, Mond at Winnington. Here, women workers are loading at Winnington Wharf.

chimneys of the soap and soda works there belched a thick smoke day and night, heavy with hydrochloric acid, which burnt the hedges, destroyed the crops and did extreme damage for many miles around in any direction the wind might carry it. The alkali waste, moreover, rich with sulphur, choked the little streams that drained the marshland and polluted the Mersey itself. For every ton of soda made, approximately double its weight of . . . a thick and evil-smelling mud had to be dumped on the marsh or poured out on waste land . . . from this nauseating sludge seeped the continual odour of rotten eggs. Finally, however, the stuff dried; and even then it remained a potent menace. For it was liable to heat in the sun, catch fire and give off the irritant and corrosive gas, sulphur dioxide.'

Hutchinson was eager to listen to Mond about sulphur recovery because an Alkali Inspectorate was about to be established by Parliament and the manufacture of useful by-products from hitherto harmful waste would be bound to win approval from the new body. Around this time Mond had a significant meeting with Henry Brunner, the older brother of his future partner. The Brunners were sons of a German-Swiss pastor who kept a school near Liverpool: Henry had completed his education in Zurich, where he became thoroughly fluent in German, while his brothers John and Joseph were sent out to find work as clerks in Liverpool.

Mond's sulphur recovery process was successful at Hutchinson's works, although the nitric acid one failed, and Hutchinson agreed to put it into large-scale operation. The two men disagreed over royalty payments, however, and Mond returned to work in Germany and Holland. Then Hutchinson died and was succeeded as head of the business by Henry Brunner, who resolved the royalty dispute and installed machinery to work the Mond process. In 1867, after marrying Frida, Mond came to settle near Widnes, where in October 1868 Frida had their second son, Alfred, the future Lord Melchett. Mond's process became widely accepted within the industry and in May 1869 he told the River Pollution Committee that his system, if adopted throughout Britain, would save almost a quarter of a million pounds a year on imports of sulphur from Sicily.

Anticipating a favourable report from the committee, Mond and his Hutchinson partners proposed forming a company from among the alkali manufacturers to take over the management of his patents. Five companies were by this time using his sulphur recovery process, but the proposal received only a lukewarm response from the industry. Mond made up his mind to start up in business on his own account. John Brunner, then Hutchinson's office manager, suggested they set up together. With industrial output recovering in Europe after the Franco-Prussian war, and a consequent rise in demand for soda products, it was an auspicious time. The only question was, which side of the business offered the best opportunities? Mond's fertile mind had been busy with other projects than sulphur recovery. In 1870 he patented a method of chlorine manufacture. He debated with his partner whether to manufacture fertilizers or ammonium sulphate from gasworks liquor. Ideas flew back and forth between them. At this point Mond heard about a revolutionary alternative to the Leblanc soda process which had been developed by a family firm called Solvay near Charleroi in Belgium. Early in 1872 he travelled to Belgium to see it at work, and immediately perceived that this was the system of the future. The Solvay process was far cleaner, simpler and more efficient than Leblanc's. Brine-soaked ammonia was carbonated with carbon dioxide in towers eighty feet high; this resulted in sodium bicarbonate which was heated to produce soda ash. The process manufactured larger and purer amounts of soda ash with less waste and no poisonous byproducts.

Mond proposed a licensing agreement with the Solvays, together with a free exchange of research and development; a remarkable example of international cooperation for its time. Ernest Solvay and his partners agreed, and Mond promised to have a plant in production in England within two years, after which time Solvay would be free to negotiate any agreements he wanted with other English manufacturers. Two years, Mond calculated, would be enough to give him and

Brunner a lead in exploiting the new ammonia soda process, which had already shown its paces in the Solvay balance sheet: the company had just declared a dividend of 100 per cent.

Brunner, Mond in Production

To get under way, Mond and Brunner needed £10,000 capital, of which Mond was able to find only £1,000, though he pledged his patents as collateral. Brunner raised another £4,000 on his own account and by November 1872 had persuaded a Manchester civil engineer named Charles Holland to put up the balance of £5,000 at five per cent, plus the right to a third of the new company's profits up to a maximum of twenty-five per cent of his capital.

Looking for a suitable site, the partners went on long country walks around Northwich – then, as now, the centre of the Cheshire salt industry. They needed a source of brine which could be pumped straight into the works, Solvay's process making it unnecessary to convert it first to solid salt. Limestone supplies were nearby in Derbyshire, while railway links to Liverpool and the Midlands provided easy access for supplies of the principal raw material, ammonia. In March 1873 they found what they were looking for, an estate belonging to the distinguished diplomat Lord Stanley at Winnington, with a part-Tudor, part-Georgian mansion from whose windows they could see the Cheshire salt-pans smoking. The house, Winnington Hall, had not been lived in by the Stanley family for about twenty years. It had most recently been used as a girls' school at which Sir Charles Hallé had given recitals and John Ruskin had lectured on art. The whole 627-acre estate, including a railway siding, was bought for £16,108 and, since the land was already mortgaged for £12,000, the partners had ready liquidity. By May, Mond had established an 'office' in the Angel Hotel at Northwich, and on 12 May he sent his first letter on notepaper headed Brunner, Mond & Co., Manufacturers of Carbonate of Soda (Pure Soda Ash), Winnington Park, Northwich.

Mond had at first wanted to demolish Winnington Hall, but John Brunner, unable to find suitable accommodation locally for his large family, persuaded his partner that if repairs were done to the house they could both live comfortably in it. Their first office was the old harness-room, where they sat on opposite sides of a double desk; later, a cowshed was converted to a clerks' office and the loft above it pressed into service as a drawing-office. The partners hoped to start production by September, while the price of soda remained high, but Mond had trouble with suppliers and also with the local workmen, who were hostile to the idea of another soda works fouling the surrounding farmland, and who distrusted this guttural foreigner with his rough black beard, outlandish clothes, dictatorial ways and sudden outbursts

Winnington Hall, Cheshire, Lord Stanley's country estate where John Tomlinson Brunner and Ludwig Mond founded their soda-ash business in 1873. The house later became an elite ICI managers' club.

of temper. Neighbouring landowners, too, were preparing to use the new Alkali Act to prosecute if they got the chance.

On top of all this, there were troubles with the manufacturing process itself, not yet perfected by the Solvays. 'Everything that could break down did break down,' John Brunner recalled in later years, 'and everything that could burst did burst.' Boilers exploded and one man died of burns. Mond never forgot the experience and for years afterwards refused to allow pressures of more than 100 pounds in his works, or to have steel pipes of more than two inches in diameter, restrictions which hampered a great deal of modernization.

Brunner, Mond were in full production by the middle of 1874, selling their first soda ash at a loss of £5 a ton. They found it difficult at first to get contracts because customers saw no reason to change from the old Leblanc product with all its impurities: they were simply accustomed to buying the stuff by the bucket, regardless of its purity. To persuade them, Mond, who was a brilliant salesman, demonstrated the economy of the purer product by giving away smaller buckets. In their first two years Brunner and Mond concentrated on the American market, but this was unfortunately overstocked and demand did not pick up until new factors influenced buying habits, including a change in American taste from bitter beer to lager, thus bringing an increased demand for bicarbonate of soda.

Money began to run short. Mond resorted to the only device left to him, selling his sulphur patents for the whole of France. By 1876,

Merseyside murk in the 1890s: Widnes in Lancashire, one of the first chemical towns. 'From the chimneys of the soap and soda works there belched a thick smoke day and night, heavy with hydrochloric acid,' wrote Ludwig Mond's biographer. Mond devised a process to recover sulphur and cut down on pollution.

however, the partners had made enough to pay off most of their debts; they celebrated by increasing the money they drew each week as salary from £10 to £30. They also began to consider the possibility, always close to Mond's heart, of enlarging their range by finding new methods of reclaiming waste materials, methods which would lead in the 1880s and 1890s to important new spin-off businesses.

The two families, while living in close proximity in those early years, did not enjoy an intimate relationship. John Brunner's wife died in 1874, leaving him with six young children, and he remarried soon afterwards a woman of whom Frida Mond severely disapproved. Frida maintained a strictly German household, importing Froebel toys for the children, insisting that only German be spoken at home and hiring a governess from Bremen. Ludwig Mond was kindly but demanding with his children as with his employees, insisting that family meals, for example, be used for self-improvement. Mond's biographer quotes one breakfast exchange: 'May I have some sugar?' 'Yes, if you tell me where it comes from.'

Manufacturing Dynamite

If Brunner, Mond encountered difficulties in setting up an alkali business with its image of industrial pollution, Alfred Nobel endured far worse problems in getting a factory established at all in Britain to manufacture the new dynamite. Not surprisingly, English gunpowder manufacturers rejected the invention out of hand. There was deep public mistrust of nitroglycerin and, in 1869, an Act of Parliament forbade the manufacture, import, sale or transport within Britain of any substances containing it.

One of Nobel's most implacable opponents was Professor Frederick Abel, chief chemist to the War Office, whose work on stabilizing guncotton had helped to make it Britain's most widely used explosive. Abel was also, as it happened, the government's senior adviser on the passage of the Nitroglycerin Bill. Personal demonstrations by Nobel before a group of eminent scientists eventually persuaded the government to modify the bill, but Nobel was still unable to establish a manufacturing plant in England. So he turned to Scotland, where he found financiers and mine-owners both willing to back the new product. After searching for a suitably remote spot, yet close to river and railway links, he found it at Ardeer, on the Firth of Clyde near Ardrossan. The place was a sandy heath with 'hardly enough nourishment for a rabbit', as he remarked. In 1871 the British Dynamite Co. was registered with its headquarters in Glasgow and a share capital of £24,000. At the opening of the factory, Nobel said: 'Well, gentlemen, I have given you a company that is bound to succeed even if there is the grossest mismanagement on the part of the directors.'

By the 1880s both Nobel's company and that founded by Brunner and Mond were prospering. The Ardeer plant covered 850 acres and produced 1,000 tons of dynamite and 1,400 tons of nitroglycerin each year. It had its own port at the mouth of the river Garnock for the transport of raw materials and manufactures, and a private railway line linking up with two main-line services to the south, the Glasgow and South-Western Railway and the Caledonia Railway. Factories for the manufacture of related products such as sulphuric acid, fulminate of mercury and detonators were established in 1877 and 1880. Safety measures were exemplary for the time and explosions rare, though there was a tragedy in 1872 when Nobel's general manager, John Downie, blew himself up through a careless accident while destroying a cargo of faulty dynamite on the quayside at Crookhaven in Ireland.

Nobel remained a restless and lonely individual who, like Mond, preferred the excitement of research to the daily slog of business management. The task of running his burgeoning companies was made more difficult by the hostility his products tended to engender wherever they were manufactured. He now lived mostly in Paris, looking, as

Left, Sir John Brunner, Ludwig Mond's partner, who was known in Parliament as 'the Chemical Croesus'. Right, Sir Harry McGowan and Sir Alfred Mond whose 'Aquitania Agreement' founded ICI. Mond became the first chairman.

he said in the last year of his life, like 'a civilized monkey'; a slender stooping figure with unkempt beard and moustache, jutting eyebrows and large, protruding ears. It was in Paris, in the small but well-equipped laboratory of his elegant mansion on Avenue Malakoff near the Etoile that he made the discovery which was to secure the fortunes of the Nobel business around the world.

He had been searching for an explosive that would have the blasting force of pure nitroglycerin with the handling qualities of dynamite. He thought one way to do it would be through a mixture of nitro and gun-cotton, but ordinary gun-cotton did not have the necessary absorptive qualities. One day, Nobel happened to cut his finger in the laboratory. He applied a collodion solution to the wound and as it throbbed throughout a wakeful night, the thought occurred to him that a preparation similar to collodion – nitrocellulose with a lower degree of nitration – might work in absorbing the nitroglycerin. At four in the morning he went down to his lab and by the time his assistant arrived for work he had made the gelatinous compound he was looking for.

Blasting gelatin, which was marketed under various names including Nobel's Extra Dynamite, Saxonite and Gelignite, was the ideal explosive. It was actually more powerful than pure nitroglycerin but was virtually insensitive to shock and strongly resistant to moisture, thus enabling it to be used for underwater blasting. It could be produced

Early explosives manufacture at Nobel's works in Ardeer, southwest Scotland. A workman of the 1890s supervises the volatile process of nitrating glycerin.

relatively cheaply. For decades it remained the most successful explosive in the world, though like dynamite it ran up against Britain's tough explosives laws and it was not until 1884 that Ardeer received its full manufacturing licence. By that time, even Nobel's old adversary Frederick Abel had to concede that blasting gelatin was 'in every respect the most perfect explosive known'. It was only a fleeting gesture by Abel, however; in the 1890s the two were to be embroiled in a bitter legal conflict over patents.

The Boom in Explosives

A new company, Nobel's Explosives Co. Ltd, was formed to operate the patent for blasting gelatin and to take over the entire assets of the British Dynamite Co. The latter's stock had multiplied tenfold during the four years of its existence, giving Nobel's Explosives a share capital of £240,000. The business rapidly grew to a point where it controlled the British market for explosives and had a huge export trade outside Europe, chiefly in South Africa, Australia, East Asia and South America, where subsidiaries were set up. By the end of the 1890s, Ardeer was producing around 5,000 tons a year, roughly a tenth of the world's consumption of explosives.

From 1873 to 1885 Nobel was trying to organize some semblance of cooperation between his often conflicting subsidiaries. In France all his patents and factories operated from 1875 under one umbrella company, the Société Générale pour la Fabrication de la Dynamite et des Produits Chimiques. In Germany, his factories competed fiercely among themselves. Nobel disliked and distrusted Germans and had no faith in their willingness to cooperate on an international basis beyond simple price agreements. 'It will be difficult, I fear, to lower the pretensions of our German friends', he wrote to the chairman of his Glasgow firm. 'Bismarck has made them so great that they cannot afford to be moderate.' Nevertheless, in 1886 – about the time that John D. Rockefeller in the United States was bringing together all his oil interests as the Standard Oil Co. – Nobel succeeded in forming the Anglo-German Trust. This was a holding company – a novelty at the time – which brought together the Glasgow firm, two companies in Hamburg, one in Cologne and one in Dresden, along with their subsidiaries. For a quarter of a century, until the First World War, the trust operated as a mutually profitable cartel. In 1915, with its companies supplying two countries at war with each other, it was broken up and its assets divided among the original shareholders, the Glasgow company reverting to the name of Nobel's Explosives Co.

Alfred Nobel's last big invention, in 1887, and the one that led to his patent war with Abel, the famous 'cordite case', was ballistite, a virtually smokeless blasting powder made of equal parts of nitroglycerin and nitrocellulose, with the addition of ten per cent camphor. The technology of weaponry in the late nineteenth century was far outstripping that of propellants, and great rewards awaited the inventor who could match the new guns with a better product than gunpowder, which was smoky, fouled the barrels and was ruined by water. Nobel's ballistite had a greater force than black gunpowder, left no deposit, did not deteriorate with keeping and was cheap to make. Frederick Abel at this time was on a British government commission appointed in 1888 to investigate new discoveries in explosives, particularly those which might have military potential, and to report to the War Office on possible improvements.

Nobel was asked by the commission to give confidential details of his invention and did so, supplying samples for their inspection. His formula was criticized: camphor was too volatile, said the commission. But Abel, the government chemist, was already trying to improve on Nobel's formula, along with a colleague, Professor James Dewar, FRS, a distinguished Cambridge scientist noted for his work on the liquefaction of gases (and incidentally a friend of Ludwig Mond's). The Abel/Dewar compound consisted of fifty-eight per cent nitroglycerin, thirty-seven percent nitrocellulose or gun-cotton and five per cent vaseline, made into a jelly by the addition of acetone. The resulting mass was pressed out in cords and given the name 'cordite', under which it was patented in England and several other countries. The English patent was made over to the government and Abel and Dewar secured sole rights for cordite to supply the British armed forces. It was not until Nobel's Explosives offered the War Office its own smokeless powder based on the ballistite patent that the affair came to light.

Against Nobel's personal wishes, the company insisted on fighting the case through the courts. Proceedings stretched from 1892 to 1895, going to the Court of Appeal and finally to the House of Lords. Nobel's lost, and were ordered to pay costs of £28,000. The fatal flaw turned out to be a detail in the wording of the ballistite patent, which stipulated 'nitrocellulose of the well-known soluble kind'. The court held that this did not cover what had been considered 'insoluble' nitrocellulose at the time of Nobel's patent, though later scientific knowledge would establish that solubility in nitrocellulose varies with its molecular size and nitrogen content.

The case caused a sensation with the press, and was vigorously debated, with the scientific establishment on the whole lining up behind Nobel and the political and military authorities backing Abel and Dewar. Nobel received some moral satisfaction during the final hearing when Lord Justice Kay said while he had been forced on formal legal grounds to agree with his two colleagues in overruling Nobel's case, he could not but sympathize with the holder of the original patent. 'It is quite obvious that a dwarf who has been allowed to climb up on the back of a giant can see farther than the giant himself . . . Mr Nobel made a great invention . . . a really great innovation, and then two clever chemists got hold of his specifications for the patent, read them carefully, and after that, with the aid of their own thorough knowledge of chemistry, discovered that they could use practically the same substances with a difference as to one of them, and produce the same results one by one.'

Nobel felt wronged and betrayed by the verdict, and it had an effect on his health, which was always precarious and plagued by 'nitro' headaches and chronic bronchial troubles. As his assistant and later biographer, Ragnar Sohlman, said: 'It was not so much the loss of money that aroused his resentment as what he took to be the unwarrantable setting aside of his achievement as an inventor, to which he was always sensitive.' Both ballistite and cordite found their own markets in different countries, and Nobel's British company found it necessary to manufacture cordite in its own interest, for which it paid Nobel a royalty equivalent to half that paid for ballistite. It was some recognition of his contribution.

Nobel died in 1896, still a bachelor although he had a final sad obsession with a woman twenty-three years his junior who milked him of affection and money before having a child by a young Hungarian army officer whom she later married. Nobel's will set up the famous Nobel Foundation with its prizes for achievement in the arts, sciences and the pursuit of peace. The fortune he left, the equivalent of £2 million sterling, was by the standards of the time immense. Yet to this lonely, brilliant, introspective man it probably gave most satisfaction that his estate included 355 patents.

The Mond Nickel Process

In 1881, Ludwig Mond, having floated his company with a capital of £600,000, was also longing to return to his first love, research. He had been complaining that 'we are no longer making chemicals, we are making money'. Now he set himself to tackle two main problems: to find a cheaper and more certain supply of ammonia than they were able to obtain from the Liverpool gasworks, and to extract a use for the chlorine which was either run off into the river or left as solid waste from the Solvay product.

There were three possible sources of ammonia. It could be distilled from bones and waste leather, hence its old folk name of 'hartshorn'; it could be distilled from coal; or it could be extracted from the air by 'fixing' the nitrogen. This proved too difficult, requiring temperatures as high as 1400°C and glass retorts of a strength to withstand them: and it was not until 1908 that the problem was cracked by the Germans Haber and Bosch. The coal method, however, led on to other important discoveries. Burning low-grade coal in a mixture of air and steam, as well as yielding ammonia, produced a valuable, hydrogen-rich gas which could be 'scrubbed' and marketed as a source of heating power, or as a smokeless fuel for gas-powered engines. 'Mond Gas' was patented and licensed and out of it grew the Power Gas Corporation which supplied a multitude of factories and furnaces in the Black Country. Mond dreamed of his clean gas abolishing pollution in the heavily smoke-laden area, and of turning the Black Country green again, but it was never used widely enough to accomplish that.

Mond's attempts to make a bleaching powder out of chlorine waste were carried out alongside experiments to develop the Victorian dream of a gas battery that would convert gas directly into electricity without intermediate engines or generators. Out of work on this came Mond's last major discovery, the Mond nickel process of 1897, on which was founded a whole new international business. The discovery, achieved while he was trying to prevent the decomposition of nickel valves by ammonium chloride, was a completely new phenomenon in science; that a gas (carbon monoxide) and a metal (nickel) could combine to form a new gaseous compound. This was tetracarbonyl, a colourless liquid that boils at 43°C and solidifies at 25°C, forming needle-like crystals.

The discovery of nickel carbonyl took time to achieve a successful commercial application, but its industrial significance was twofold: it acted as a toughening agent for steel (Americans used it for armour-plating and to replace heavy copper coinage), and it was a highly effective way of separating nickel from ores containing small amounts of precious metals lost by other methods of recovery. In Ontario, which had great deposits of nickel, the ore also contained copper sulphate and a proportion of metal such as gold, platinum, silver and iridium. The Mond process isolated the precious metals and also obtained nickel of 99.9 per cent purity.

By the time the Mond Nickel Company, later merged with the International Nickel Company of Canada, was formed in 1900, the Brunner half of Brunner, Mond had largely withdrawn from the day-to-day running of the business in his pursuit of public life, though he was to remain chairman until 1918, nine years after Ludwig Mond's death. John Brunner had entered Parliament in 1885 as Liberal MP for Northwich, remaining a conscientious backbencher for the next twenty-five years, and was made a baronet in 1894. In the last decade of the nineteenth century, both Brunner and Mond were rich and influential public figures. On his entry into Parliament, Brunner had been dubbed the 'Chemical Croesus', while Mond became a patron of the arts in England and Italy. He filled his St John's Wood mansion with Italian Old Masters and bought the Palazzo Zucchari in Rome, near the Spanish Steps, to house another large collection of works of art.

Alfred Mond, Ludwig's second son, married Violet Goetze in 1892, when he was training to be a lawyer. He became a director of the family firm in 1894 but had no desire to make a career of it. On witnessing his father's discovery of nickel carbonyl in the laboratory in 1897, however, he became excited by the possibilities of science harnessed to business, and plunged with enthusiasm into building up the Mond Nickel Co., of which he was made chairman, and into expanding its activities into mining and refining in Canada. His legal abilities, a natural flair for management and a driving intellectual curiosity would eventually make him an outstanding business strategist, but politics remained for him, as for Brunner, the main focus of his life. He entered Parliament in the Liberal landslide of 1906, gaining Chester for the Liberals: it had been a Conservative stronghold for twenty years.

Unlike some other politicians of German extraction, Mond did not suffer personally or professionally during the First World War, though a neighbour of his in Lowndes Square was deeply suspicious of his habit of keeping carrier pigeons in his garden. He rose to become First Commissioner of Works in the wartime coalition under Lloyd George and Minister of Health in 1921–2 before returning to Brunner, Mond as chairman in 1926 after the bruising Lever lawsuit and the resignation of Roscoe Brunner.

The characters of Sir John Brunner and Ludwig Mond had a formative influence on the company they founded, and indirectly but powerfully helped to shape the corporate ethos of Imperial Chemical Industries. Mond's passion for laboratory research and his incessant seeking after new markets that could be created out of scientific discovery gave Brunner, Mond an edge of innovation while Brunner's radical instincts and non-conformist background moulded the company's reputation as a progressive employer in the tradition of the Rowntrees, Cadburys, Wedgwoods and Courtaulds. Brunner, Mond brought to ICI several pioneering concepts in industrial relations. It was the first company to introduce (in 1884) a week's holiday with pay for every worker who had completed a set number of shifts in the year. The holiday week's pay was subsequently doubled to enable workers to go away for a proper break, and at a time of their own choosing, not when it suited the employer. Sir John Brunner also introduced the idea of an industrial 'parliament' at which workers had a chance to question the boss in person; a tradition that was enshrined in ICI from the beginning. In Victorian Britain, such an idea smacked of an invitation to anarchy, if not outright subversion or insubordination. There are even now not many companies that practise it in the Britain of the 1990s.

3

IMPERIAL HORIZONS

ICI began as a business enterprise on 1 January 1927 with 33,000 employees working in five main industrial areas – alkali products, metals, explosives, dyestuffs and general chemicals including chlorine, acids and synthetic ammonia, the foundation of what was anticipated to be a huge fertilizer business. It was one of the largest industrial enterprises of the day, and Britain's biggest exporter of alkali. Its horizons seemed limitless and were based on the confident assumption that the British Empire would provide a vast captive market for nitrogenous fertilizers, in which the group had its biggest single stake, the £20 million complex at Billingham put up by Brunner, Mond. When the Registrar of Joint Stock Companies objected to the use of the word 'Imperial' in the company's title, Mond and McGowan despatched an outraged letter to the President of the Board of Trade, Sir Philip Cunliffe-Lister, which succeeded in overruling the Registrar. 'We would like to state,' they wrote, 'that the name was chosen after the most careful consideration and study, and for very special reasons . . . We are "Imperial" in aspect and "Imperial" in name . . .' No other combination of business activities, they argued, would ever be so important to the Empire. 'The developments which this Company has in view, we may confidentially inform you, will be of enormous value, both from the point of view of national defence and of the economic position of the Empire . . .'

To Wendell Swint, the European manager of du Pont, Sir Harry McGowan spelled out the new company's aims even more grandly. A note by Swint recorded in December 1926: 'Sir Harry explained that the formation of ICI is only the first step in a comprehensive scheme which he has in mind to rationalize the chemical manufacture of the world', adding that this envisaged working arrangements between the three great chemical powers: IG Farben, ICI and du Pont and Allied Chemical in the USA. IG remained the force to be neutralized, with its enormous resources, the scale of its business operations and its research (it never employed fewer than 1,000 chemists) and the overwhelming reputation of German chemical superiority. (Even after the defeat of the Nazis, American commanders in Germany would describe the IG

Trademarks of the four companies merged to form ICI: the Nobel motif of wavy lines survives in ICI's corporate logo today.

The first board meeting in 1927, with McGowan and Mond seated front centre.

as the most powerful combine in Europe.) In 1926, it produced all Germany's magnesium, nickel and synthetic rubber and nearly all its dyestuffs; the bulk of its nitrogen and synthetic petrol; half its pharmaceuticals and more than half its photographic supplies. It was pre-eminent in explosives as well, and enjoyed close relations with the government.

Unlike ICI, IG concentrated on such innovative lines of chemistry as plastics, oil from coal, solvents, resins and insecticides rather than on the old heavy commodities, such as soda ash and chlorine. Its trend of development was already foreshadowing the 1950s. It never spent less than £2.75 million a year on research even in 1932, the pit of the depression, whereas ICI never spent much more than £1 million at the best of times, and in 1932 spent only just above half that. Exports represented well over a third of IG's turnover, and it had strong overseas links in its manufacturing subsidiaries and associates. In no other industry had Germany been able to regroup its resources so formidably within seven years of total military defeat in 1918; a phenomenon which would repeat itself after 1945 when IG Farben, broken up by the Allies, quickly recovered strength in the shape of its 'big three' constituent companies, Bayer, Hoechst and BASF.

As for the third great chemical power in the world, the United States, ICI had inherited alliances with both Allied Chemical and Dye Corporation and du Pont from Brunner, Mond and Nobel respectively. Through Brunner's, the new company had a substantial stake in Allied, which partnered it on the alkali side: Nobel Industries had an agreement on patents and processes with du Pont, which, like IG Farben, based its product strategy on scientific research and had little interest in bulk chemicals producing a low margin of profit.

For a while, the division of background interests persisted between Alfred Mond, who regarded Allied as the more important American partner and who still believed in trying for a triple alliance with ICI, Allied and IG, and his board colleague McGowan, who was determined that the old Nobel–du Pont relationship should not be jeopardized by the formation of ICI. In the end, negotiations with the Germans, chiefly over technology exchange in oil from coal and dyestuffs, came to nothing when IG put forward a group of unacceptable demands including restriction of British dyestuffs activities to the UK alone. Du Pont became the principal partner in foreign policy. Under an extended Patents and Processes Agreement, the two companies undertook to exchange technical information on a long list of products and the world was divided between them into 'exclusive licence territories'. Du Pont reigned in the Americas, excluding Canada, and ICI retained the Empire markets, again excluding Canada, which had its own jointly owned company, Canadian Industries Ltd. The licensing system effectively cut out competition between du Pont and ICI in each other's territories and would eventually provoke the mammoth US *v.* du Pont and ICI anti-trust suit of 1944. In the 1920s and 1930s, however, such agreements seemed perfectly normal. It was, as ICI's historian observed, 'a cartel-maker's world'.

Magnificence on Millbank

At home, ICI's grand purposes were soon suitably enshrined in a monumental headquarters building on Millbank, facing the Thames near the Houses of Parliament. In pre-Roman times, before London was a city, the site had been part of a trade route to and from Europe crossing the Thames at its lowest fordable point. The spot had been picked out as the four chief executives of ICI's founding companies sat in their small room over nearby Smith Square planning the shape of the new company. Within two weeks of ICI's registration as a company on 7 December 1926, the excavators were moving in to prepare the foundations.

The new building, constructed of British steel, English stone and Scottish granite, went up faster than any other structure of its size in Britain: it was built by John Mowlem in just over two years, and the first five floors were occupied by staff in August 1928. It was the first building in the world to be lit by 'artificial daylight' provided by tungsten lamps in pale-blue globes (an innovation which did not succeed

ICI's headquarters on Millbank was a monument of art deco in 1928. Here craftsmen work on carvings in the unfinished building.

The chairman's office in 1928. It remained in use, unchanged except for the furnishings, until 1985.

and was replaced in 1933); it also had its own artesian wells which continued to supply water until the 1950s, and an efficient dust-extracting system connected to 180 plug-in points throughout the building. All the metal fittings were of a copper and nickel alloy called 'Silveroid', made by the Mond Nickel Company. The same material was used to coat the magnificent twenty-foot-high main doors of Imperial Chemical House, made of cast bronze and modelled with panels in bas-relief illustrating the application of science to industry.

Some of the most distinguished men of their day were to sit in ICI's imposing circular boardroom on the eighth floor, preserved today as a monument to art-deco style, although most of the building's interior was entirely remodelled in the late 1980s. They included, at various times, Lord Birkenhead, formerly the famous advocate F.E. Smith; Sir John Anderson, who was to play an important part in the company's secret wartime role in developing the atom bomb (and give his name to an air-raid shelter); and the Marquess of Reading, the former Rufus Isaacs, who had been Lord Chief Justice from 1913 to 1921 and Viceroy of India from 1921 to 1926. Isaacs' son had married Alfred Mond's daughter Eva in 1914.

From the first, the company appeared to be regarded more as a public service than a powerful new enterprise – 'almost a branch of the Constitution', as Dr Reader expressed it. Mond's high-flown rhetoric at the company's launch on 30 November 1926 did not seem out of keeping: 'We are on trial before the eyes of the entire world, and especially the eyes of our fellow citizens and of the Empire. We are not merely a body of people carrying on industry in order to make dividends, we are much more: we are the object of universal envy, admiration and criticism, and the capacity of British industrialists, British commercialists and British technicians will be judged by the entire world from the success we make of this merger.' McGowan injected a note of Scottish practicality, but his message was the same: 'Primarily of course the duties of a Board of Directors are to make dividends for their shareholders, but in forming this combine we are doing something for the Empire.'

'Every Man a Capitalist'

In labour relations, the new company started with the gleaming reputation of Brunner, Mond's tradition of 'co-workers in industry', and the works councils which gave employees direct access to their managers; but, above all, with the concept of profit-sharing, which for Mond lay at the heart of the co-partnership idea. 'The best answer to socialism is to make every man a capitalist,' he wrote in 1927. In pursuit of this he introduced the ICI Workers' Shareholding Scheme, which enabled employees to buy the company's ordinary shares at 2s. 6d. below the market price, and to pay by instalments for the shares. Free shares were also granted, on a sliding scale linked to pay. 'You cannot make the world more prosperous by making the rich poorer,' he remarked on introducing the scheme, which was open to anyone earning less than £2,000 a year. 'What you want to do is to make the poor richer.'

Imperial Chemical House was not yet finished when Mond, by this time Lord Melchett (he was ennobled in May 1928), convened the first meeting of ICI's Central Works Council there on 19 April 1929. Eight hundred workers' representatives from all the company's factories were brought to London by special train and charabanc to meet the directors. Melchett told them: 'I look on you as my friends and partners, without whom I could do nothing and without whom the shareholders would never see any dividends.' That evening, he took all eight hundred to see the current variety show at the London Coliseum, and at the end of it they sang and cheered him.

ICI's labour policy, progressive though it was in many respects, was founded on linking the loyalty of workers directly to management. The unions, already weakened and demoralized by the General Strike and the long-drawn-out coal strike which ended in bitter defeat for the miners, could not be expected to welcome this, nor did they. Ernest Bevin fiercely opposed the company's 'staff grade' scheme by which hourly paid workers with five years' service might gain promotion to a weekly wage and greater security – but at the discretion of the directors. Bevin claimed this would 'drive a wedge between the work-men'; he wanted the unions to be recognized as the proper hinge between the workforce and the board. Nor did the unions approve of the layered system of ICI works councils, which had consultative rights with management on every issue except the hard-core, essential ones of wages, hours and conditions of employment.

Union hostility remained unabated towards ICI until 1947, when the works councils were recognized in return for a negotiating pro-cedure with shop stewards having their say on pay and conditions. Sixty-seven years on from Melchett's ringing declarations of co-partnership, twice-yearly 'ICI parliaments' are held at Harrogate, one for weekly paid earners and one for salaried staff, and many issues are thrashed out informally over drinks and dinner with the line managers before the question-time sessions with the board of directors. The system has generally stood the test of time well. From 1926 to 1993, the company had never been shut down by a total strike and, as one long-serving chlorine worker said on a BBC television documentary about the chemical industry, 'In all my years with the ICI, I've never known a dispute that couldn't be settled by a works council.'

A Sense of Place

'The ICI', as it was familiarly known, became the dominating presence in a score of chemical towns or suburbs where previously Brunner, Mond, Nobel, United Alkali or British Dyestuffs had been the major employer – Winnington, Runcorn, Widnes, Billingham, Northwich, Stockton, Ardeer, Blackley. The functions of the new ICI groups re-mained broadly rooted in those places which had been associated with them under the old individual companies. Alkali Group was based at Winnington, the original Brunner, Mond headquarters; General Chemicals was at Runcorn; Fertilizers at Billingham; Dyestuffs at Blackley and Explosives at Ardeer, the site chosen by Alfred Nobel for his first British works in 1871. Each had its distinctive character within the corporate ethos, one fostered particularly in and by the managers' clubs like Winnington Hall and Billingham's Norton Hall.

Winnington Hall represented something uniquely collegiate in Brit-ish industry. Housed in the country mansion that had once belonged to Lord Stanley of Alderley, and which John Brunner and Ludwig Mond had been forced to buy with the land they wanted for their first Solvay works, it had an Oxbridge and public-school atmosphere where dress and manners were informal and 'conviviality consorted genially with high ability', as Reader described it. Norton Hall at Billingham, Brunner, Mond's showpiece of the early 1920s, was modelled along similar lines; Peter King, one of ICI's research directors in the 1970s, recalled how many inventive ideas came out of sessions in the bar at

THE BRIDGE

'The Bridge': the cover of ICI's first house journal in 1928 symbolized the company's progressive ideas for linking workers and management, a philosophy inherited from Brunner, Mond.

Norton Hall. The easy-going common-room atmosphere contrasted with the stiffer formality of Dyestuffs and General Chemicals ('Gen. Chem.'), where the background of the scientists tended to be grammar school and provincial university and men wore black coats and butterfly collars and addressed each other as 'Doctor' or 'Mister' even if they had been colleagues for thirty years.

Recruiting the Best

From the beginnings of ICI, Alfred Mond was determined to maintain his father's philosophy of attracting the best scientific talent of the day to work on industrial problems. That was the German style and the only way, Mond believed, in which to match or outclass the technological achievements of IG Farben. Brunner, Mond had its own well-established head-hunting system master-minded by Major Francis Freeth, the man who had conceived the daring raid on BASF's nitrogen secrets in 1919, and this was continued in the early months of ICI. Freeth, a brilliant if erratic character, a destructively heavy drinker until he forced himself into total abstention in his fifties, ran an idiosyncratic method of talent-scouting based on personal contacts at Oxford and his own judgment of ability. He had failures, naturally, but a remarkable record of successes as well, measured by the number of Freeth-picked men who ended up in leading positions in ICI or even rose to be chairman, like Sir Peter Allen.

Freeth recruited for Alkali Group; other groups had their own selectors during the company's first year of existence, after which a central management selection process was devised by Henry Mond, Alfred's son, and P. C. Dickens, a Wykehamist and an Etonian respectively. One scheme which did not survive the depression was to start talent searches in the public schools. ICI hoped to take twenty to thirty boys a year – potential chemists, physicists, engineers or managers – who, after reading the appropriate subjects at university, would be offered posts four years later at salaries of £350 to £400 a year. One laudable object of the scheme was to break down the prejudice against industry in the public schools and older universities – a prejudice which remains solidly ingrained sixty years on. Dickens wanted public school boys and their parents to 'appreciate the possibilities of obtaining good and well-paid work outside the so-called learned professions, which are overcrowded'.

Certainly ICI could offer good pay, some of the highest in British industry in the late 1920s and early 1930s. The chemical industry also had a certain glamour about it at that time, in the way, as one old ICI hand has said, that some of the newer electronic industries had in the 1980s. 'The best chemists and engineers flooded into ICI,' recalled Sir Peter Allen, who was recruited by Freeth from Cambridge in 1928 to work in Alkali Group and who later became involved in the first commercial development of polythene and Terylene on his way to the boardroom. 'Out of the people at Winnington the first two or three years I was there, about eight or nine made the main board. It was surprisingly free and easy, we were all on first-name terms or the Edwardian surname, and people were encouraged to be enterprising.'

Investing in Research

The emphasis on quality went through the organization from scientific brilliance to the equipment on the bench. The discovery of polythene would probably not have happened had Freeth not brought over a glass-blower from Holland who could work to much finer standards than were common in Britain to produce retorts capable of withstanding such high-pressure work with gases. That craftsman 'trained a whole generation throughout ICI,' said Allen. Freeth also imported Dutch mechanics whose skills outshone those of even first-class English fitters. 'They set standards for the laboratories. When we came along with demands for apparatus to contain 2,000 or 3,000 atmospheres, that was unprecedented. Nobody had ever had an apparatus of that pressure before, and the fact that the glass-blower had sealed glass into metal so that it wouldn't blow out, and mechanics who could fine-tune their lathes to give you the clearances you needed for these enormous pressures was a huge advantage then . . .

'Just on polythene, you would find no better experimental engineer than Dermot Manning, for example. Clifford Hunter [another of Allen's colleagues from early polythene days] had one brother who was head of the Shirley Institute in Manchester, another who was assistant to the Astronomer Royal and a third who was a distinguished surgeon. Hunter himself was a Whitworth scholar in engineering from London University. Those were the sort of people we could attract.'

To fertilize the new company with scientific talent, Mond followed another German practice, setting up a Research Council with the universities through which leading academic scientists would be invited to brainstorming sessions with ICI scientists: outsiders who attended were paid fifty guineas plus expenses for every meeting, generous indeed in 1927. The scheme was intended to provide ideas for promising lines of work in ICI laboratories, and one academic member, Professor Robert Robinson, was certainly to be influential in this direction, not least in suggesting the line of research which led to the discovery of polythene and in the early development of pharmaceuticals. Other academics who took part included Professor F. A. Lindemann, later Churchill's chief scientific adviser Lord Cherwell. Continuing the grand tone of purpose that characterized the formation of ICI, Mond explained in his letter of invitation to the visiting professors that 'the object with which Imperial Chemical Industries was organized . . . [is] to place the Chemical Industry of the Empire in a position second to none in the World'.

Within a year, ICI's expenditure on research rose from £221,000 to £350,000, and recruitment of chemists and engineers burgeoned in the spring of 1928. Billingham was to be the main focus for the talent, especially for work on oil from coal, Mond's persisting dream, which he commended to the Research Council in late 1927 as 'by far the most important problem'. The received wisdom of the day was still that the world's oil resources would be virtually played out by the mid-1950s.

By 1930 George Pollitt, the founding manager of Billingham, estimated that research expenditure was running at well over £1.2 million, but he stoutly defended the necessity. For ICI to show a good return on capital, he argued, it was 'necessary that new and temporarily very profitable processes should be discovered and put into operation at regular intervals'. To critics who suggested that market investigation should take place before what would now be called 'blue-sky' research, Pollitt countered: 'The really lucrative processes are likely to be those manufacturing products which are entirely novel, and it would be unfortunate indeed if research . . . were barred because an investigation indicated there would be no market.' The Research Council was axed in 1937 but grants continued to be made for specific purposes, including several thousand pounds over the years 1937–9 as 'grants or salaries paid to German refugees'. These were listed as 'Prestige payments giving only an indirect benefit to ICI'. The refugees were mainly Jewish scientists driven out by Hitler, and it was a project on which the ICI chairman, Lord McGowan, collaborated directly with Lindemann.

Depression and Disaster

The research programme, like everything else, was torpedoed by the depression. But even before the Wall Street crash – indeed, within three years of ICI's formation in such an atmosphere of grand hopes and imperial horizons – everything was going wrong. The success of ICI had been largely predicated on the Brunner, Mond nitrogen plant at Billingham – fruit of the Oppau raid – supplying an ever-increasing demand for fertilizers throughout the Empire. One of the first decisions made by the ICI board was to commit £20 million to Billingham, partly by the sale of Nobel's General Motors shares. Markets of a million tons a year of nitrogenous fertilizers in Britain alone were talked about. But the world market forecasts were wrong. The world already had far too much ammonia plant; it was one of the first industrial status symbols wanted by developing countries, and the expertise of ICI, IG Farben and Allied Chemicals was available in abundance to provide it. The massive staff cuts made by Orlando Weber (the 'Fire

Chief') at Allied had sent dozens of highly qualified engineers onto the world market with ammonia-plant skills to sell. It was no longer the advanced technology everyone had sought in 1919.

Furthermore, market-sharing agreements between ICI and IG Farben had failed to materialize. Meeting after meeting – on a cruise liner in the Mediterranean, in Paris and in London – broke up in disagreement until, early in 1929, with the world market for nitrogen worsening, they did agree each to keep to its own market; ICI in the British Empire and IG in most of Europe, with both organizations pledging not to increase their capacity. In October 1929 the collapse of the money markets in New York multiplied the consequences of the nitrogen over-supply for farm products of all kinds. It was clear that Billingham had been built and extended far in excess of any realistic level of demand. In barely two years, £20 million of investment looked like disappearing up its new factory chimneys.

Indeed, ICI came perilously close to bankruptcy by the end of 1929. Jobs drained away and Lord Melchett wrote to Ernest Solvay, the son of his father's old partner, to ask him to rescue ICI by buying stock in it for Solvay et Cie. In 1931 ICI's profits fell to their lowest ever level, less than £4 million on capital employed of nearly £100 million. Salaries and wages were cut by five per cent across the board, and were agreed without the kind of industrial bloodletting which led, in the case of the pay cuts in the Royal Navy, to the Invergordon Mutiny and Britain's fall from the gold standard. By 1932, six years after its formation, the company had lost ten per cent of its capital employed.

Could the massive investment at Billingham be rescued? The answer, Melchett persisted in believing, could lie in oil from coal. Research at Billingham had always been targeted towards using its resources for the hydrogenation process. It was never a sound commercial prospect, but Melchett was personally committed to it for reasons connected with his former Welsh mining constituents, and government could be (and was) persuaded that it had both a social and a defence value.

In 1935 the Prime Minister, Ramsay MacDonald, came to open the Billingham petrol plant. As a symbol of regeneration from the dole queue it had the same kind of impact as the restarting of work on Ship 534 – the then-unnamed *Queen Mary* – at John Brown's yard on the Clyde had made in 1934. But ICI's future, and the exciting scientific developments which were to secure it, would come not from heavy chemicals and bulk commodities like fertilizers, soda ash or even oil from coal, but from up to then neglected groups in the company like Dyestuffs and Explosives, where research would really pay off.

Melchett died in 1930, aged only sixty-two, having seen the collapse of the Billingham fertilizer dream and none of his emphasis on research yet bearing fruit. But it was on that foundation that an entirely new kind of chemical industry would develop, built on plastics, man-made fibres, pharmaceuticals and agricultural chemicals. It would require a world war to push that industry into high gear, but the first great discovery – appropriately for the Mond tradition, in a laboratory at Winnington – would not have been possible without the Mond belief in the value of research and men like George Pollitt who protected research programmes even when, as in 1933, they seemed to be leading nowhere in particular.

4

INTO THE AGE OF PLASTICS

The word 'plastic' to describe synthetic substitutes for such natural materials as wood, metal, rubber and leather was not part of everyday speech in the early 1930s. Indeed, it had only been coined in that context in 1927, in an ICI report on the 'Plastic Materials Industry'. When ICI set up its infant Plastics Division in the summer of 1933 its first chief executive, Adrian Hodgkin, having accepted the appointment from Henry Mond, second Lord Melchett, was overheard to murmur to Melchett as he left the boardroom: 'By the way, what are plastics?' 'God knows,' replied Melchett, 'but you might show a little enthusiasm.'

Early Plastics

Plastics of a kind, though not known as such, had been around since 1862, when Sir Alexander Parkes' new material, a form of nitrated cellulose known after its inventor as 'Parkesine', was exhibited for the first time at the International Exhibition in London. Some of the objects made from Parkesine and shown that year can still be seen at the offices of the Plastics and Rubber Institute in London. The better-known 'Celluloid', invented by the American John Wesley Hyatt in 1869, was also a nitro-cellulose compound. Less flammable acetate resins were patented by Cross and Bevan in 1894 and phenol-formaldehyde resins by the Belgian Leo Baekeland in 1909. Under the trade name of 'Bakelite', the latter became familiar objects in the homes of the 1920s, chiefly for small household wares like beakers and trays and, later, casings for early wireless sets. When Sir Peter Allen, who would later play an important role in the development of polythene and become an ICI chairman himself, joined the company in 1928 he had no idea of the huge potential of plastics; they were associated for him with 'rather grubby ashtrays'. 'They had very limited uses and very limiting properties. You couldn't get Bakelite in white or a decent colour, for example. The ureaformaldehydes, which *could* carry colour and in which you could get white wares, were very susceptible to water. If you washed up your plastic saucer a hundred times, it cracked because of water penetration.'

As usual, it was the Germans who were in the vanguard of plastics research. Soon after the war, in 1922, Hermann Staudinger published his findings into the structure of natural rubber, suggesting that it was composed of giant long-chain molecules. With this new understanding, scientists were able to begin developing much more flexible, truly plastic materials. The development of polyamides by W. H. Carothers of du Pont, from which he discovered nylon, had its origins in Staudinger's research. In Britain, however, the 1927 report by ICI's Plastic Materials Committee was still thinking of materials based on nitro-cellulose (which was almost explosive) or formaldehyde and urea, which the Billingham plant was well equipped to provide. 'The Committee', said the report, 'considers the Plastics industry as a whole to be one of great potentialities, using raw materials and processes which belong essentially to the chemical industry of this country, the chief of the raw materials being products of fundamental importance to ICI.'

The market seemed to support the committee's faith. Ugly as Bakelite was, and vulnerable to cracking as was the colourless urea-formaldehyde compound marketed as 'Beetle' by the British Cyanide Company, there was a rising demand for electrical gadgets for the home which could be made of plastic. Cars were made with Bakelite steering wheels and dashboards, and even in the depression new housing estates were going up requiring electric light switches, door knobs, kitchen fittings and a variety of 'fancy goods'. In Britain, celluloid was made by the British Xylonite Co. Ltd, established in 1877. Bakelite was made chiefly by two subsidiaries of the Bakelite Corporation of America, in which ICI had an indirect interest. Several smaller companies were also manufacturing Bakelite and casein formaldehyde products. The ICI plastics committee did not envisage huge growth – perhaps 6,500 tons of saleable products by 1930, worth about £1.4 million. But it wanted ICI to secure its place as a supplier of the raw materials.

ICI first tried to take over British Xylonite but was firmly rebuffed. In 1932 its advances were also rejected by Bakelite Ltd. As third choice it turned its attentions to a firm called Croydon Mouldrite Ltd, a manufacturer of phenol-formaldehyde powders which was controlled by the British Goodrich Rubber Company and was regarded as the most important British competitor to Bakelite. Having acquired a majority stake in this for a modest £33,500, it then set about organizing a Plastics Division (in truth just an executive committee at that stage) to coordinate the research that was going on at Billingham into urea-formaldehyde, at General Chemicals into vinyl resins, at Ardeer into nitrocellulose and at Dyestuffs into phenol-formaldehyde. In 1938, all the strands, including the discovery of methyl-methacrylate ('Perspex'), would be pulled together into a full-blown Plastics Group, but long before that, and quite independently of any conscious interest in the industrial potential of new plastics, one of the key discoveries of the twentieth century was made by accident in a laboratory at Winnington, home of the Alkali Group.

Paving the Way for Discovery

Winnington, where Ludwig Mond had set up his ammonia-soda works in partnership with John Tomlinson Brunner in 1873, was steeped in the Mond philosophy that research paved the way for industrial progress rather than have it serve needs already perceived by the market. In 1889, making his presidential address to the Society of Chemical Industry, Ludwig Mond said: 'The statement is frequently made that "Necessity is the mother of invention". If this has been the case in the past, I think it is no longer so in our days . . . We can now foresee, in most cases, in what direction progress in technology will move, and, in consequence, the inventor is now in advance of the wants of his time. He may even create new wants, to my mind a distinct step in the development of human culture. It can then no longer be stated that "necessity is the mother of invention": but I think it may truly be said that "the steady methodical investigation of natural phenomena is the father of industrial progress".' (In 1958, twenty-five years after the discovery of polythene at Winnington, that final declaration was inscribed on a commemorative plaque in the Winnington Research Department.)

Francis A. Freeth, Winnington's research director from 1921 to 1927, was a committed believer in what is now called 'blue-sky' research, the open-ended pursuit of answers to which the questions had not yet been asked – in terms of industrial application, anyway. He was apt to make flamboyant statements not calculated to endear himself to management. 'What are they doing,' he inquired of the Brunner, Mond directors in the early 1920s, 'examining last month's costs with a microscope when they should be surveying the horizon with a telescope?' But Freeth's free-wheeling and often eccentric style was based on meticulous, practical grounding. During the First World War, when the Allies had not yet got the German atmospheric nitrogen process, Freeth contributed vitally to the production of ammonium nitrate for high explosives, using his knowledge of the 'phase rule' – methodical investigation of natural phenomena by tediously repeated analyses and calculations. Between 1919 and 1922, Freeth spent time at the University of Leyden in Holland, the home of one of Europe's finest physical laboratories, to study how their experimental techniques were being applied to liquid gas systems at high pressure and low temperatures. He imported one of Leyden's finest glass-blowers and two highly skilled Dutch instrument makers to help prepare the equipment at Winnington for his work on ammonia-soda and oil from coal. The vessels they made for high-pressure work, far in advance of any techniques possible in England at that time, paved the way for the experiments in which a revolutionary new polymer was to be made. 'Without the help of these Hollanders it is by no means certain that polythene would ever have been discovered,' says Peter Allen.

Freeth, who was Brunner, Mond's and later ICI's chief talent scout, recruited two brilliant young chemists from London University, John Swallow and Reginald Gibson, and sent each in turn to study at Leyden. While Gibson was there he sought help on a minor technical problem from Dr Anton Michels, a research assistant in the Thermodynamics Laboratory in Amsterdam who was working on the design of apparatus to make precision measurements at high pressures.

Gibson joined Brunner, Mond as a research chemist in September 1926, shortly before the merger into ICI, and a year later returned to Amsterdam for a working holiday with Michels. The two men became friends and Michels spent that Christmas in Cheshire with Gibson's parents, beginning a lifelong association with ICI. At Michels' request, Gibson was sent to Amsterdam in the autumn of 1928 to work with him for the next three years. The following year two more bright graduates, this time from Oxford, were recruited by ICI, who would play key roles in the polythene story: Michael Willcox Perrin and Eric William Fawcett. Perrin was despatched to Holland to work with Michels, and Fawcett, who had been hired for the oil-from-coal project, was sent to America to work on techniques of petroleum distillation at the American Petroleum Institute in Washington.

Winnington in 1929 was 'a ferment of ideas', according to Tony Willbourn, formerly of ICI's Plastics Division. The number of graduates in its laboratories rose in two years from thirteen to sixty-six, and by mid-1930 there were eighty-two senior research staff on its strength, of whom only twenty-one were connected with the alkali business that formed the core of Winnington's activities. The Physical Chemistry group under Swallow had nineteen on its staff and the Coal-Oil Group Fourteen. A Development Group with fourteen scientists worked on a variety of other projects. 'It was splendid, exciting, but not business-oriented in the sense of being guided by careful assessment of the commercial viability of the potential new products and processes,' wrote Willbourn. Nevertheless, faith in 'blue-sky' research continued at Winnington even as the depression began to bite and budgets were cut back. A report in July 1930 by the research management team at Winnington noted that the Physical Chemistry Group was engaged on 'work involving special techniques . . . in general of a high scientific order and it is out of work of this type that the big discoveries have usually come in the past . . . we submit in our unanimous opinion that this type of work should be extended'. The recommendation was accepted, and work went ahead to see what interesting phenomena could be discovered at high temperatures, under high vacua and at high pressures.

The object was a practical one, sponsored by the Dyestuffs Group which was interested in 'pressure-freezing' as a method of isolating different dyestuffs. A young Cambridge engineer called Dermot Manning was given the task of designing vessels that could be used up to a pressure of 3,000 atmospheres: they became known, from their shape, as 'bombs'. Early in 1931 the high-pressure apparatus, made in Holland under Michels' supervision, was installed in a ground-floor front-room at Winnington known as 'Lab Z'. Gibson was recalled from Amsterdam to start work on the pressure-freezing in March 1931, and Fawcett was brought back from America to work on the coal-oil project, but as the slump worsened this was dropped and he was transferred to Dyestuffs. While in the States, Fawcett had moved on from his petroleum work in Washington to take advantage of the recently signed ICI–du Pont agreement for the exchange of technical information. At the du Pont laboratories in Wilmington, Delaware, he met and became friends with Wallace Hume Carothers, the high-flying Harvard chemist who had been recruited to find new business products and was to discover nylon in 1937. Fawcett's experience with polymers was to play a key part in what was to come.

Michels came over from Amsterdam in the spring of 1931 to talk to Dyestuffs' research committee. He speculated that pressures above 1,000 atmospheres might produce chemical reactions that would not normally happen except in the presence of catalysts. On the research committee was Professor Robert Robinson, then professor of chemistry at Oxford and one of the visiting academics who, it was hoped, would stimulate new and creative lines of work in ICI. He was intrigued by Michels' talk and suggested a number of reactions that might be studied. The first to be chosen happened to be between benzaldehyde and ethylene.

The First Polythene

The pressure-freezing experiments had come to a dead end, so Reginald Gibson began work on Robinson's programme. It was done with the apparatus in open Laboratory Z, and everything had to be assembled by hand: lab assistants needed to be fit and strong to work the pumps and turn the screw press. Joints in the pipework required force and skill to take them apart and re-seal them. Manning invented a self-sealing pressure joint which was later to make practicable the design of large reactors and high-pressure equipment generally. In his revolutionary 3,000 atmospheres 'bomb', the reactants were contained in an inverted test-tube over mercury, and the 'bomb' was then immersed in an oil thermostat heated by a gas burner. The maximum temperature before the oil fumes became unbearable was 180°C. Nothing came of these first experiments, but in January 1932 Michael Perrin and John Swallow drafted a report urging that the high-pressure chemistry work be continued. Perrin was aware that it was an auspicious time to be working in this field: activity was going on at many universities in chemical kinetics and the first attempt was made to apply the principles of quantum mechanics to chemistry. Work being done at Harvard, moreover, had shown that polymerization reactions were 'markedly affected' in the liquid phase up to 20,000 atmospheres, Perrin noted, and this 'inspired some confidence in the hope that there really were novel effects to be discovered'.

The chemical programme at Winnington was begun in February 1932, at a time when research in ICI as a whole was at its nadir. Three years before, in 1929, Freeth had composed a doggerel verse which became part of ICI history as the nitrogen collapse and the onset of depression threatened all Mond's dream of scientific excellence:

> First the test-tube, then the pail,
> then the semi-working scale,
> then the Plant, and then disaster –
> faster, faster, faster, faster!

But the fears were unfounded at Winnington. Gibson and Fawcett began work with mixtures of ethylene and carbon monoxide. These were found to react readily at 160°C and 3,000 atmospheres to give a white, powdery substance which appeared to be a type of polymer. Then one evening toward the end of November, a party of important visitors was being shown round the laboratories after working hours. They had just left the high-pressure lab when they heard a loud bang. As Perrin recalled more than fifty years later, Gibson and Fawcett had been joining up the lead from the compressor to the pipe going into the 'bomb'. 'By mistake they picked up the two coupling parts, one made of a hard, strong steel and the other of a relatively soft steel. That was submerged in the hot oil . . . The party of visitors walked through the lab with that thing cooking away and then the weaker of the two nuts began to give way and came off. Then the thing really went up! If the visitors had been in the lab at the time, there might have been hell to pay . . .' As it was, orders went out that work on gases must only be carried on in one of the new safety cubicles that had been built of brick for the coal-oil hydrogenation work in the Convertor Laboratory. Equipment was accordingly set up on a temporary basis, using a hydraulic test pump to supply the pressurized oil that had originally been intended to test the coal-oil convertors.

On the evening of Friday, 24 March 1933, Gibson and Fawcett set out to react ethylene and benzaldehyde at a temperature of 170°C and a pressure of 1,900 atm. The apparatus was left overnight and on the

Saturday morning was found to have lost some gas. The two chemists raised the pressure back over 1,900 and left it over the weekend. On Monday morning there was virtually no pressure left in the apparatus because a leak had developed in the oil line, and all the benzaldehyde had blown out of the test-tube into the oil. When they dismantled the 'bomb', Fawcett noticed that the tip of the gas-inlet tube, which had been in the reaction space, looked as if it had been dipped in paraffin wax. Gibson wrote in his notebook: 'Waxy solid found in reaction tube.' It was the first recorded observation of polyethylene, an entirely new polymer.

Fawcett carefully scraped off the substance, which weighed about 0.4g. Analysis showed it to be a polymer of ethylene of fairly high molecular weight, similar in some ways to paraffin wax but with a higher melting point and more viscous when melted. Threads could be drawn from the molten material. Attempts to repeat the experiment were only occasionally successful. The first resulted in an explosion so violent that it smashed the gauges. But in May the experiment worked again, producing 'a hard waxy solid containing no oxygen, melting at 113°C and analysing to $(CH_2)_n$ – apparently an ethylene polymer'. After that the pair had variable success: sometimes the 'waxy solid' was formed, but on other occasions they found only a black deposit of carbon, resulting from an explosive decomposition of the ethylene.

Fawcett knew that they had made an important discovery. As Tony Willbourn wrote some twenty years later: 'It was accepted wisdom among the small band of polymer scientists of the time that olefines did not come from high molecular weight polymers, but here they had just such a polymer of ethylene, the archetype of all olefines.' Fawcett pressed hard to be allowed to continue the experiments but any commercial possibilities for the new material seemed remote, so he was put on to other work involving low-pressure distillation, only to find this running into a dead end when most of the work done at Winnington turned out to have been already patented in America.

More than two years were to elapse before the ethylene experiments were resumed in December 1935, with a new team of chemists, the 'bombs' this time safely isolated in brick cubicles. Fawcett meanwhile was nursing a bitter disappointment that his and Gibson's discovery had not been allowed to develop. He was, as a contemporary described him, 'an awkward devil in many ways, not a fitter-in at all'. His determination to make the world of science recognize what had been achieved at Winnington led in September 1935 to what became known in ICI as 'the Fawcett disclosure'. It could easily have led to Britain losing one of its key wartime advantages over Germany in the development of radar, which was to prove the first major use of polythene, as it became known.

The Fawcett Disclosure

The occasion of the Fawcett disclosure could scarcely have been more public in its field. It was the Faraday Society's General Discussion at Cambridge on 'The Phenomena of Polymerization and Condensation', the first major conference on polymer science to be held in the United Kingdom. It was attended by the world's most eminent polymer scientists, including Wallace Carothers of du Pont, then working on his epoch-making discovery of nylon, and, from Hitler's Germany, Hermann Staudinger and Kurt Meyer. Fawcett applied for permission within ICI to give a paper to the conference on the polymerization of ethylene, at that time unknown and, in the words of Sir Peter Allen, 'by some incredible piece of silliness from above was told that he could'. Patents had not yet even been applied for. Luck, however, in the shape of the Germans' invincible conviction that such polymerization was impossible saved Britain's air war from disaster.

Fawcett actually went round to the University Arms Hotel the night before the conference to tell Staudinger about the ICI breakthrough. Staudinger simply did not believe him, and was not interested even in discussing it. At the conference itself, Professor Hermann Mark of Vienna poured scorn on the idea: 'That ethylene does not polymerize may be understood from the fact that the double bond in this molecule is activated only by somewhat high temperatures, at which the chains formed by this activation disintegrate again with remarkable velocity.' Then Fawcett got up and told the assembled scientists that he had in fact made a solid polymer ethylene, with a molecular weight of 4,000 by heating ethylene to 170°C, at a pressure of 1,000 atmospheres. Staudinger refused to comment, even when prompted by the conference chairman. In effect, said Allen, he was denying that Fawcett had done it. 'Of course that created a tremendous stir and the minutes of the meeting didn't record what Fawcett had said. We were lucky in that. It would have ruined our patents.' In 1937, two years after the second batch of experiments had confirmed the process and the patents were safely out, one of IG Farben's top polymer chemists, a Dr Ambros, visited Winnington and was heard to remark: 'I don't know how we missed it.'

The Germans had one other near miss at obtaining the secret of polythene. In late 1938, IG Farben expressed interest in an exchange of technology, specifically on polythene. One of ICI's main board directors, D. R. Lawson, suggested that in return for such an important piece of information ICI should press for details of a whole range of IG's advanced products, including polystyrene, two processes for PVC and the 'Buna' synthetic rubbers. Whether or not IG would have agreed to this – one imagines not – ICI's Groups Central Committee decided the time was not ripe to enter into such discussions with IG.

Thus, almost casually, in a boardroom memorandum, a significant military advantage was preserved for Britain. As Bill Reader, the ICI historian, has remarked: 'There cannot have been many business propositions in history which have broken down with such advantage to Great Britain.'

Progress on Polymerization

It had been Michael Perrin, with his colleague John Swallow, who persuaded ICI's Alkali Group board that work should resume on the promising high-pressure work on polymerization. Their report in May 1935 concluded: 'At least two cases have recently been found of practical value which seem to demand active exploitation, and the whole of this work has been of very considerable scientific interest in an almost unexplored field. It is felt that the work has now reached a stage when an increase of effort is required, directed to obtain practical results from the facts already discovered.' No special significance, however, was attached to the early experiments with benzaldehyde and ethylene: the decision to re-open the research work was made after John Paton, who joined Winnington in 1935, discovered that carbon monoxide reacted with aniline under pressure to give a hitherto unknown solid compound and of high molecular weight. The reaction between ethylene and carbon monoxide under pressure also produced a solid polymer, as Fawcett and Gibson had noticed.

On 20 December 1935 Perrin, Paton, and another chemist called Edmond Williams (later chairman of the Plastics Division) set up an experiment using ethylene alone. The temperature and pressure were the same as in Fawcett and Gibson's first experiment, 170°C and 2,000 atmospheres, but then things developed differently. Pressure started to fall, slowly but steadily. Perrin hoped that it was due to polymerization taking place but his lab assistant, Frank Bebbington, suspected that the ethylene might be escaping through a leaky joint. He periodically raised the pressure back to 2,000. When all the ethylene in the secondary compressor was used up, the 'bomb' was cooled and opened. In Perrin's words, 'it was with no surprise but considerable pleasure that I saw the vessel apparently filled with a white powder.' There were eight and a half grams of it, more than double the amount that Fawcett and Gibson had succeeded in making from all their experiments put together. For Dermot Manning, the engineer who had designed the equipment, the moment had a significance that stayed with him for thirty years. 'You can imagine our excitement,' he told an audience in 1964, 'when masses of snowy white polymer spilled out . . .'

It was some months before the team realized the chance accident that had brought success. The Germans had probably been right in their assertions that ethylene would not polymerize, but a trace of

The first plastic: early samples of polythene, discovered in a laboratory accident at Winnington in 1933 by Reginald O. Gibson. (right) and Eric W. Fawcett.

oxygen in the gas, which was bought in cylinders from the British Oxygen Company, had acted as a catalyst. As extra ethylene was fed in to counteract the leak, the oxygen entering with it had sustained the reaction. The oxygen in the cylinder gas was, however, not constant; too little; and there would be no polythene – too much resulted in decomposition. 'If the leak had not occurred,' says Perrin, 'the experiment would probably have been far less spectacular than it was, and might well only have been a repetition of the earlier ones.' Reginald Gibson, in a lecture delivered in 1980, seventeen years after his retirement from ICI, asked: 'One wonders what Perrin would have done if the explosive reaction had been encountered in those first experiments – would he have been discouraged as Fawcett and I had been, and would the waxy solid have remained only of academic interest?'

The problem of getting the right amount of oxygen fed in each time was solved 'overnight', as Sir Peter Allen recalled, by Sir Cyril Hinshelwood, one of ICI's outside consultants, who suggested that every time they bought a cylinder of ethylene they should simply extract all the oxygen it contained and put back what was needed for the reaction to work. 'Basically the oxygen discovery was the thing that got the process going,' said Allen. 'After that we could do it time and again instead of holding our fingers in our ears and wondering if it would bang or not.'

Within a short time, the new material was demonstrated to have properties of a considerable scientific interest. It was crystalline and its molecular structure could be accurately picked out by X-ray. Perrin recorded that there was immediate recognition of its industrial potential: 'It could be moulded, when heated under a slight pressure, and formed into films and threads. It did not melt in boiling water. It was chemically resistant, as would be expected with a pure hydrocarbon. Also, because of its chemical composition, it would be sure to have outstandingly good properties as an electrical insulator.' This last was to lead to polythene's critical role in the Second World War.

Patents for Polythene

By February 1936 the first British provisional patent had been filed in the names of Perrin, Paton and Williams along with those of Fawcett and Gibson. By April a brand name, 'Alketh', later changed to 'Alkathene', was registered for the material. In October 1936 Perrin confirmed to R. E. Slade, ICI's director of research, how the provisional patents had been filed. The first, dated 4 February 1936, covered 'the production of the polymer with controlled rate of heat removal and controlled oxygen content, and the variation of the molecular weight of the polymer with pressure and oxygen content. In addition the production and uses of the polymer in the form of threads, staple fibre, films, tape and moulded articles have been covered'.

Under the heading 'Uses', Perrin reported to Slade: 'It is felt that, of a large number of possible uses, attention should first be concentrated on those connected with the electrical industry, where the outstanding insulating properties of Alketh, combined with its flexibility in the form of tapes and films, and its chemical inertness, would appear to be most promising.'

Complete British patent specifications were filed in September 1937 for manufacture and conversion of the polymer into threads and films. The trade mark Alketh was registered in April 1936 and, in November 1937, the generic name polythene was introduced to describe solid polymers of ethylene. At the same time a price of fifteen shillings a pound was fixed by ICI's sales committee for the new material in the form of powder, and a price of £2 a pound for threads or films.

A detailed study of the electrical properties of polythene was undertaken by Metropolitan Vickers and, in June 1937, it was agreed that the Plastics Division of ICI – still only in essence the committee headed by Adrian Hodgkin of 'What are plastics?' fame – should take over development of its moulding uses while Dyestuffs Division looked after textile uses and Alkali Division the electrical and 'other unspecified uses'. The British patents covered the method of making 'solid products of a rubber or resin-like character', but in the United States ICI succeeded in a very strong 'composition of matter' patent, which, if a material is hitherto unknown to science, protects not only the method of making it but also the end products as well, thus cutting out any alternative chemical formulation which might produce the same results. In America both du Pont and Union Carbide mapped out their own paths to the making of polythene, but the composition-of-matter patents ensured rich royalties for ICI in the US market: between £45 million and £50 million when production geared up for the mass manufacture of moulded household goods after the war.

Polythene Finds a Role

Peter Allen, who had joined the ICI alkali works at Winnington straight from Oxford in 1928, was brought in to urge on and coordinate the development of polythene in 1936, at a stage when perhaps fifty pounds of the stuff had been made. Reflecting on it all half a century later in his lush Sussex garden, Sir Peter still had a sense of wonder at this first of the modern plastics, which in fifty years had gone from 'the amount that would fill a hollow tooth', scraped out of the test-tube by Fawcett and Gibson, to a world output approaching twenty million tonnes a year.

He remembered seeing the first piece of polythene film being made in 1937 at Winnington by a Singapore Chinese laboratory assistant named Tommy Koh. Allen, John Swallow and Edmond Williams watched him. 'He took some chips of polythene, put them in a test-tube with xylene and boiled it up; the chips dissolved to a slightly viscous solution which was then poured on to a cold square plate of glass, poured all over the surface, then put in a very mild, warm oven to dry the solvent off. We all went off to lunch. When we came back, Williams nicked his thumb-nail under a corner and stripped off a sheet about a foot square, and that was the first sheet of polythene film that was ever made.' In 1982, travelling by train through South Korea, Allen was struck by the fields of crops covered entirely in polythene film and his mind flew back to that scene in the Winnington laboratory. In 1960 the house journal of the J. Sainsbury grocery chain said it was difficult to see how the self-service shopping revolution could have been possible – 'let alone prospered, without the aid of transparent wrapping materials'. Subsequently other plastics, like PVC, were developed for packaging film.

Nobody in 1937 thought of polythene film as a packaging material (though du Pont as early as 1941 believed this would be its largest commercial market), or dreamed of its ultimate mass production in moulded form for buckets, wheelbarrows, washing-up bowls and other household wares. 'We didn't really know what the devil we were doing with it,' said Allen. But after Metropolitan Vickers had examined its dielectric properties for insulating cables, efforts were made in late

Today's self-service shopping would be impossible without polythene.

1937 to interest cable firms and the Cable Makers' Association in the product. Prolonged discussions with the CMA on a development agreement broke down in 1938.

As usual, however, it was the percipience of one individual which paved the way to development. Bernard Habgood was a member of ICI's Dyestuffs' technical staff who had first-hand knowledge of the submarine cable industry and was an expert on rubber and gutta-percha, the two natural products then used for insulating land and underwater cables respectively. Habgood observed that polythene seemed very like a synthetic gutta-percha, better than the natural product because it had a higher softening point and wouldn't oxidize or deteriorate under water. In May 1938 a sample was sent to the Telegraph Construction and Maintenance Company, a specialist cable manufacturer, and by September they had asked for 100 tons to be delivered by the middle of 1939. The early work done by TC & M, led by John (later Sir John) Dean, was outstanding in establishing polythene's value as a cable insulator.

Polythene was eventually used to insulate the first round-the-world telephone cable but, at that stage, as Allen recalled, 'We were just experimenting, and then war broke out. There was an immediate requirement for anything that could illuminate in the blackout. We found that polythene was a very good carrier for luminous powders subjected to ultra-violet light, and one of the things we were doing in the first weeks of the war was devising strips of polythene to put round policemen's helmets, making luminous dog collars and things like that. Then radar took hold and from then on we were slaving like mad to make more and more . . .'

From an eighty cc reactor in the original experiments at Winnington, development moved to a three-quarter-litre size in November 1936 and, by January 1937, to a nine-litre vessel capable of producing 10 tons a year. By September 1938, ICI had designed a 50-litre reactor thought to be capable of making 50 tons a year: Allen asked for permission to raise capacity to 300 tons a year. The board cautiously allowed him to go to 200 tons. The first full-scale polythene plant, a 100-tonner (two 50-litre vessels) went into production on 1 September 1939, the day Germany invaded Poland and war became unavoidable for Britain. Polythene was about to meet its hour in history while, for ICI as a whole, the war would have a profound and catalytic effect on its development in many areas – in plastics, man-made fibres, pharmaceuticals, agricultural chemicals and, for a brief but momentous period, in giving birth to the atomic age.

5

THE CRUCIBLE OF WAR

On a dark, wet day in the first winter of the war, Michael Perrin, who was about to be deployed on ICI's most secret project – 'Tube Alloys', the code name for Britain's work on the atom bomb – called on the professor of physics at Birmingham University, M.L.E. Oliphant. Professor Oliphant had been experimenting with uranium compounds in the exploratory work on a 'super bomb' which had been put into high gear by the Chamberlain government in the spring of 1939.

Perrin remarked on the dismal weather and Oliphant said: 'I've been sitting here watching the planes go over,' which surprised Perrin because the cloud cover was so low, and then he realized Oliphant was talking about radar. They were looking, Oliphant said, for the most suitable dielectric material for insulation. Perrin told him about polythene, and he thought it might be just what was wanted. As soon as he could, Perrin got in touch with one of his co-patentees, Edmond Williams, and said, 'Look, I can't tell you anything about this, but get hold of as much polythene as you can and take it to Professor Oliphant in Birmingham'.

Polythene, the accidental invention which had languished for more than five years while ICI's scientists wondered what to do with it, exactly met its hour in radar. The process of locating the position of objects in space by the use of short radio waves, deriving its name from an acronym of Radio Direction and Range-finding, had been developed on both sides of the Atlantic in the late 1920s and early 1930s and perfected for military purposes in 1935 by R. A. (later Sir Robert) Watson-Watt. Before war broke out in September 1939, Britain was already equipped with a chain of radar masts to give early warning of approaching aircraft, but the masts were awkwardly high and obvious targets themselves for air attacks. To enable radar sets to be fitted into warships or aircraft, it was first necessary to reduce the wavelength and hence the size of the 'mirror' needed to concentrate the electromagnetic beam. At the outset of war no one could generate electromagnetic waves at wavelengths measured in centimetres – 'centimetric radar'. That problem was solved in the first winter of the war by two

British scientists, J. T. Randall and H. A. H. Boot, who discovered the cavity magnetron which could generate a wavelength of ten centimetres or less. But the strength of the signals being bounced back from the target was small, and without exceptional insulation they risked being lost in the feeders from the aerial into the equipment.

Neither of the two materials then widely used for electrical insulation – rubber and gutta-percha – was good enough to make centimetric radar a practical proposition. Polythene was. In the words of Watson-Watt, it had 'a high dielectric strength, it had a very low loss factor even at centimetric wavelengths, it could fairly be described as moisture-repellent and it could be moulded in such a way that it supported aerial rods directly on water-tight vibration joints backed by a surface on which moisture film did not remain conductive. And it permitted the construction of flexible, very high frequency cables very convenient to use.'

The first ton of polythene made in ICI's full-scale manufacturing plant was delivered for experimental radar cables shortly after the outbreak of war. The plant was quickly doubled in capacity and the second unit came into production on Dunkirk Saturday, 1 June 1940. All possible output was then channelled to radar use; although polythene-insulated sets were not ready in time for the Battle of Britain that summer, the decision had already been taken to standardize all future radar cables on the use of polythene.

Radar sets with polythene insulation were light enough to install in aircraft and could work on ever higher voltages and on frequencies eventually as short as three centimetres, giving a clear, detailed picture with the different textures of water and solids sharply defined. The first sensational use of mobile radar was at the end of the Blitz on London, when RAF night fighters began to locate and shoot down the German bombers, and then at the Battle of Cape Matapan against the Italian fleet in March 1941, one of the most decisive British naval victories since Trafalgar. It was largely a night action and the radar sets installed in Admiral Cunningham's battleships of the Mediterranean Fleet enabled the British guns to be so accurate that the Italians lost three heavy cruisers, a six-inch gun cruiser, three destroyers and a battleship, while the British lost only one naval aircraft and suffered no casualties or material damage to the fleet.

Radar sets on RAF aircraft monitoring the exit of the German pocket battleships *Scharnhorst* and *Gneisenau* from Brest in February 1942 unluckily proved defective and the raiders escaped, but centimetric radar, when introduced in 1943, was a decisive advantage for the Allies. Admiral Doenitz, visiting Hitler in May 1943 to tell him that the Battle of the Atlantic would have to be called off for a time, said: 'What is now decisive is that enemy aircraft have been equipped with a new location apparatus . . . which enables them to detect submarines and to attack them unexpectedly in low cloud, bad visibility or at night' (Mark Arnold-Forster: *The World At War*). Doenitz had told Hitler that in the previous month, German losses had risen from fourteen submarines – about thirteen per cent of those at sea – to thirty-six, or about thirty per cent. Such losses were too high, said Doenitz: 'We must husband our resources, because to do anything else would simply be to play the enemy's game.' In Arnold-Forster's words, 'the tide had turned'. March 1943 had been the worst month of the Atlantic war for the Allies, with forty-three ships sunk in the first twenty days. April and May were the worst months for Doenitz: no Allied ship was lost to U-boats in the Atlantic between the middle of May and September 1943, and the German navy never regained supremacy. Subsequently, airborne centimetric radar insulated by polythene guided Allied bombers in the night raids on Hamburg and Berlin.

The Germans, who had twice missed their chance in the 1930s to pick up the British process for polythene and had not managed to develop their own formula in time for radar use, were obliged to employ a bulkier insulating material and their radar was consequently less effective. Before the Japanese attack on Pearl Harbor on 7 December 1941, Lord McGowan, the ICI chairman, wrote to Walter Carpenter, the head of du Pont, offering the whole of ICI's polythene technology and a team from du Pont duly visited Britain. But du Pont and Union Carbide were already working on polymerization by a different route and a year after McGowan's offer, du Pont decided against using the British process, which they considered too erratic. Before then, however, the Bell Telephone Company had experimented with polythene-insulated cable on the Washington–Baltimore section of its telephone network. The raw polythene was shipped over from ICI early in 1940 for processing by du Pont and the cable was made by Western Electric.

Polythene Comes of Age

Experiments in the moulding of polythene were made during the war, chiefly for battery boxes in submarines, where a casing was required that would withstand the shock of depth charges. Sir Peter Allen recalled: 'We got the biggest moulding ever made in plastic up to that time, about three feet six by eighteen inches, and it withstood the shock admirably. But we couldn't get it rigid enough so that it wouldn't bulge. We never did solve that problem, so the Navy settled for a laminated box instead.'

In 1940, a 1,000-ton plant was built at Winnington to produce polythene to be converted to chlorinated polythene, something like PVC (polyvinyl chloride), which had been a German and American development. It would have been a useful rubber substitute for Britain when Malaya fell in 1942, cutting off supplies of natural rubber, but the process was too erratic to give a consistent product. The Ministry of Aircraft Production agreed to construction of the plant, however, because the solution made a very serviceable dope for tautening the fabric then used in aircraft bodies. 'I don't think any aeroplane was ever treated with it, and the dope idea was soon dropped,' said Allen. 'But the plant got built. The right thing was done for the wrong reasons.' By 1945, the Alkali Group had the capacity for producing about 5,000 tons of polythene a year.

Ironically, it was to be a German chemist, the brilliant Karl Ziegler of the Max Planck Institute at Mülheim, who in 1950 discovered the way to make polyethylene of a high molecular weight at normal temperatures and pressures, and the high density of this material, with its simpler arrangement of molecules, opened the way for the mass production of polythene bowls, buckets and bottles that were to sweep the world in the late 1950s and early 1960s. By this time, of course, the original patent had long since expired and two American oil companies, Phillips Petroleum and Standard Oil of Indiana, independently developed low-pressure processes. With their ready access to domestic oil resources, American companies were well placed to develop oil-based plastics – the wave of the future – instead of using a feedstock based on alcohol extracted from molasses, as the British had done. At the end of the war, ICI was still thinking that the future of polythene lay in the insulation business, and it was forced to license the Ziegler process to keep pace with developing technology. However, the 'composition of matter' patents still ruling in the US helped to ensure a healthy flow of royalties back across the Atlantic.

Sir Peter Allen, looking back in 1985 to the early days of polythene development, spoke of it as one of the key discoveries of the century: 'From zero, or as much as would fill a hollow tooth, to nearly twenty million tons in fifty years – that exceeds all base metal tonnages. With nylon and polyester, it was certainly an epoch-making discovery. Plastics as a whole most certainly have changed our lives.' (Sir Peter Allen, chairman of ICI 1968–1971, died in January 1993.)

Du Pont's delayed rejection of the British polythene process angered many ICI people responsible for developing what they considered an invention of comparable importance to du Pont's nylon. They were suspicious that the American firm might try to reduce the rate of royalty on the grounds that they themselves had done much to develop the process side; as Peter Allen wrote at the time, 'that we only invented the product and a half-baked way of making it'. But before long the whole ICI/du Pont alliance, with its agreements over licensing and market-sharing, was facing far worse strains in the eight-year lawsuit filed by the US Justice Department against ICI and du Pont under the Sherman Anti-Trust Act. Dragging on from 1944 to 1952, this brought Washington investigators to search ICI files in London and ended in a comprehensive dismantling of patent and process agreements between the two companies, destroying any exclusive rights which ICI still held in the United States. Judge Sylvester T. Ryan, whose summing up in the case dismissed as 'irrelevant' the question of how public interest was served by these arrangements, hammered the final nails into the coffin of the prewar cartel system. But in the booming chemical industry of the 1950s no one was prepared to waste time mourning its death.

Profits from War

The war had done much to lay the foundations for that boom, though all industrial companies concerned with war materials were subject to an Excess Profits Tax. Images of 'profiteering' from rearmament had surfaced as early as 1933 in a cartoon by David Low in the London *Evening Standard* which depicted a group of conspiratorial plutocrats labelled with the names of Krupp, Vickers and 'Imperial Poison Gas Industries Ltd'. In 1935 ICI and other companies gave evidence to a Royal Commission on 'The Private Manufacture of and Trading in Arms'; at the time Low's cartoon appeared they were making only two per cent of their turnover from war materials and were not manufacturing poison gas at all. That came later – more than 1,300 tons of assorted gases were made in the early months of the war but the stockpiles were never used.

Nevertheless, when Britain began to rearm from 1936 onwards, ICI was bound to play a leading part. As its official historian, W. J. Reader, remarked, 'Almost any branch of the chemical industry could be converted from peaceful to warlike applications'. And ICI dominated Britain's chemical industry. Ammonia supplied the basis of nitric acid, essential for explosives; the technology of dyestuffs could be applied variously to explosives, poison gases or pharmaceuticals. ICI also offered the largest pool in the country of scientific talent combined with industrial resources. As war became increasingly probable, the company negotiated various 'agency' roles with the government – a system designed to avoid profiteering by which government paid the costs of plant for war production which would be useless in time of peace. With twenty-five such factories producing material ranging from aircraft alloys to mustard gas and detonators, ICI was the government's largest industrial agent in the Second World War. Strategically, it was of vital importance, maybe even indispensable, as Dr Reader observed. 'Without the resources which ICI commanded,' he wrote, noting particularly those of General Chemicals, Explosives, Alkali and Metals Groups, 'the British industrial effort in the Second World War would have had to take a very different form.'

The biggest agency plant of all was a hydrogenation works at Heysham, Lancashire, in which the government invested more than £6 million and which ICI's Fertilizer Group ran in partnership with Shell. Oil from coal was still perceived as the alchemist's stone: in 1938 a senior official of ICI was advised by du Pont that a long-term policy based on coal (for heavy chemicals including plastics) was 'sounder than one based on oil, as there are periodic doubts whether the oil resources have anything but a limited life'.

The Heysham plant never in fact contributed much in the way of petrol to the war effort, but it developed a remarkable aviation fuel additive called Victane which could make fighter planes fast enough to catch the flying bombs, though at great expense to their engines. The plant was sited on the Lancashire coast rather than at Billingham, up till then the centre of the company's oil-from-coal work, because Teesside was thought to be within dangerously easy reach of the German bomber bases. As aircraft range increased, of course, almost everywhere was at risk. In the very early stages of rearmament, the government held highly secret talks with ICI over Billingham's vulnerability to German air attack and it was decided to spread its key activities to more remote areas. Plans were accordingly implemented in 1937 and 1938 to put up smaller ammonia plants in Dowlais, South Wales, and Bishopton in Scotland.

On the outbreak of war Imperial Chemical House was turned over to the Board of Trade and the Ministry of Aircraft Production. ICI head-office departments dispersed to outlying areas fringing London – Slough, Welwyn and Mill Hill. Two directors established offices in their homes in Surrey and Essex. ICI's sales grew enormously during the war, and so did its profits, though these were greatly reduced by wartime taxation. As the country's biggest fertilizer manufacturer, as well as producing ammonia, bleach, chlorine, dyestuffs, paints and a vast range of other industrial and agricultural materials – quite apart from any involvement in munitions – ICI was far better prepared to benefit from the accelerated technology of war than its predecessor companies had been in 1914. This time, for instance, as German dyestuffs were prevented by naval blockade from reaching their export markets and the prewar cartel with IG Farben collapsed, there would be no shortage of khaki and blue dyes for service uniforms.

Aside from purely war materials, the government became ICI's biggest customer for many commodities, and ICI scientists moved in on areas of strategic wartime planning such as agriculture. The company advised on mustering farmland resources for maximum productivity of food and feedstock; it set up a campaign with government backing for grassland management, and it became expert at lobbying in Westminster and Whitehall on behalf of its own ideas for emergency innovations. Among these was a scheme for feeding cattle straw pulped with caustic soda and then washed, as a substitute for maize or barley. So expert did ICI become in these techniques of persuasion that Reader considers 'in certain matters of wartime farming ICI . . . came close to directing the policy of HM Government'.

The war gave a great push to innovations and discoveries within the company on which much postwar business would be built. As told in detail in later chapters, important breakthroughs in weedkillers and pesticides were made in ICI's plant-protection laboratories at Jealott's Hill, Berkshire, and the infant pharmaceutical business (begun in 1936 amid unsuitably murky surroundings in Blackley, the Manchester suburb where Dyestuffs Division had its headquarters) developed out of wartime necessity such world-beating drugs as the anti-malarial 'Paludrine'. 'Chemically, it is a good and exciting time to be alive,' wrote Peter Allen in his diary in 1943. Not only were new discoveries being made, but hitherto undeveloped ones, like polythene were coming into their own. Among the latter, the ICI discovery of the 1930s to make its greatest impact on the war – and to open up entirely new markets in later years – was 'Perspex'.

Perspex – a Key Invention

Perspex, the trade name for transparent sheet made from methyl methacrylate, or 'Resin M', as it was first code-named in ICI, was the result of a brilliant process of synthesis invented in 1932 by Dr John Crawford, a chemist working in the explosives division based at Ardeer, the old, original Nobel plant on the Firth of Clyde. Its great wartime role as the material for aircraft canopies had in fact been the spur for its invention. Reginald Mitchell, the designer of the new fighter plane later to be known as the Spitfire, was searching in the early 1930s for a suitable transparent material to enclose the pilot's cockpit in a sliding canopy. 'Glass was suicidal and celluloid had terrible problems of opacity,' Crawford recalled. A talent scout for Mitchell visited the Ardeer plant, where work on resins was going on. The next part of the story was related in 1986, when Crawford was eighty-five, in a letter from his New Forest home to the secretary of a local Spitfire association: 'The nature of my work in ICI made me aware of what was afoot in the way of new plastics, and a German firm, Rohm and Haas of Darmstadt in the Rhineland, with a daughter company in Delaware, were experimentally developing their "Plexiglas", which their research chemists had uncovered in the mid-twenties in the course of a routine investigation. Chemically, it was the polymer (PMMA) of methyl methacrylate (MMA), and was highly transparent, workable, mechanically strong and light-resistant. The tricky process for converting the water-like MMA into solid PMMA sheet was successfully devised by the Germans, and it seemed that Plexiglas was protected by a barrier of patents. There was, however, one snag for the Germans – MMA could be made only at much expense and difficulty by an academic process'.

Crawford set to work in the summer of 1931 to devise an effective and practical manufacturing process for MMA. Another ICI chemist, Rowland Hill of the Dyestuffs Division at Blackley, independently produced a polymer of methyl methacrylate, but it was Crawford who discovered the most economic commercial process, mixing acetone cyanohydrin with sulphuric acid, adding methanol to the products and isolating the 'ester' by steam distillation. The reaction needed to be carried out with specific catalysts present, like copper and sulphur. The working out of the process was widely recognized as a brilliant piece of chemistry and, with some modifications, Crawford's process is still the basis for large-scale manufacture of acrylic plastics throughout the world.

Lord McGowan ordered the construction of a plant for the new resin, which was named 'Perspex' from the Latin 'to see through' and is today defined in the Oxford Dictionary as 'a tough, unsplinterable plastic material, much lighter than glass, used for transparent parts of aircraft, etc.'. The trademark was registered on 16 November 1934 and the product was first incorporated into the new Spitfire in 1936.

The obvious civilian market for a splinterless glass substitute which, unlike cellulose nitrate, did not go yellow in sunlight, was for car windscreens, but ICI was so nervous of losing its bulk sales of soda ash to the glass manufacturer Pilkington that it put a voluntary ceiling on Perspex sales in the ten-year agreement it signed to supply the Triplex safety glass company, which was eventually acquired by Pilkington in 1965.

The war not only hugely increased demand for Perspex in aircraft but also inadvertently discovered an entirely new market for it as an optical material. Surgeons treating wounded pilots discovered that fragments of Perspex were tolerated by the body's tissues, even when they got into the eye. An ophthalmic surgeon named Harold Ridley, observing the lack of inflammatory reaction, went on to pioneer the use of a special grade of Perspex, known as CQ, for intraocular surgery, replacing the natural lens of the eye after operations such as those for cataract. Perspex became the chief material for contact lenses until the advent of alternatives to the hard lens, now known as 'soft' and 'gas-permeable' lenses, which use a different formula of plastic.

The product remained a key invention for ICI in its enormous versatility; it is today used all over the world for signs, light fittings, glazing, dentures, technical models, sanitaryware and lightweight furniture, and ICI is Europe's largest producer of acrylic sheet. Despite the almost simultaneous discovery of polythene within ICI, it was the first of the modern plastics to be in commercial production by 1939 as an entirely new business for the company.

Man-Made Fibres

Alongside the infant plastics industry, the other great development of the 1930s in man-made materials had taken place in fibres, when du Pont announced its discovery of a new synthetic textile fibre called nylon, at the New York World's Fair in October 1938. This was the triumphant culmination of a great gamble for the American chemical giant, the payoff to ten years of pure 'blue-sky' research, and it founded a whole new industry without which most modern clothing and a huge variety of other synthetic textile products would be inconceivable.

The origins of artificial fibres go back to 1832, when a Frenchman named Branconnet discovered nitrocellulose by treating cellulose products, such as wood, cotton and paper, with nitric acid, but he did not try to make filaments from it. The first commercial rayon is credited to another French inventor, Count Hilaire de Chardonnet, who patented an artificial silk made from cellulose nitrate in 1885. Around 1892 British chemists were experimenting in the field; two men named C. F. Cross and E. J. Bevan patented viscose yarn and Nobel Explosives at Ardeer tried out methods of making nitrocellulose fibre. In 1920, Nobel became interested in fibres derived from alginic acid, extracted from the huge quantities of seaweed on the coast of Western Scotland, but a much more promising idea, brought to Ardeer in 1935 from outside the company, was a wool-like fibre based on vegetable protein from East African ground-nuts. 'Ardil', as the new fibre was known, eventually reached the market in 1951 but, though as warm and soft as wool with many attractive properties, it never became widely popular. Its main problems were that it had much less wet-strength than wool and could never be made pure white, its natural colour being a brownish-cream.

By this time, nylon was sweeping the world. Although the Germans had been working on production of a true synthetic fibre since 1910, it was a brilliant young chemist from Harvard named Wallace Carothers who first achieved it. Carothers had been talent-hunted by du Pont to undertake a programme of pure, fundamental research without any targeted commercial objective, but in the hope that out of it would come new business products to replace reliance on heavy chemicals. Carothers and his team were encouraged to pursue any line of research they thought promising. In 1928 they decided to concentrate on polymers of high molecular weight achieved by chemical condensation. Among these were polyesters, from which Carothers tried to produce a fibre but decided that it was not worth pursuing. Instead, he settled on the polyamide group, condensation products of dibasic acids and diamines. Over 3,000 different polyamides were synthesized and one, code-numbered 66, was chosen for development, largely on the basis of its cheap and available raw materials, adipic acid and hexamethylene diamine. Carothers found that the molecules, arranged end to end, could be drawn out into fibres of unusual strength and were superior in many other properties to natural fibres or chemically modified ones like rayon.

By 1937, experimental stockings made from 'nylon 66' yarn were being knitted in the du Pont laboratories and a bare five months after the announcement at the World's Fair, ICI took out a licence to manufacture the new fibre in Britain and several of the Dominions. Realizing that it needed the experience of a specialized textile firm, ICI formed a partnership with Courtaulds, then the world's largest producer of viscose rayon and, under the name of British Nylon Spinners, the new company was registered in January 1940, on the same day that food rationing began. It immediately turned to manufacturing nylon for parachutes, a role that became critical to the war effort when Japan's entry in December 1941 cut off large supplies of natural silk.

Terylene – the First Polyester

In 1941, ICI was presented on a plate with the discovery that had eluded Carothers at du Pont and incidentally also IG Farben, which had been working along similar lines. Where those two giants with all their batteries of scientific resources had failed to produce the world's first polyester fibre, it was the discovery of two chemists working in the small research laboratory of an obscure Manchester company called the Calico Printers' Association. Geoff Myers, who spent thirty-three years with ICI's Fibres Division, calls it 'one of the romances of science'. One of them J. R. (Rex) Whinfield, became excited by news filtering out of Carothers' work in 1935 and had urged then that Calico Printers get into the field of synthetic fibres. Five years went by, however, before they followed his advice. Then Whinfield, assisted by a colleague called J. T. Dickson, plunged into work on the line which had been abandoned by Carothers because he found the molecular structure unstable (it was accordingly excluded from the du Pont patents). Polyesters are formed by an acid and alcohol condensation, and Carothers had failed because he was working with acids known as aliphatic acids, which have a long-chain molecular make-up. Whinfield chose one of the so-called 'aromatic' acids, with a different structure including a benzene ring. This was terephthalic acid, an intermediate of dyestuffs, and the alcohol used to react with it was ethylene glycol, familiar as the basis of car anti-freeze. As Whinfield suspected, the resulting molecular chain was closely packed and strong, and highly resistant to melting.

The main problem, and perhaps one that had turned Carothers off the scent, was that terephthalic acid was a notoriously difficult product to react, being extremely impure. Dickson devised a way to purify it and the two men managed to produce a few grams of a polymer with a melting point of 249°C which could be drawn into threads. These turned out to have most of the properties of nylon with some unique ones of their own. The fibre was less affected by water than nylon (although this could be a disadvantage when dyeing), and it could be crimped to give the feeling of a woollen yarn, something which was much more difficult with nylon. Indeed, there are those who think that if Carothers had succeeded with polyester he might never have bothered to go on and investigate the polyamides which produced nylon.

As it happened, the one area where the new fibre was no match for nylon was that in which nylon first revolutionized the clothing industry and gave its name to a generic product – women's stockings. Polyester yarn suffered from 'creep' which caused stockings to bag at the knees and to retain their shape instead of springing back. But it was exceptionally resistant to wrinkling and could be heat-set in pleated skirts, which became one of Terylene's great early successes. It also had versatile uses as a furnishing fabric and for industrial products like sails and ropes. Unlike rayon or cellulose acetate, it was also highly resistant to sunlight through glass and made excellent curtains. Net curtaining became one of its biggest markets.

Whinfield had already chosen the name Terylene for his invention when the CPA brought it to ICI – then 'just a few grams of dirty-looking stuff like treacle', as Bob Melhuish, who handled ICI's patent negotiations, remembered it forty-five years later. Under that name it had been patented by Calico Printers Association, but all wartime patents, which were filed in great secrecy, automatically came to the attention of the Ministry of Supply in case of possible war use. Terylene was extensively studied at the National Chemical Research Laboratory on the banks of the Thames at Teddington, south London. The verdict was: an interesting material, but it could not be developed in time for war use. One huge technical problem was the development of suitable techniques for melt-spinning. The Ministry of Supply knew that ICI had melt-spinning technology through its 1939 Nylon Agreement with du Pont: if any company could develop the new material quickly, ICI could.

In 1943, two years after the CPA had patented his invention, Rex Whinfield was working for the Ministry of Supply. A meeting was arranged between him and John Swallow, one of the ICI scientists involved in the original high-pressure work on polythene who by this time was research director of Plastics Division. The meeting at Welwyn resulted in further ICI work on the new fibre and in 1944 the company was confident that polyethylene terephthalate, as the compound was known, could produce an outstanding synthetic fibre for which there might well be a large market. It could even be cheaper to produce than nylon, which was derived from benzene; cheap ethylene from oil

J. R. Whinfield, who cracked the secret of the first polyester fibre, Terylene, and patented it in 1941. It was discovered in the laboratory of a small Manchester printing works after eluding the massed resources of du Pont's team working on nylon. ICI developed it into a worldwide business.

cracker technology was now a more tempting option than the old process of distilling it from molasses. But it would probably take about four years to develop to marketing stage.

ICI went into patent negotiations with the CPA, which wanted to form a joint company. ICI shied away from that; it already had one joint company with Courtaulds, and CPA was seen as a much less suitable partner, unable to keep up financially. Doubtless also, ICI saw many advantages in going it alone on Terylene. It finally made a licensing agreement with CPA to last twenty years from 1946 at a royalty rate starting at 7½ per cent and progressively declining to 3 per cent as sales went up from 1 million pounds a year to more than 10 million. In addition, CPA were granted the right to a smaller rate of royalty in any peripheral field of invention which the war had prevented them from developing. ICI took Whinfield and Dickson on to its staff and a pilot plant was set up to produce fifty tons a year until full-scale production got under way.

Any potentially marketable new synthetic fibre was bound to excite the attention of Courtaulds, ICI's partner in British Nylon Spinners. But ICI had refused Calico Printers' wish to form a joint company and could hardly be seen to hand over development to another joint company, even if it had wished to do so, which was certainly not the case. Some ICI men thought the company already had a poor deal over nylon, making the polymer and 'practically giving it away' to Courtaulds through BNS, while Courtaulds reaped half the profits. (The intermittently stormy relationship between the two companies came to a head in 1962, when ICI tried without success to take over the fibre manufacturer.) The BNS board fought long and hard to share the rights to Terylene, attempting in the process to block ICI's use of the du Pont melt-spinning technique for making nylon, but after much acrimonious bargaining and legal discussion, ICI won the day and the sole rights to the world's first polyester.

The first piece of Terylene fabric was woven at the Shirley Institute in Manchester in August 1946. In November that year, Rowland Hill and K. W. Palmer of Dyestuffs examined the prospects for synthetic fibres in Britain over the next twenty or thirty years and concluded that it was 'a field tremendous in scope; a field that, measured in terms of capitalization, might be as big as ICI and Courtaulds are together at the present time'. The optimism, despite heavy development costs, seemed justified: new fibres of many kinds were rapidly developing, like du Pont's acrylic 'Fibre A', sold as 'Orlon'; ICI's own 'Ardil' and many others. Du Pont, which had bought the CPA's American patent application, developed its own Terylene-style yarn, called 'Dacron'. Subsequent developments in the acrylics field would bring household names like Monsanto's 'Acrilan' and Courtauld's 'Courtelle'. Huge tonnages were confidently anticipated and fibres seemed to many to be a more promising business area than plastics (polythene at this stage was still largely restricted to its use as an electrical insulator). It was an understandable, if wrong judgment in the context of the time and of transatlantic developments like the massive $175 million said to be earmarked by du Pont for nylon investment in 1946.

The first commercial sale of Terylene in Britain was on 4 October 1948 to the Nottingham firm of Dobson and Braine for the manufacture of lace curtains. In 1950 Lord McGowan, still chairman of ICI at the age of seventy-six, led the board to the decision to invest in a £10 million plant at Wilton to produce 5,000 tons of Terylene a year: development costs up to that stage had amounted to £5 million. A 'Terylene Council' was set up within the company to direct development planning: among its members was Richard Beeching, then an ICI executive who went on to become chairman of British Rail and the axeman of unprofitable branch lines.

The Wilton plant, controlled by Plastics Division, went into production in 1954. It was supplied with its raw polymer by another Wilton factory under Dyestuffs' control. So rapidly did the business grow that by 1956 the Terylene Council was transformed into a fully fledged Fibres Division. Terylene pushed ICI into the fibres business and was the driving force behind its abortive bid for Courtaulds, its single biggest customer for Terylene. In 1961, ICI was the world's second

largest chemical company, three and a half times the size of
Courtaulds, which nevertheless was the world's largest manufacturer of
man-made fibres. ICI, wrongly as it turned out, thought it needed to
involve itself more in the textiles business as it sought new markets for
Terylene, and it saw a merged ICI-Courtaulds as a formidable British
rival for the other great international fibres groups, particularly in order
to stand up against European competitors like Monsanto should Britain go into the Common Market. But it reckoned without ferocious
opposition from Courtaulds board. The bid failed but ICI gained control, as a sort of consolation prize, of the jointly owned British Nylon
Spinners and in 1965 merged it with the Fibres Division to make a
completely new company, ICI Fibres Ltd.

Polyester, of which Terylene was the world's first and most successful example, is today the most widely used synthetic fibre in terms of
tonnage. What gave it supremacy was its ability to blend better than
nylon with natural fibres like cotton (still commanding over fifty per
cent of the world's fibre consumption) and wool. This opened the way
to the whole 'easy-care' revolution in clothing. There had been drip-
dry garments made of 100 per cent synthetic fibre, but they lacked the
comfort and appeal of natural fabrics. A fifty/fifty or sixty-seven/
thirty-three polyester blend was the answer.

In the late 1950s, ICI bought the rights to a new process of
'bulking' or crimping the yarn which for the first time in this technique
did not make the garment elastic in its properties. ICI named the new
yarn 'Crimplene' and it became immensely successful for easy-care
clothes until the late 1960s, when fashion changed and Crimplene, the
invention of an Italian named Mario Nava from the Macclesfield district, became associated damningly with a frumpy, middle-aged image.
Terylene is so versatile and adaptable a fibre that Bob Melhuish can't
see it being superseded in its field. 'The prospects of another breakthrough like that are very, very remote,' he said in his Harrogate home,
close to the main British centre of Terylene production.

Rex Whinfield, who first cracked the secret of its manufacture in a
Manchester back-street laboratory, finished his career on the board of
ICI Fibres, acting as a kind of ambassador for the product he had
fathered. He retired in 1963 and died in 1966, a gentle, modest man
with a large, impressive head, remembered with affection by old colleagues. Although never developed for wartime use, Terylene was
undoubtedly the most influential of the inventions of that period in
terms of postwar business for ICI. Its patents were extended in 1957
for five years beyond the usual sixteen-year term because of the secrecy under which wartime regulations had demanded all patents
should be filed.

The plastics and man-made fibres invented in the 1930s and pushed
into high-gear development because of the war were to have an

immense, transforming effect on society in the 1950s and 1960s. Along with other discoveries they formed what might be termed the 'convenience revolution' of modern life. But there was one discovery of the 1930s which overshadowed all others in its portents for the world; one in which ICI as Britain's leading science-based industrial group was to play a small but highly significant role – a most remarkable one for any commercial enterprise.

6

ICI's Atom Bomb

Soon after the outbreak of war, an ICI scientist drafted a paper which now has the charm of an historical curiosity: 'The year 1939 is likely, in the future, to be remembered not so much for the start of the present war than as the date of the discovery of a new phenomenon in physics which has been given the name of "nuclear fission" . . . The importance of this discovery lies in the certain proof, which it provides, that the enormous store of sub-atomic or nuclear energy available in matter can be released and controlled for practical use. It may mark the introduction of a new technical era in civilization and lead to the development of a source of power which will allow for the re-orientation of world industry.'

The tone seems innocently Utopian to a generation which has grown up under the shadow of nuclear war and is now fearful in addition of industrial accidents like Three Mile Island and Chernobyl. But such opinions were widespread in the scientific community at that time, even though it was already clear that the first practical use of atomic energy would be as a weapon of massive destruction.

Final proof of the possibility of nuclear fission in the first nine months of 1939 had sparked off a tremendous burst of theoretical and practical work in laboratories around the world. Over a hundred scientific papers on the subject appeared, their sober and measured presentation masking a ferment of excitement.

The first steps towards this momentous discovery had been taken at the end of the nineteenth century with the work on radioactivity done in Germany by Roentgen, the discoverer of X-rays, and in Paris by Pierre and Marie Curie. Further key links had been added to the chain by Ernest Rutherford, John Cockcroft and James Chadwick in Cambridge, Enrico Fermi in Rome and Irene Curie and Pierre Joliot in Paris. The latest burst of discoveries, to which the ICI paper referred, originated with the German chemist Otto Hahn, the Austrian physicist Lise Meitner and her nephew O. R. Frisch and, independently, Pierre Joliot, proving at last what had long been suspected, that the release of atomic energy from uranium was possible. The papers embodying all this work were available for anyone to read – many of them were published in the distinguished journal *Nature* – and speculation, particularly in the popular press, had ranged freely over the implications not only for industry but also for weapons. The words 'super bomb' were much in evidence.

In the spring of 1939 the British government, alerted by the urgent prodding of G. P. Thomson, professor of physics at Imperial College, London, began to give serious consideration to the defence implications, including the availability of pure uranium compounds, and the Air Ministry was entrusted with the business through Sir Henry Tizard's Committee on the Scientific Survey of Air Defence. The general feeling was one of scepticism, but experiments were begun by Thomson and by Professor Mark Oliphant at Birmingham University, who were supplied with uranium by Britain's only source of the metal, a firm called Brandhurst and Co. Meanwhile, estimates of just how much would be needed to achieve the 'critical mass' necessary to start a chain reaction leading to an explosion varied wildly between the pound weight envisaged by some sensational newspaper reports and the one or more tons which the government's chemical defence committee thought might be required.

The £5 Million Atom Bomb

On the outbreak of war in September, Tizard's committee was reconstituted as the Committee for the Scientific Survey of Air Warfare, which reiterated the belief that it was highly improbable that any practical bomb could ever be made out of uranium, though there were fears that Hitler's scientists were working on the problem. Work went on without any great urgency – Tizard and the government considered other scientific defence problems far more pressing – until a paper written in Birmingham changed the whole official attitude almost overnight. This was a report produced by Professor Rudolf Peierls and O. R. Frisch. Frisch had worked prewar with the brilliant Niels Bohr in Copenhagen; he was on a visit to England when war broke out and decided to stay in Birmingham with Peierls, a young refugee from Nazi Germany who was then professor of mathematics and physics at the university.

Together the two men had worked over a key paper published by Bohr just two days before the outbreak of war, in which he had put forward his theories that fission was more likely to occur in the light isotope of uranium, U235, than in U238, which forms almost 99.3 per cent of natural uranium. The problem would be to separate them.

Speaking forty-six years later on a Channel 4 television documentary, *Our Bomb*, Peierls, now Sir Rudolf and the 'grand old man of British physics', as the programme described him, recalled: 'Our main motivation was that we suspected the Germans might have had the same ideas and might in fact be further advanced, and such a weapon in the hands of Hitler would have been very frightening. We knew there could be no defence; the only thing to do would be to have the weapon yourself and use it as a deterrent.'

Bohr's paper came to be regarded as one of the classics of nuclear fission and, using it as a basis, Peierls and Frisch produced some revolutionary new theories which they set out in three typed foolscap pages. These propounded a critical size for the bomb, estimating that one of five kilograms' weight would produce an explosion equivalent to several thousand tons of dynamite, and proposed separating the isotopes by thermal diffusion to produce a lump of pure U235 rather than, as had previously been suggested, increasing the proportion of U235 in the metal from one part to ten parts in 140. Frisch and Peierls also suggested making the bomb in two or more sections, to be kept separate until the moment for explosion, and they gave a warning about the dangers of radiation, which they predicted would be fatal to living beings for a long time after the bomb had gone off.

While some of the details in this paper were wrong – not surprising since many of the 'nuclear constants' were still unknown – much of it was almost eerily accurate. Professor Oliphant, immediately recognizing its importance, sent a memo to Thomson, who in turn discussed it with him and with John Cockcroft at the Ministry of Supply. Interest in the bomb project was now rekindled, and made still more urgent by the information that some French scientists had managed to smuggle out of occupied France the world's entire stock of heavy water.

Doctors H. von Halban and L. Kowarski were two of Professor Joliot's colleagues in Paris, and they had been carrying out experiments for some time with heavy water, which resembles ordinary water in appearance and chemical behaviour but has a particular hydrogen isotope which makes it efficient in slowing down neutrons, a vital part of the process of atomic explosion. Even in ideal conditions it is only present in ordinary water at 0.015 per cent and producing it on a large scale is slow and expensive. Before the war there had been only one plant capable of making it, situated in Norway, and from there the entire stock, 185 kg in twenty-six cans, had been successfully transferred to France and then brought by Halban and Kowarski to England under the escort of the Earl of Suffolk, who organized the escape from France of scientists and much valuable scientific equipment, including industrial diamonds. Once safely in England, the heavy water cans led a colourful existence, being kept at different times in Wormwood Scrubs prison and under the protection of the Librarian of Windsor Castle, Sir Owen Morshead.

By now the question of making an atomic bomb had progressed from being one of many subjects concerning Tizard's committee to having a special uranium committee of its own, known as the MAUD committee. MAUD is not the acronym it was designed to appear. The name originated in a telegram sent by Niels Bohr to Frisch when Denmark was overrun by the Germans, and which ended with the words 'tell Cockcroft and Maud Ray Kent'. This was thought to be some cryptic reference to radium or uranium, and hence its adoption by the uranium committee: only after the war was it discovered that it referred to a woman named Maud Ray, living in Kent, who had been nanny to the Bohr children.

The Maud Committee was one of the most important and secret government bodies of the whole war. Thomson was its chairman, and the original members were Professors Chadwick, Oliphant, Cockcroft and P. B. Moon, subsequently joined by others including Professor P. M. S. Blackett, responsible for scientific research at the Ministry of Aircraft Production (MAP) and Professor Francis Simon of the Clarendon Laboratory in Oxford. There was some initial havering about the constitutions of Maud's policy committee and the technical sub-committee, and of the wisdom of employing scientists like Frisch who were of German origin. However, it started work in April 1940, and from then on feasibility studies on the bomb rapidly gathered momentum. Chadwick, who had made the major discovery of the neutron in 1932, was put in charge of organizing the physics research, which was distributed among other universities including Cambridge and Bristol and was mainly concerned with isotope separation, a subject of enormous complexity which also involved chemistry. Professor William Haworth of Birmingham University took over the direction of chemical work on the production of gaseous compounds of uranium, and of pure uranium metal.

At only the second meeting of the Maud Committee, ICI was called in. It was an inevitable development. As the company's official historian commented: 'For transforming scientific theory into industrial fact, in the conditions of wartime Britain, ICI's resources were unmatched . . . ICI alone had the scientific and industrial range needed to comprehend and coordinate the central processes, especially the separation of U235 from uranium.'

The company immediately set up a secret War Committee, consisting of Lord McGowan, Lord Melchett, J. G. Nicholson and G. P. Pollitt, all of whom had been members of the original ICI board. The ICI personnel who worked most closely with the Maud Committee itself were an executive manager, Wallace Akers, the head of research, R. E. Slade, and Slade's assistant, Michael Perrin, who had been involved in the discovery of polythene in the early 1930s. As the war progressed, many other ICI employees became unwittingly caught up in the scientific development of an atomic weapon; only the most senior were aware of the tremendous significance of what they were doing.

At the beginning there was no formal agreement between ICI and the Ministry of Aircraft Production. The company's concern was chiefly with the production of U235 by an industrial process which started with the manufacture of a gas, the mixed hexafluorides of U235 and U238. The next stage was the separation of the U235 hexafluoride and finally its recovery in metallic form through combining it with fluorine. Uranium hexafluoride, or 'hex' as it was nicknamed by the Americans and later by the British, was a most unpleasant and intractable material to work with, extremely corrosive and quick to solidify when its temperature fell below 120°F, or if it came into contact with many other compounds, including water. However, no adequate substitute could be found, and one of ICI's first assignments was to provide a few grams of the substance for experiments. They did this free of charge, the research manager of General Chemicals funding it out of some spare research money. One of the research chemists working with hexafluorine was Dr Charles Suckling, who after the war was to make one of ICI's most successful pharmaceutical discoveries (see Chapter 8). He says now that at the time he had no idea of the significance of what he was doing. The Secret War Committee, however, and Akers, Slade and Perrin were in no doubt.

By September 1940, Chadwick was urgently asking for production of hex on a larger scale: he needed three kilograms immediately. There were some difficulties within ICI about quoting a price, because no one was certain whether it would be followed up by further orders; a deadlock broken only by a personal approach to Melchett by Simon and Professor Lindemann, later Lord Cherwell, who was briefing Winston Churchill on developments. Far more difficult were the problems of making the stuff on anything like a commercial scale. ICI did have a plant for making pure hydrofluoric acid, which was required in the process, but it had been out of commission for some time and needed expensive repair and modification.

By December 1940, however, the contract for the three kilograms was placed, at an agreed price of £5,000, and production got under way: ICI estimated that a plant could be built within eighteen months capable of producing around 450 kilograms a day. The most difficult part of the operation was the separation of the hexafluoride of U235 from the mixed hexafluorides of both isotopes; Maud and ICI eventually agreed that the best bet lay in a separation process which depended on the small but crucial difference in weight between the isotopes. If a membrane with microscopically small holes could be constructed and the hex pumped through it, the U235 would pass through at a marginally slower rate than the heavier U238 and could thus, with infinite care, be collected separately, still in a gaseous form. From this the solid metal could then be recovered.

One problem was that a full-scale gaseous diffusion plant would present a large and vulnerable target to German bombers. Another, more immediately pressing, was producing the metal membranes – millions of square feet would be required, with a predicted density of 160,000 to the square inch. The technical problem was solved by the research manager of Metals Group, S. S. Smith. Following the analogy of the printing processes in photography, where pictures are built up from hundreds of thousands of minute dots, he asked Michael (now Sir Michael) Clapham, who was then managing an ICI subsidiary called the Kynoch Press, if very small holes could be etched on metal. Kynoch made some unsuccessful efforts in this direction, but a further idea of Clapham's produced a satisfactory result by means of an electrode deposition process that was used for lithographic plates in the works of one of his former employers, a small printer in Bradford called Lund-Humphries. This process was successfully adapted for mass production.

By now ICI was confident enough to produce a report for the Maud Committee dated July 1941, which envisaged that a bomb could be in production by the end of 1943 at a capital cost of £5 million (see Appendix). The paper ended with the company declaring itself ready to take 'executive charge' of the work on behalf of the Ministry of Aircraft Production. Work at Birmingham under Professor Haworth was still progressing, and ICI began to make pure uranium metal by the new method they had devised, thus releasing the Birmingham team from manufacturing to experimental work. In May 1941 the company's work had been put on a more formal basis because by then it was recognized that ICI's assistance would be needed on all sorts of other problems, in particular the construction by Metropolitan-Vickers of a twenty-stage diffusion plant. In June, ICI signed a contract, whose final value was £8,700, to render advice and help with experiments as required.

ICI's management was very enthusiastic about the Maud work, viewing it as a straightforward requirement of public duty, but their commercial instincts were also aroused by the heavy-water or 'boiler' research still being carried out by Halban and Kowarski. It was becoming increasingly clear that the two men were reaching the end of the work they could usefully carry on in Britain and might have to go to America, where resources were more plentiful. The patent situation was one of extreme complexity, but ICI saw the heavy-water research as leading to the development of 'a new source of power of great importance in peace and war'; one which could have the greatest possible effect on world industry. It was essential, the board believed, that these ideas should be 'developed for the British Empire' by a British firm.

ICI was fully prepared to be that firm, and it was this which led a practical businessman like McGowan to believe that a private commercial enterprise like ICI could take over responsibility for the development of nuclear power in Britain, including an atomic weapon. The idea seems inconceivable today, and in the event made no headway then, but it remains a odd footnote in business history that it should have been seriously entertained at all.

While Maud pondered the whole question of heavy-water supply, and the future position of Halban and Kowarski, ICI offered to take over their research in its entirety, and if it proved necessary to move the work to the US, to make arrangements with du Pont or its subsidiary, Canadian Industries. These proposals were included in the final reports of the Maud Committee, and the Minister of Aircraft Production, Colonel Moore-Brabazon, seemed to be in agreement.

By the end of July 1941, the Maud Committee had finished its work and produced its report. In essence its conclusion was that 'It will be possible to make an effective uranium bomb which, containing some 25 lb of active material, would be equivalent as regards destructive effect to 1,800 tons of TNT and would also release large quantities of radio-active substances which would make places near to where the bomb exploded dangerous to human life for a long period'. The final arbiter was to be the Defence Services Panel of the Scientific Advisory Committee under Lord Hankey. It consisted of a group of five eminent British scientists including three Nobel prize-winners and Sir Henry Dale, President of the Royal Society. Three of them were connected with medicine, one was a physicist and one a professor of chemical technology. After a detailed study of the report, they concluded that the project was feasible and Lord Cherwell, who had concerned himself closely at all stages, recommended to Churchill that the bomb should be built. Churchill sent Cherwell's memorandum to his Chiefs of Staff with an accompanying minute whose words have become celebrated: 'Although personally I am quite content with the existing explosives, I feel we must not stand in the path of improvement, and I therefore think that action should be taken in the sense proposed by Lord Cherwell: and that the Cabinet Minister responsible should be Sir John Anderson.' The Chiefs of Staff were unanimous in agreement that work on the bomb should proceed apace, and proceed in Britain rather than abroad.

The man named by Churchill to be in charge of the whole project, Sir John Anderson, was a former Home Secretary and in 1941 Lord President of the Council. He was a chemist by training who had carried out work on uranium as a young man at the University of Leipzig and had sat briefly on ICI's board for a few months in 1938. Akers from ICI was appointed under him as working head of the project, and a technical committee of scientists was set up, with ICI's research director Roland Slade among them. The whole project, which was now moved from the Ministry of Aircraft Production to the Department of Scientific and Industrial Research, needed a name – a coded name which did not give any hint of its overwhelming importance.

Sir Michael Perrin recalled how the name was chosen. Perrin and Akers had been discussing what to call themselves and their thoughts turned to 'tanks', a name chosen in similar circumstances for the development of the new weapon in the First World War. 'We went over to Anderson and suggested "Tank Alloys". Anderson thought for a bit and said, "No, that won't do . . . I think you can assume that there will always be a tube in anything and I suggest you call yourselves the Directorate of Tube Alloys. It's quite meaningless, but it sounds as if it's got some kind of importance".' And so Tube Alloys it became.

Anderson was a strange, aloof man, inclined to a certain frosty grandeur in his manner and style of writing. One of the Americans with whom he dealt on atomic matters said that his memoranda read as if they were written by a member of Lord North's cabinet. Perrin first encountered this daunting personality when he took a small piece of uranium which had been made by General Chemicals Division round to show to Anderson, not knowing of Anderson's youthful work on the subject. 'He took it in his hand and looked at it very carefully each way round for about a minute without saying anything, not a change in his face, and then he looked up at me and said, "Yes, Perrin, you know the first time I saw metallic uranium was when I made some in order to measure its specific heat for my thesis on the chemistry and properties of uranium at one of the German universities." He looked rather fierce, as if to say, "Why are you wasting my time?" Then suddenly his face changed and he said, "But it wasn't nearly such a nice piece as this. Thank you very much." And he put it away carefully in a drawer of his desk.'

ICI's bid to take over the whole development of nuclear energy 'for the British Empire' was rejected out of hand by the Hankey Committee: indeed, it is doubtful if anyone in the company, apart from Melchett and McGowan, had really thought that they could. Anderson himself was firmly against the idea. Halban, after protracted negotiations with ICI over his salary and a share in the profits from his work, eventually went to Montreal and took part there in the Canadian side of atomic development, which was quite extensive. Still, the appointment of Wallace Akers as Anderson's deputy in charge of the project on a day-to-day basis meant that the company continued to be closely involved at the highest level. An official of the Ministry of Aircraft Production noted that the situation 'verges on the Gilbertian. The Government decides to turn down ICI's request to be allowed to run the development and then asks ICI to let them have the chief protagonist of the ICI request to manage the matter for the Government'. Akers encountered some initial resistance to his appointment from the civil servants whose ranks he had temporarily joined, on what he optimistically thought was a part-time basis. His personality and drive soon won over colleagues in Britain, but it was to be a different matter in the States where he and Perrin made frequent visits on the thorny subject of Anglo-American nuclear cooperation. (On one such journey Perrin took with him a sample of heavy water, which gurgled noticeably in its container and excited much curiosity among his fellow passengers.)

The Uneasy Collaboration

Much has been written about the Anglo-American relationship in the development of nuclear energy, and it can only be sketched in outline here. The early signs from across the Atlantic had been encouraging, with Dr Vannevar Bush, director of President Roosevelt's Office of Scientific Research, and Dr J. B. Conant, president of Harvard and Bush's deputy, both wholeheartedly in favour of collaboration between the two countries on atom-bomb research. In 1941, Roosevelt offered to pool American resources with British on a joint development. But the British, who were ahead of the Americans at that stage, rejected the offer, still being concerned to keep Halban's work under British control. The consequences of that rejection were swift and irreversible. When Simon, Akers and Halban went to America in January 1942 to visit the various centres where American research on the project was being carried on, they realized with a shock how far and how fast the Americans had moved in a few months. They were well ahead on the processes for producing fissile material, had done a great deal of work on plutonium as an alternative to uranium and were in almost every respect in advance of the British.

In Britain at this time the crucial diffusion-plant models were still far from perfect and, as the months went by, the British team became reluctantly aware that not only were they being outstripped scientifically by the Americans but also that collaboration was becoming progressively eroded. One important reason for this was that the US military authorities had assumed a much greater degree of control over the project than the British at first realized. In particular, the chauvinistic Major General L. R. Groves of the Engineer Corps had been appointed principal executive of a newly formed Military Committee directing the American project, with the result that a far stronger emphasis on security began to be felt at once. Groves didn't care much for the British, but he was deeply suspicious of the many scientists of Central European origin associated with them, such as Peierls and Klaus Fuchs (correctly in the case of Fuchs, as events turned out). He had considerably increased the compartmentalization of the work in America, so that many of the theoretical physicists who were working on the secret military applications were almost hermetically sealed off from contact with each other and with the outside world.

In addition, the Americans found it hard to believe that Akers, though working in the capacity of a government official, was not also seeking to further the interests of his own company. This was quite untrue, and deeply resented by Akers and his British colleagues, but nothing could shift the American suspicion. Things might have gone quite differently, Perrin believed in later years, if the internationally known James Chadwick rather than Akers had gone to the States in the first place, but Chadwick, always fussy about his health, feared and disliked travelling, and by the time he did cross the Atlantic it was too late. Akers worked tirelessly and selflessly in the interests of cooperation, but to no avail; Groves seemed almost to carry on a personal vendetta against him, taking exception even to the fact that Akers used ICI offices when in New York, which was an obvious and convenient course for him to take. By the beginning of 1943, Anglo-American collaboration was virtually at an end.

Churchill made every effort to restore cooperation, realizing that after the war nuclear weapons would be, in the words of the atomic-energy historian Margaret Gowing, 'the supreme symbol of power, and that if Britain had no part in this she would have very little say in the other major issues facing the world'. In August 1943, he succeeded in persuading Roosevelt at Quebec to share American atomic research and resources in the common war effort. The Quebec Agreement used the code name invented by Sir John Anderson, Tube Alloys, and so did the so-called Hyde Park Agreement a year later, which consisted of a brief, confidential *aide-mémoire* initialled by Churchill and Roosevelt at the President's New York home, Hyde Park. This rejected the suggestion that 'the world should be informed regarding tube alloys [*sic*] with a view to an international agreement regarding its control and use', and said the matter should continue to be one of 'the utmost secrecy'. When a bomb was finally available, the note continued, 'it might perhaps, after mature consideration, be used against the Japanese, who should be warned that this bombardment will be repeated until they surrender. Full collaboration between the United States and the British Government in developing tube alloys [*sic*] for military and commercial purposes should continue after the defeat of Japan unless and until terminated by joint agreement'.

According to Sir John Colville, Churchill's private secretary, when Senator McMahon, the architect of the McMahon Act which destroyed postwar Anglo-American nuclear collaboration, visited Churchill after his return to office in 1951, he was shown Churchill's copy of the secret *aide-mémoire* and said if he had known of its existence he would never have proceeded with the McMahon Act.

America Takes Over

Wallace Akers was the obvious choice as technical adviser to the Combined Policy Commission set up under the terms of the Quebec

Agreement, but General Groves remained hostile to the ICI man and Chadwick was appointed instead. Practical work had meanwhile been continuing in various parts of ICI, largely undisturbed by these high-level international affairs. Much of it, from the end of 1941, had focused on heavy water: ICI had been interested in heavy water for some years before the war, but had withdrawn from work on it when the Norsk Hydro in Norway managed to produce it by a much cheaper process. During 1942, the company considered alternatives to the electrolytic method used in Norway, which used vast amounts of electricity. Distillation was one possibility, and the American theory was also studied which involved preferential exchange of heavy hydrogen between gas and water, using a catalyst. Neither proved promising, and although it would have been possible for the British to build a full-scale electrolytic plant, the cost of the electricity required would have been prohibitive. By the end of 1943 it was clear in any case that to contemplate production of energy for bombs as well as for industry would take more manpower and material resources than Britain at that stage of the war could possibly afford. Then, when the Quebec Agreement restored some degree of collaboration, news began to flow back to Britain about the success of the Americans with their own gaseous diffusion plant, their developments in nuclear physics and, above all, the work going on at Los Alamos under the code name 'Manhattan Project'.

Soon there was a regular brain drain to the States. Requests for British Scientists and engineers were speedily met, even though Groves' policy of working in independent pockets of research meant that they were never given the full picture of what was going on. Four ICI scientists went as part of a team of thirty-five working on electromagnetic projects in America, and J. P. Baxter, the research manager from General Chemicals who had made that first piece of uranium metal out of his spare research budget, went to Oakridge, Tennessee, in the summer of 1944. This vast plant was where the fissile material was made, and Baxter's great knowledge and experience of uranium chemistry made him such a success that he became general manager with overall responsibility for all the plant's research, development and production. Peierls, Fuchs and Frank Kearton (later Lord Kearton, the chairman of Courtaulds and British National Oil Corporation) were among British scientists and engineers attached for a while to the so-called Kellex Corporation in New York, the anonymous-sounding business set up by Kellogg's, the cereal manufacturers, to cloak work on the atomic project.

By the spring of 1944, ICI was once more working on the processes for separating U235. ICI Metals had already made a workable membrane on a laboratory scale and were now trying to demonstrate that it could be produced in quantity. A small factory in King's Lynn was taken over for the purpose, but it suffered delays and was not ready until after the war. Work had also continued on uranium metal at General Chemicals, using calcium as a reduction agent (the Americans used magnesium). Getting the exceptionally high degree of purity required proved very difficult, as did the process of converting the small ingots into rods. However, by the spring of 1943 a pilot plant was in operation producing up to 1,000 pounds of uranium a week. General Chemicals also carried on with experiments on producing hexafluoride, but production never got beyond the laboratory scale, and when ICI Billingham needed the gas for its own experiments, cylinders of it had to be sent over from the States.

Plans for a full-scale diffusion plant and hopes that Britain – in particular the teams at Billingham and Oxford – might be able to contribute substantially to the American effort both faded after the Quebec Agreement. But in May 1944, when Britain began considering the question of its own, postwar nuclear industry, ICI was invited to produce estimates for a low-separation diffusion plant. These were made and revised in great detail, drawing considerably on work already done by the Americans. But in April 1945, the project was halted, frustrating the engineers and scientists who were convinced they had at last solved all the remaining technical problems. The Directorate of Tube Alloys believed that gaseous diffusion could now be carried out efficiently and relatively cheaply and that the whole process could be revived after the war. When the work was wound up at Billingham, everything was left in a finished and accessible state, ready to be started up at any time. These hopes were not to be realized.

By June, 1944, the government had authorized ICI to spend £950,000 on Tube Alloys research; £870,000 had in fact been spent. This total was greater than for all other spending by ICI on government wartime research put together and, by the time the war ended, ICI was the only large organization in the country competent to design an atomic-energy plant. Yet in 1945 a domestic nuclear industry scarcely existed at all in terms of plant and installation, though the resources were all there in scientific and technological expertise. Its bid to become what emerged as the UK Atomic Energy Authority had been stifled at birth, but ICI provided two men to key appointments in that authority when it was set up by the Attlee government after the war. One was Christopher Hinton, a chief engineer of the Alkali Division, who was one of the chief engineers responsible for the design of the reactors at the Atomic Energy Research Establishment on the old RAF station at Harwell. The other was Michael Perrin, who became Deputy Controller (Technical Policy) to Lord Portal of Hungerford, former Chief of the Air Staff who was appointed the Atomic Energy Authority's first Controller of Production.

Perrin had had an eventful war with Tube Alloys; in 1944 he was involved in an Anglo-American mission code-named Operation Alsos which went into Germany, took possession of documentary evidence on the country's nuclear programme and removed a group of ten senior scientists working on it. They were spirited into England and kept in a 'safe house' belonging to British intelligence until after the bomb was dropped on Hiroshima. They had no idea why they were there, nor that the whole house was wired for sound and that Perrin was receiving a full translation the next day. At their first dinner, Perrin recalled, one of them said wonderingly: 'This is quite extraordinary. If it had been the other way round and we had been your people taken to Germany, we wouldn't have dared to talk of anything we were doing or had been doing.'

7

A Do-It-Yourself World

'1951 should be a year of fun, fantasy and colour, a year in which we can, while soberly surveying our great past and our promising future, for once let ourselves go.' So declared Gerald Barry, Director-General of the Festival of Britain at a press conference in October 1948, two and a half years before the festival was due to open. Fun, fantasy and colour had certainly been lacking in Britain for many years, and nowhere was this more evident than in the home. The whole country seemed shabby, down-at-heel, needing a new dress or a coat of paint; little more than the most essential maintenance had been carried out during the war and immediate postwar years, and production of the new synthetic materials like nylon, polythene and Perspex had been almost entirely earmarked for military use. Clothing was still rationed under a coupon scheme. Furniture – what little there was of it – was mass-produced and sold under the 'Utility' label (sales were originally restricted to new brides and people who had been bombed out of their homes) in a pitifully limited range of styles and colours. Kitchens were still equipped with the enamel or galvanized metal bowls and buckets, the stone sinks and heavy cast-iron stoves which had remained un-touched in design and materials for decades.

But even as Gerald Barry was speaking, a housing boom was getting under way; within ten years, ten million people, or one in every five in Britain, would be living in new, postwar houses. New towns (fourteen of them had been visualized by the Abercrombie Plan for London in 1944), new factories and new housing estates all demanded a new internal environment, and it was the research chemist who provided the materials for it.

Nylon, the first true synthetic fabric and ICI's Terylene, the first polyester, made immediate inroads on the sales of traditional fabrics such as wool, cotton and silk as soon as they came on the civilian market. Both nylon and Terylene attracted dirt, but could be washed easily; expensive materials in light colours which needed correspond-ingly expensive dry-cleaning lost much of their snob appeal in conse-quence. Detergents were first marketed for the housewife under brand names in 1951 – they had been developed during the war as substitutes for soap – and the result was a wash-day revolution as coppers, wash-boards and metal buckets boiling on the stove in steam-filled kitchens became a thing of the past for many people. Reflecting in 1986 on the greatest changes in his lifetime, ICI's top research scientist Professor Derek Birchall singled out the disappearance of wash-day – which might in fact stretch to four days if the weather prevented outdoor drying on the line. At the other end of the economic scale, domestic servants were a dying breed in the postwar years, and washing ma-chines and refrigerators revolutionized the middle-class kitchen at the same time as sitting-rooms began to fill with furniture designed on what everyone called 'contemporary' lines.

Along with the washing machines came colourful, lightweight, easily washable and unbreakable buckets, bowls and brushes, all made from polythene. Virtually all ICI's wartime output of polythene had been absorbed by the demands of radar, and by the end of the war the Alkali Group had plant capable of producing around 1,500 tons a year, most of it manufactured at Wallerscote and Winnington. If these plants were to be kept going it was obvious that new, peacetime outlets would be needed. At first, though, there was a good deal of mistrust of the various plastic materials on the part of the public, much of it engen-dered by unfortunate experiences with the early plastic mackintoshes. These were made from polychlorothylene recovered from scrap cable insulation (the wrong material, wrongly made up) and easily became brittle and split. But in the kitchen, it was a different matter. The first polythene bowls began appearing in the shops as early as 1948. More expensive at that time than the traditional enamelled ware, they nev-ertheless quickly became popular as their advantages were realized – bright, clear colours, long life, resistance to chipping or rusting, quiet in use and much safer when washing up precious glass or china.

There were a few initial disasters when they were put on the stove to boil water, but people soon learned to use them properly. When they were first made, only one per cent of the UK production of polythene was used for domestic products, but designers were quick to find uses for the new material – bread-bins, storage boxes, jars, brushes – and by 1957 forty per cent of a much larger production was in use for house-hold goods. ICI never got into the manufacture of moulded polythene: it sold the raw material in bulk, usually in the form of chips. 'Small firms could always make things cheaper than we could, so we never really got into the fabricated forms,' said Sir Peter Allen. 'Otherwise you end up owning the entire business down to the shop in the high street selling wheelbarrows.'

As early as 1941 du Pont had predicted that polythene film would form the largest market for the new plastic, and the sales of this new material expanded enormously with the rise of supermarkets and self-service, and indeed helped to bring about the shopping revolution of the 1950s. In 1960, the house journal of J. Sainsbury and Co. remarked: 'It is difficult to see how self-service could have been possible, let alone prospered, without the aid of transparent wrapping.' For the first time, customers could see what they were buying, even though it was pre-packaged. The Sainsbury journal also noted that 'all counters from which unwrapped food is served are covered with Perspex canopies, another tribute to the plastics industry.' Plastic bags and carriers were the next to be developed, and polythene was used to coat cardboard for milk and soft-drink cartons.

By 1953 it was an important raw material for consumer products, but the manufacturing process still required very high pressures. That year, however, various independent discoveries enabled polythene to be made at low or ordinary pressure. The most influential process was that of Professor Karl Ziegler at the Max Planck Institute in Mülheim. He discovered how to make high polymers of ethene at a pressure only a little above normal, though the process required expensive and complex catalysts which had to be suspended in an organic solvent. ICI, no doubt to its chagrin as the begetter of polythene, had to license the Ziegler method to keep abreast of technology. At much the same time, two American oil companies, Phillips Petroleum and Standard Oil of Indiana, discovered other methods of making polythene at very low pressures (less than 100 bars, compared with the 1,000 and 3,000 bars needed by the original process). These also used solid catalysts, different from those employed by Ziegler.

The new materials were different from their predecessors. They were high density, stiffer and less flexible, and could not be used, for example, for cable insulation or the new 'squeezy' bottles for washing-up liquid which were developed in the early and mid-1950s from the older versions of polythene. But they soon found an important market in the manufacture of rigid bottles for milk, bleach and other liquids, and such things as milk-bottle crates where lightness and strength were necessary. Both types of production method have been developed and improved ever since, which, among other things, has helped to keep the price down. Today polythene in its different formulations is one of the most inexpensive and versatile materials in everyday use. One incidental result of the explosion of polythene uses was to teach the public that there was more than one form of plastic. Another type of plastic, polyurethane foam, was always less visible but in its own way had a comparable impact on the way we live.

Revolution in Refrigeration

Polyurethanes were invented by Otto Bayer in Germany just before the Second World War in an effort to produce a synthetic fibre that could compete with du Pont's nylon; they were developed by IG Farben at Leverkusen during the war, principally as foams for insulating material in V2 rockets and some aircraft and military vehicles. The details of polyurethane technology were brought back to Britain after the war by the Allied commission on German wartime industrial development, and ICI's Reg Hurd was one of the chemists who played a major role in its progress after that. After serving in the British and Indian armies, Hurd took a degree in chemistry and in 1950 joined the Resins Technical Service of ICI in the Dyestuffs (later Organics) Division. Resins, as well as being used in paint manufacture, are also needed to make polyurethane foams: put together with polyisocyanates, they react giving a foaming cellular structure which is produced by bubbles of carbon dioxide being trapped in the polymer as it is formed. The early types were made from a resin known as 2:4 toluylene di-isocyanate, or TDI. Rigid foams fill up complex cavities and bond strongly to most surfaces, giving immense strength: sandwiches of foam and plastic or aluminium skins can support an adult's weight. Hurd's early work at ICI was concerned with testing TDI foams for injection into aircraft wings to give them resistance to anti-aircraft fire. Injected as it foams, TDI sets solid inside the wing, enabling a missile to pass right through it without shattering the structure. Repairs can then easily be done by plugging the hole with more foam.

TDI rigid foams had one serious drawback, however. In the enclosed spaces where they needed to be applied, they gave off vapours which caused the eyes of people handling them to water and sometimes produced asthmatic attacks. (The flexible version used for furniture upholstery could be made in ventilated factory conditions.) Hurd and his colleagues used to make batches of the stuff using a domestic Kenwood mixer. On one occasion he noticed a woman stirring the mixture was becoming blue in the face and wheezing. It was then that he decided to try to produce 'a less hazardous technology', and in particular to prove that it was possible to make foams from a different polyisocyanate, Diphenyl Methane Di-isocyanate, or MDI. It was known that MDI was much easier and safer to handle, but conventional wisdom had always been that it was impossible to make foam from it. Its only significant use at this period, in the early 1950s, was as a solution in xylene for bonding rubber to metal, and it was only in this form that ICI made it.

Hurd began in a small way, with just himself and two 'very good lab assistants', but with the great advantage that his boss in the division, Dr Hampton, was interested in resins and both encouraged and funded his work. Hurd recalls that the use of MDI to make a foam was thought impossible because 'the two isocyanate groups used in TDI have a different reactivity. When you look at MDI, the two groups do not have that difference, and it was assumed this would prevent MDI from making foam. And indeed if you take pure MDI it still won't make foam'. What Hurd used was crude MDI; he argued, correctly as it turned out, that if the reactivity of the resin mix was changed, it was possible to compensate for the lack of reactivity in the MDI.

There seemed little commercial interest, however, so he set about making his own variants of polyester resins. 'They are quite simple to make, nothing exotic in the chemistry.' Having done this, he found that they did indeed foam much more easily with TDI than the usual resins, and he went on to see if they would foam with MDI. He took some commercial MDI solution, distilled off the xylene, 'And sure enough I could make a foam with it'. Yet it was still only of minor interest, and there were many other things going on in the department with surface and fabric coatings. Hurd remembers that all he did at the time was to write to the research department and tell them for the record that, 'It *is* possible to foam with MDI'.

The timing of his discovery, however, was much more crucial than Hurd and his colleagues at first appreciated. The world was at the outset of a boom in refrigerated cargo ships and the whole refrigeration industry, and the principal form of insulation used in the cold stores in the ships was cork. This could smoulder for long periods and had been responsible for many fires, notably the burning of the Canadian Pacific liner *Empress of Britain* in Liverpool Docks. While TDI foam was recognized as having excellent insulating properties, it could not safely be used in the cargo holds of ships because of the toxic vapours it gave off while being injected in confined spaces. So Hurd and a young colleague called Abbotson demonstrated to two or three shipping-insulation manufacturers that it was possible to make rigid foam with a 'safe' isocyanate; that the MDI foam was less liable to be ignited during welding on ships' plates, that it was a more efficient insulant and gave added strength in cargo holds.

'Then we had a bit of luck – and luck comes into all inventions,' Hurd recalls with satisfaction. There was an Open Day at the Refrigerated Cargo Research Council, a body which had been set up by shipowners to try to improve design and performance in insulation materials and techniques. ICI was invited to lay on a demonstration of its new foams, and the shipowners were immediately intrigued. At this stage, says Hurd, they were still 'making the stuff in a bucket stirred with a stick – not even using the Kenwood mixer – because it was so simple to make'. Someone suggested to Hurd that he should give a lecture on MDI foam at the next International Refrigeration meeting at Nantes, in 1957, which attracted shipping people from all over Europe. The response was immediate and positive, particularly from the Dutch. Within two years of that lecture, ICI was providing foam to fill cold stores, refrigerated transport and carbon dioxide tankers; chemical plants and pipelines were also being insulated with rigid foam.

The technique revolutionized the refrigeration of ships: P & O's *Oriana*, for example, carried 100 tons of rigid polyurethane foam when she went into service in 1960 – three of her holds were insulated with it, as well as a provision room, bulk stores and brine room. Four hundred of her doors were filled with it, saving weight without impairing their strength. The *Canberra*, which went into passenger service in 1962, had over 100 doors constructed with the foam filling, as well as deep-freeze rooms and cold stores. In the construction industry, too, the foams made an immediate impact. They are now extensively used as a thermal insulant, can be bonded (without a separate gluing operation) to a variety of facing materials and can be used as a core in curtain-wall panels (as in the Piccadilly Hotel, Manchester), or in flooring (as in Salisbury Cathedral).

By the early 1960s, MDI rigid foam had gone into buildings for heat insulation in Europe, Canada and Australia. Growth was helped by ICI's development of simple, inexpensive machines which pumped the correct mixtures of the liquid chemicals to a self-cleaning mixing head which prevented the head from seizing up during reaction. But before commercial success could be assured, customers had to be persuaded that the remarkable properties of the foam would last for the lifetime of a ship or a building. A mathematician on ICI's staff helped by proving that classical physical theory supported the experimental data.

From the consumer's point of view, the development of MDI foams revolutionized the manufacture and price of domestic fridges and freezers, making them a possibility in far more homes than before. By the early 1960s they were becoming a standard fitting in British kitchens instead of a luxury item, and frozen food gained sweeping popularity: between 1955 and 1957 sales of deep-frozen food doubled, and by 1960 they had doubled again. The frozen-food cabinet appeared in every corner store and a dramatic change in eating habits took place: frozen chicken, fish fingers, peas in or out of season and strawberry mousse became as much staples of the British diet as tinned salmon, baked beans and pineapple, products of the earlier invention of canning.

It was in Italy that the potential of polyurethane foam for consumer durables and white goods was first recognized. The traditional method of making fridges had been to construct a strong steel outer casing and an enamelled steel or heavy-duty plastic lining, and to insulate the cavity between the two with a fibrous material such as fibreglass or polystyrene. The Italians quickly designed a much better combination of a thin, respectively cheap plastic interior 'skin', an insulating layer of foam which gave added strength to the lining, and a thin outer steel casing. The foam layer itself could be made much thinner than the materials it replaced, and the thickness of fridge walls could accordingly be reduced from three inches to 1.25 inches, enabling the manufacture of more compact yet more capacious fridges for small kitchens, and permitting sleeker, more modern styling. This was one factor contributing heavily to the success of Italian fridges in the 1960s, when they swept the European market with a cheaper and better product more suited to small modern apartments. Other countries soon followed the Italian lead and, by the end of the 1960s, a large proportion of fridges were made by this method: today, almost all use foam in their construction for insulation and strength.

Germany's Bayer company pioneered TDI flexible foams, which revolutionized the furniture industry, and ICI was quick to follow Bayer's lead here and in other variations on the chemistry such as high-performance synthetic rubbers and coatings. By 1960 ICI's Organics Division had set up a new Application Research and Technical Service Group under Dr Jack Buist to carry out development over the whole field of urethane chemicals. Hurd became one of two technical section managers. During the 1960s the team introduced developments which greatly extended the market for MDI foams: continuous lamination processes, for example, and variations on the chemistry which produced applications as diverse as soles moulded directly to shoes and impact-resistant car bumpers.

Chemists were entranced by the versatility of polyurethanes. As John Rigg, former chairman of Organics Division, put it: 'You can take these two components [resins and isocyanates] and play tremendous tunes on them.'

Hurd transferred to management in the early 1970s. His original two lab assistants had expanded into a staff of 140 in Manchester and 60 in Brussels as the full commercial potential of MDI chemistry was recognized. It was an exciting time. Hurd, by the 1980s a dapper, white-haired man living in retirement on the edge of Derbyshire's Peak District, quoted T. E. Lawrence: 'It was the morning freshness of the world to be.'

In the mid-1980s he was still actively concerned with foams and questions of their toxicity and flammability, and lent his expertise to the study of such disasters as the 1985 British Airtours crash in Manchester and the fire which destroyed a Woolworth store in Liverpool in 1979, in both of which the role of foam-filling came under severe scrutiny. While not playing down the dangers of some flexible foam used in seating, Hurd stressed that the rubberized fibres and latex which preceded polyurethanes can be just as hazardous in fires. On a personal note, he reflected on the changes wrought in everyday life by flexible foams: 'Today you have soft seats all over the house; when I was a lad, you didn't. They were too expensive, or they didn't last, or the springs came through.'

Colour Comes to Stay

Almost simultaneously with the discovery of MDI foams came another, equally exciting and commercially attractive innovation for ICI. One of the things people most remembered about the 1951 Festival of Britain was colour, of which war-scarred Britain had been starved. Everything, as the social historian Henry Hopkins wrote, had seemed either 'gravy-brown or dull green'. But certain bright shades were still unobtainable in cotton except by using dyes which either faded or washed out.

The first synthetic dyes had been discovered in England in 1856 by William Henry Perkin, but Germany quickly seized leadership in the dyestuffs industry and by the outbreak of the First World War, the Germans commanded nearly 90 per cent of the market worldwide. The collapse of the European dyestuffs cartels after the Second World War enabled Britain to expand her export markets, but up to the late 1940s there had been no major discoveries in the industry since the azoic dyes which had been developed in 1912.

Nylon and polyester fibres demanded new and improved dyes and dyestuffs chemists were falling over themselves trying to be the first in the field. Within ICI alone, something like 3,000 new potential dye structures for all fibres were being synthesized and screened ever year, though very few reached the technical and commercial standards required. These could be summarized as offering a worthwhile advantage over existing dyes; the ability to be made in a good shade range of bright and softer colours; capable of being patented; relatively cheap to make; fast in sunlight and when washed; and generally easy to use. In the case of polyester, a limited number of dyes were available, but they were neither truly fast nor offered really satisfactory colours. They were known as 'disperse' dyes because a very fine dispersal of the colour was needed to dye the fibres.

In the 1950s, synthetic fibres were still only in their infancy. Polyester did not come on to the market in bulk until 1954, and the quantities still being sold of wool, cotton and viscose rayon far outstripped it. Ten million tonnes of cotton and viscose rayon were produced each year, and one million tonnes of wool; nearly three quarters of all this production was dyed or printed, and dyestuffs manufacturers, ICI included, had to make continual advances in technology or be left behind in the race.

In spite of the small impact of synthetic materials on the fabric market at that period, there was a tremendous confidence in them within ICI, especially in the fledgling Fibres Division, and a widespread feeling that cotton and natural fibres would soon lose ground against them. Today, it is possible to apply the perspective of hindsight. 'Synthetics were being promoted beyond their natural horizon,' says John Rigg, who was in charge of European sales for the Dyestuffs Division in the mid-1950s. This was a period when it was scarcely possible to buy a cotton shirt in a chain store, even though nylon was notoriously uncomfortable in hot weather. The synthetics manufacturers were vigorous in promoting their own products, and no one in the cotton industry was effectively mounting a counter-attack.

Nevertheless, work continued on dyes for natural fibres and within the 'Dyehouse' – a research department of Dyestuffs Division – a small group concentrated on finding a new bright wool dye which would be satisfactorily colourfast when washed. They had a totally new idea in mind: to modify the structure of some known groups of dyes so that they would actually undergo a chemical reaction with the wool fibres. Instead of the previous types of water-soluble wool dyes, which were only attached to the fibres by weak physical forces – allowing the dye molecules to be readily washed away – the ICI chemists were trying to produce a 'co-valent' link. This would be a true chemical bond between dye and fibre, making the colour part of the fibre itself.

One of the chemists, Dr W. E. Stephen, had prepared derivatives of azo dyes with what he thought would be potent fibre-reactive groups, among them derivatives of trichlorotriazine, or cyanuric chloride. Stephen's initial tests, however, were disappointing. The senior technologist in the wool-dyeing section, Ian Rattee, was not impressed by results from the first samples which Stephen sent him. But one morning in 1953 when Stephen and Rattee were reviewing progress, Stephen pointed out that what they were trying to bring about between the acid-chloride groups in the dye and the amino groups in the wool was what is technically known as the 'Schotten Baumann' reaction. This only takes place in the presence of a strong alkali, which would have disastrous effects on wool. But, as Rattee now reasoned, the classic Schotten Baumann reaction also took place with hydroxyl groups as well as with amino groups. Cotton contains hydroxyl groups in abundance; moreover, cotton is not affected by a great deal of alkali.

Rattee suddenly realized that these dyes might work well with cotton, producing the long-elusive co-valent link between dye and fibre to give water-soluble dyes which would be colourfast even when wet or being washed. Cotton dyes were not in Rattee's province, but he knew they were a much larger business target than his own efforts with wool, so that same day he proceeded to test Stephen's dichlorotriazinyl dyes on cotton. They worked. A feverish excitement gripped the team of research chemists and technologists when it was realized that a search that had lasted sporadically for sixty years was perhaps at last coming to an end.

But the success so far had only been in minute quantities, under laboratory conditions; there was a long way to go before the dyes could be marketed for large-scale use in textile mills. Further small-scale experimentation followed, and within six months three promising dyes had been chosen for more concentrated development – a red, a blue and a yellow. At this stage the research managers had to approach the divisional board, who swiftly grasped the thrilling implications of the discovery. In order to maximize the lead time over competitors which would be provided by patents, the usual ultra-cautious development procedures were pared to the bone, and the board sanctioned the production of half a tonne of each of the three colours, of which only gram weights had been made up till then in the lab. Details for scaling up the process to produce these relatively vast amounts had still to be worked out.

There remained one major stumbling block – hydrolysis. It was, paradoxically, the very reactivity with the hydroxyl groups of cotton which made the new dyes so successful; but water and alkali also contain hydroxyl groups, and any reaction between the dye and the water before or during the dyeing process resulted in a loss of dye through hydrolysis. Stephen developed a buffering process which controlled the pH factor of the system during isolation, drying, storage and re-dissolving. The problem was not considered to have been finally cracked until the dye powders had withstood storage times of between eight and twelve months, and success here was the key to the commercial success of what ICI christened its 'Procion' reactive dyes.

At first it was thought that the reactive dyes were most suitable for continuous fabric dyeing (as opposed to batch dyeing). Bulk trials were organized in the continuous dyeing machines of friendly customers in the UK, who were themselves greatly excited by the new discovery. Each experiment used several thousand metres of fabric, so they had to be very carefully controlled.

The first trial was a dismal failure, though it was later discovered that the machine used had mechanical faults and the fabric had given trouble even when dyed by conventional methods. The second series of tests, in a different location, proved resoundingly successful, and the decision was taken to press ahead with all the multiple operations which precede any dye being launched on to the market: research, patenting, works production, planning, engineering and many others. Since the end of the war, the home market had not been big enough to support such a heavy expenditure on R & D, so Rigg and his export sales team were heavily involved from the start. Soon teams of ICI sales and technical men – they were known as travelling 'Procion circuses' – set off to make sales presentations to all ICI's major markets abroad.

In such a rushed timetable, there were bound to be some difficulties. The blue dye caused doubts because in order to be competitive with traditional blue vat dyes, it would have to be sold at a loss of as much as £1 per pound (at 1958 prices). But it was argued, rightly, that it was only a matter of time before a cost-effective blue would be developed. The three-dye range was launched in March 1956, and sales almost immediately took off, at first in industrialized countries such as Japan, the USA and Scandinavia, then in countries such as India, Brazil and Pakistan, which were major users of cotton. In the 'Dyehouse', meanwhile, research had not slackened and within a year of the original launch a further eighteen brilliantly coloured 'Procion' dyes were successfully developed.

From the beginning the division had been looking for ways of extending the application of these revolutionary products, in particular their possible use in batch dyeing and fabric printing, in both of which they proved effective. Batch dyeing was made possible by a discovery which enabled it to be carried out as a cold dyeing process, a commercially attractive proposition which was eagerly adopted by manufacturers. Fabric printing, which calls for the mechanical application of the colour to precisely defined areas of cloth in order to form the pattern, was at first more difficult. Various 'thickeners' composed of gums and starches are mixed by the textile printer to produce a viscous paste which can then be applied exactly where a sharply printed patch of colour is wanted. Unfortunately, both the thickeners and the cotton were rich in hydroxyl groups, so the dyes reacted in a similar way with them until a new, cheaper and non-reactive thickener was discovered, based on sodium alginate, made from seaweed.

Another problem was caused by the use of red dye in fabric printing. When prints containing red were well washed and then stored, a certain amount of hydrolysis took place, especially in damp atmospheres made acidic by pollution, like that of Manchester. The red colour 'bled' or flushed beyond the limits of the printed design. The alginate-based pastes also proved to have too short a life to be useful. For a time it looked as though the reactive dyes would not be able to be used in printing, until further research showed that less reactive monochlorotriazine dyes could replace the dichloro dyes in this process. They needed a hot rather than a cold dyeing process, but they gave good colour fixation and their lower reactivity meant that the colour pastes remained stable for much longer, so that 'bleeding' or flushing was stopped.

By 1961, demand for 'Procion' dyes was running at 600 tonnes a year, and ICI's market forecasters were predicting sales of two and a half times that amount within three years. New and specially designed plant had to be built, and a modern plant at Trafford Park, Manchester, with a capacity of 1,500 tonnes a year came on stream in 1963. Another, at Grangemouth in Scotland, was under way by 1967. Procion dyes made small but significant earnings within three years of first marketing the product and earned a true surplus over and above the large sums spent on development and plant by about 1971 or 1972 – only sixteen years after the dyes were first recognized as a workable discovery.

Along with these advances went work on other types of dye. Like everyone else, ICI was eager to win the race for an improved range of polyester dyes. Here, says John Rigg, the problem was one of finding those colour molecules which penetrated into the fibres and had the required fastness. Cotton polyester was a runaway success in fabric development, combining the easy-care benefits of man-made fibre with the comfort and appeal of natural cotton. But it presented a peculiarly difficult problem to the dyer, who needed a single technique capable of dyeing two different types of fibre, each of which required a different class of dye.

The new colourfast reactive dyes and those for polyesters made a considerable impact on the world market for dyestuffs; today, expansion is much slower, and is largely dependent on the growing aspirations and prosperity of the developing world. The industrialized countries, meanwhile, can buy clothes in any colour that fashion and taste demand, secure in the knowledge that their brightness and fastness are beyond doubt.

Paints Lead the DIY Revolution

The postwar explosions of colour in clothes and domestic utensils were matched by comparable advances in the paints which decorated homes and offices, and in ease of use which transferred much of the business of decorating from the professional to the do-it-yourself enthusiast. ICI had been concerned with paints and lacquers almost from its inception; 'Dulux' was a brand name used by it and also by du Pont in the early days of ICI's existence, and was the first of the alkyd-based paints, which were a breakthrough from the old, lead-based types. In those days, however, decorators and their suppliers were the main customers; even in the early 1950s, the advertising slogan was, 'Say Dulux to your decorator', rather than a direct approach to the consumer, which it was feared might annoy the professionals. But by then the do-it-yourself revolution was just around the corner or, more accurately, just poised to cross the Atlantic. Interest in the home and its appearance was growing, fostered by the new crop of women's magazines and by television, which was promoting a return to the home hardly seen since Victorian times. From 1950 onwards, football and dog-racing began to lose their crowds and cinemas to lose their audiences and close down; more than 800 shut in Britain between 1954 and 1959 and admissions halved in the same period. Sales of draught beer in pubs slumped while those of bottled beer, which could be drunk at home, soared. Men and women alike focused more of their activities on the house, the car and, from about 1950, on the do-it-yourself kit. The American concept greatly eased the financial burden of the new patterns of living, combined with rising labour costs. Nearly three quarters of all wallpaper

By 1953, Dulux was on the retail market. It rapidly became a brand leader.

sold by the second half of the 1950s was direct to the public; sales of portable electric drills rocketed and even furniture began to be sold in kits which claimed that 'all you need is a screwdriver'. Abandoning the community spirit fostered by the war, people became increasingly closeted in their homes and were busy improving them with wallpaper and paint.

By 1953, Dulux was on the retail market. It rapidly rose to become the brand leader, and ten years later the famous Old English sheepdog was used in the advertisements for the first time, chosen as a symbol of 'family'. The breed at that time was relatively uncommon, but under the influence of the ads has become widely popular; indeed, puppies are often advertised for sale as 'Dulux puppies'. Decorating materials seemed to improve month by month; the home handyman (and, increasingly, handywoman) was served by developments such as Berger's non-drip 'Magicote' and Polycell's wallpaper paste that even the clumsiest enthusiast could apply successfully. Brilliant white paint was a notable success for ICI in the mid-1960s and still, some thirty years on, enjoys a substantial market share; two-thirds in the case of gloss paint and between 50 and 60 per cent of emulsion, which was itself a dramatic technical advance over the prewar distemper. The arrival of brilliant white marked a pinnacle for ICI's Paints Division at Slough, giving the company some forty per cent of the entire paints retail market in Britain and about twenty per cent of the trade market. By 1981 the picture had changed as competition grew more aggressive, particularly from Crown. In 1983, ICI launched a successful counter-attack with its range of off-whites with a hint of colour. Within six weeks, a variety of competing products was in the shops, but in 1993, Dulux still retained about a quarter of the total UK market.

Dulux paint is one of the very few products ('Weedol' garden herbicide is another) which go directly from ICI to the customer in the high street. The brand has 'a very emotional pull', according to Philip Hanscombe, managing director in 1986 of the Paints Division. 'Many people think of ICI as Dulux; the brand gives the company a humanity.'

The division is always chasing innovation: paint is one of the most competitive areas in which ICI operates. 'We roam the world looking for new ideas,' said Hanscombe. One American innovation that was successfully developed to a new formulation in the Slough laboratories was solid emulsion in a box, totally mess-free and ideal for painting ceilings. The formula took two years to develop but Hanscombe believed it could be as important to the DIY market as vinyl silk proved in the early 1970s. ICI feels reasonably confident that it is ahead of the competition, given the technical complexities of the paint's production. 'It could still have fifty per cent of the market in ten years' time,' predicted Hanscombe. Appropriately for the DIY market, new paint products at ICI are tested by a consumer panel drawn from around 4,000 people retained for the purpose; about 1,200 tested solid emulsion at home before its launch in February 1984. It's one of the few paint products, given differing national tastes, that has a large-scale export potential into France and Germany, where the division maintains manufacturing plants. (Since 1986, when ICI acquired Glidden Paints of America, the company has ranked as world leader in paints manufacturing.)

Plastics, synthetics and do-it-yourself products have certainly changed the surface of life and its convenience in the years since the Second World War. But much deeper changes and benefits have come from the area in which ICI took its single most far-reaching decision to diversify away from bulk chemicals in the 1930s. Wartime and postwar discoveries in pharmaceuticals have improved not merely the quality of life but the chance of life itself for millions of people.

8

THE HEART OF THE MATTER

Alfred Mond had wanted ICI to be a research-based company whose innovations would match those of its great German rival, IG Farben. But the collapse of its cornerstone business, the nitrogen market, in the late 1920s and the world depression that followed, forced deep cuts in its research budgets, which did not begin to rise again until the mid-1930s. By this time the whole chemical industry was undergoing profound change, away from the old nineteenth-century bulk commodities towards 'fine' organic chemistry, and ICI's research policy began to change direction in response. Pesticides, pharmaceuticals, synthetic rubber, fibres and plastics were among the new developments clamouring for attention, and Dyestuffs, something of a Cinderella compared with the influential Alkali and General Chemical groups within ICI, now put forward determined attempts to work on them. Pharmaceuticals, with its close affinity in technology to the chemical synthesis used in dyestuffs, was one area that the scientists at Blackley successfully claimed for their own.

After much debate within the company's upper management, ICI finally took the plunge into active work on pharmaceuticals in 1936, under the prodding of C. J. Cronshaw, research director of Dyestuffs who later became the division's chairman and in 1943 a main board director. Further powerful support for diversifying into pharmaceuticals came from influential academics advising the company, several of whom felt angry that the British appeared to be leaving everything in drug research to the Germans and the Swiss. Among them were Warrington Yorke, Professor of Tropical Medicine at Liverpool University; Robert (later Sir Robert) Robinson, Professor of Organic Chemistry at Oxford University; and Carl Browning, Professor of Bacteriology at Glasgow University, who had worked with Paul Ehrlich in Germany.

An ICI board minute of 11 June 1936 authorized an initial 'grant' of £15,000 a year for five years from October 1936 for 'research by the Dyestuffs Group in regard to synthetic organic pharmaceuticals', with special emphasis on two areas: original research to discover new remedies, and the making of 'certain pharmaceutical products already

114

imported into this country from abroad'. Seven young doctorate chemists were seconded from different sections into the experimental effort. All were well aware that if they had not made any significant advances by the end of the five-year period the project would be cancelled.

One of the seven was Dr Frank Rose, who had joined the Dyestuffs Division in 1932, aged twenty-three. Rose was to have a most distinguished career in chemistry and be elected a Fellow of the Royal Society. In 1986, although long retired from ICI, he was still working with undimmed enthusiasm as a consultant in a tiny office crammed to the ceiling with papers, in the headquarters of Pharmaceuticals Division at Alderley Park in Cheshire. (He died two years later.) When he began work in the infant pharmaceuticals group in 1936, their laboratories were at the Dyestuffs plant in Blackley, north of Manchester. (A process section was set up at Huddersfield in the following year.) Blackley was about the least suitable environment imaginable for pharmaceutical work. Rose vividly remembers it as 'absolutely filthy – all the smoke from Manchester, all the coal, the perpetual smell of naphthylamine. You couldn't open a window for black smuts. It was just like a Lowry picture, but it was convenient for the textile industry, which was why it was there'. The atmosphere was heavily polluted with zinc and arsenic and frequent viral infections made it difficult to keep the laboratory animals alive for the periods of time necessary to carry out toxicity tests.

Rose was an azo chemist: the newly discovered sulphonamide drugs were based on azo compounds, which have two adjacent nitrogen atoms between carbon atoms. The Bayer laboratories at Elberfield had produced the first sulphonamide drug 'Prontosil' in 1932. Originally made as an azo dye for furs, its anti-bacterial properties were noticed more or less by accident during experiments with rats which had been infected with streptococci. This pioneering work was followed up by French, British, American and Swiss chemists, among them Ernest Fourneau of the Pasteur Institute in Paris, who found that the anti-bacterial action of 'Prontosil' was due to its breakdown in the animal body to a colourless compound named sulphanilamide. Unlike the azo derivative 'Prontosil', this was a known compound and could not be patented, so any manufacturer could produce his own formulation. An 'Elixir of Sulphanilamide' which went on sale in America in 1937 contained a proportion of diethylene glycol as a solvent: in the two months it was available it resulted in at least seventy-six deaths from liver and kidney damage. It was this which caused the enactment of a Food and Drug Act by the US Congress to prevent similar tragedies, and this Act, together with the food and drug legislation that followed it, effectively stopped the US from suffering such disasters as the thalidomide maiming which happened later in Europe.

In Britain the first major development in the field of sulpha drugs came with May and Baker's '693' compound, or 'M & B' as it became popularly known. After clinical trials the first patient received the drug in March 1938, and it soon brought about a dramatic reduction in the number of deaths from lobar pneumonia. By 1940, Rose and his colleagues had discovered a route to the related pyrimidine derivative sulphadimidine, which was much less toxic and was rapidly adopted by British doctors. By this time, however, Rose was more preoccupied by the work which resulted in his major discovery, 'Paludrine'.

The War Against Malaria

Efforts to reproduce the natural anti-malarial properties of quinine in synthetic form dated back to the late 1890s, in particular to the work of Paul Ehrlich at the Moabite Hospital in Berlin. More experiments had been done in Austria: Professor Julius Wagner-Jauregg of Vienna won a Nobel prize in 1927 for his work in the field. But the main thrust of early anti-malarial research was carried on in the Bayer laboratories at Elberfield, where it was focused on Ehrlich's untried idea of preparing derivatives of a dyestuff, methylene blue, as potential drugs to combat the disease. (Ehrlich had relinquished this line of work in the 1890s largely because of his inability to infect small animals with malaria in the laboratory.) By 1925, Bayer chemists had synthesized a promising compound which was tested initially on syphilitic patients suffering from 'general paralysis of the insane', who had been deliberately infected with malarial parasites as part of their treatment. The success of the Bayer compound led on to trials with patients who had acquired malaria by natural means, and after more clinical tests throughout the world, it was given the approved name of 'pamaquin' in the UK. It came on to the market under the trade mark 'Plasmoquine'.

The first British work on pamaquin – whose full chemical structure was not revealed by Bayer until 1928 – was done by, among others, Robert Robinson at University College, London, and George Barger at the University of Edinburgh, working under a research programme initiated by the Joint Chemotherapy Committee of the Medical Research Council and the Department of Scientific and Industrial Research. Robinson, who had been a strong supporter of ICI's entry into pharmaceuticals, was one of a number of academics who formed the company's advisory Medicinal Products Panel. For some time any new drug discoveries were submitted to the panel for biological assessment within university departments, though this ultimately proved impractical. Nothing superior to pamaquin came out of the work done by Robinson and Barger (nor from similar research in other countries), but it set the stage for the gigantic wartime effort that was soon to follow.

Meanwhile thousands of compounds continued to be synthesized at Elberfield in an effort to produce a drug which could bring about a complete cure for malaria. Eventually the Germans produced a branded drug called 'Atebrin' with the approved name of mepacrine (quinacrine in the US). Mepacrine acted like quinine – and unlike pamaquin – in its ability to kill the malarial parasites in the erythrocytic phase of malaria, when they penetrate the red cells, ultimately rupturing them and causing the well-known symptoms of chills, fever and sweating. Mepacrine could suppress these and was often able to bring about a cure of those types of malaria where the parasites did not persist in the cells of the patient's liver.

One reason why the Germans had focused so much effort on quinine substitutes was the difficulty Germany had experienced in the First World War in obtaining supplies of the natural product. As war loomed again in the late 1930s, it became evident that this time round it could well be the British who would be cut off from supplies if, as seemed increasingly likely, the Japanese gained control of the East Indies, the main source of chinchona bark from which quinine was extracted. The Association of British Chemical Manufacturers in 1938 issued a confidential list of essential drugs which would have to be produced domestically if and when war broke out. Pamaquin and mepacrine were both included, along with a number of barbiturates, hypnotics, sedatives and anaesthetics. By this time, the work of ICI's pilot team had progressed far enough to establish that pharmaceuticals would take a permanent place in the company, although it was not yet marketing any drugs. So ICI joined the other leading British pharmaceutical manufacturers, including Glaxo, BDH, Boots and May and Baker in the war research effort.

'We were assigned to "Plasmoquine" and the anti-malarials,' recalled Frank Rose. The ICI work was done in great secrecy, directed by a Consultative Committee chaired by Dr Harry Hepworth. Initially, there was no record of its meetings at all, not even in the main board minutes of ICI or those of Dyestuffs Division. It was decided that ICI should take four or five of the German drugs and work out some sort of manufacturing processes, at least in embryo form, so that they could be rapidly adapted for wartime use.

For about six months the team of seven ICI chemists stopped looking for new drugs and concentrated mainly on 'cracking the German patents'. Today, the structure of synthetic drugs has to be divulged, but this was not so in the 1930s, when the British Pharmacopoeia, Rose recalled, only listed about twenty synthetic compounds: now about three quarters of its contents are synthetics. One of Rose's colleagues, a brilliant chemist named Frank Curd who was killed in a railway accident in 1948, set out to discover the structure of mepacrine from the thirty or so examples of the German patents, with such success that ICI had a pilot plant in production by September 1939. Large-scale manufacture at Grangemouth was under way by the time the Japanese entered the war in 1941. This supplied British and later American forces with mepacrine for malarious areas, which still, at that time, included Malta and virtually the entire Mediterranean – one reason why so few people took summer holidays there. By 1943 the Americans, with some information from ICI to help them, were making their own mepacrine at the rate of a ton a day.

At first, mepacrine was considered as merely a synthetic substitute for quinine, but its use in the field on large numbers of servicemen in the Far East soon revealed that the synthetic was in fact more effective. Curiously, the Japanese continued to use the less efficient quinine. Even so, it was clear that an improved drug was desirable. A major drawback to mepacrine was that it did not solve the problem of relapses: it also turned the skin yellow, and about a third of the people who took it suffered gastro-intestinal upsets as well. 'It was quite a common sight in port towns like Liverpool to see sailors and soldiers walking about with their skins completely yellow,' said Rose. More seriously, patients tended to become anaemic since the drug didn't begin to tackle the disease until the parasites had actually invaded the red blood cells, and about one fifth of the red cells of the body could be occupied by parasites at any one time.

By 1942, Dr Garnet Davey had joined ICI as a parasitologist. In 1969 he was to become research director of Pharmaceuticals Division, but in his retirement in Dorset he said in 1986 that he would never have gone into industry at all had it not been for the war. 'I was cursed with academic snobbery, like so many people in this country.' He had been drafted into the Ministry of Supply at the beginning of the war, to work on radar (in spite of being a zoologist by training who had lectured on the subject at Cardiff University). Davey worked in ICI with birds, which could be infected with malaria: at first with canaries, many of them obtained from the Yorkshire miners who used to breed them for use in detecting methane gas underground, and later on with chickens. By chance, the ICI team learned from Africa that some soldiers who had caught malaria and, simultaneously, a streptococcyl infection, had been treated for the latter with sulpha drugs such as 'Sulphamethazine' (sulphadimidine) which Frank Rose had synthesized. 'Not only was the strep infection cured, but there was a decrease in the malarial condition as well,' recalled Rose.

Rose and Curd now began to design potential anti-malarial drugs based on this fact, incorporating into the pyrimidine molecule some of the structural factors present in mepacrine. These were synthesized in the laboratory by Curd, and sent to Davey for tests in his 'chick' assay. To their joy, number four (compound 2666) was active. A quick toxicity trial showed it to have unexpected side-effects such as acute

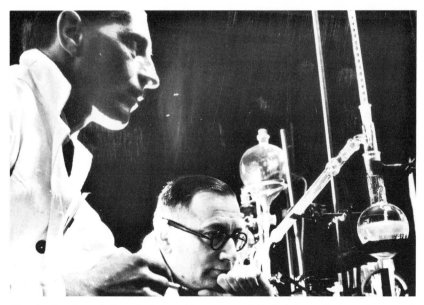

Frank Curd and Frank Rose, discoverers of Paludrine, the wartime anti-malarial drug still high in the field 40 years later.

frontal headaches, but a start had been made, and the chemical effort was broadened and intensified.

A later pyrimidine derivative (3349) was actually effective in human malaria trials, but the ultimate success came with Rose's synthesis of analogues based on the chemical system, biguanide. Clinical trials at the Liverpool School of Tropical Medicine, in which the research team at one point deliberately infected themselves with malaria, 'identified' the compound 4888, named proguanil or 'Paludrine', as the best of the group.

'I made up a few pounds and had them flown out to Cairns in Australia,' said Rose. At Cairns, Brigadier Hamilton-Fairley (father of the cancer specialist killed by an IRA car bomb in London), had set up a hospital to deal with the expected flood of malaria cases from the war in the Pacific anticipated to take place in 1945. Hamilton-Fairley reported favourably and ICI 'made tons of it for the Pacific campaign, which never happened because the Americans dropped the atom bomb'. The two names on the patent were Rose and Curd. (ICI scientists were asked at an early stage if they wanted to profit financially from royalties earned by their inventions, as the German chemists did, and they voted against it.)

Paludrine was used extensively in the Malaysian campaign after 1945 (it was the name given to the Good Fairy in one ENSA pantomime) and is still in use for prophylaxis in those parts of the world where the parasites have not developed a resistance to it. 'Very few drugs have lasted forty years like this one,' said Rose with some satisfaction, 'and I think I can say we never killed anyone. Paludrine has an inbuilt safety device – if you take too much of it, it makes you sick. Whenever you get a new drug, sooner or later someone will try to commit suicide with it, but you can't do that with Paludrine.'

Above all, Paludrine was colourless and proved to act in the early stages of the disease before the malaria parasite invaded the bloodstream.

An important offshoot from the anti-malarial work at ICI was the antiseptic 'Hibitane', the result of further research by Rose and his colleagues using 'the same sort of chemistry'. At first designed as an anti-viral compound, Hibitane is now widely used as a hospital antiseptic and ranks as one of ICI's four or five top-selling pharmaceutical products.

Measuring Drug Absorption

The discovery in 1940 of the medicinal section's first drug, sul-phadimidine, led to some innovative work on drug absorption done first by Rose and later taken up intensively by his colleague Alfred Spinks. Rose had been intrigued and puzzled by apparent discrepancies between anti-bacterial activity *in vitro* (in the test-tube) and *in vivo* (in living animals, or tissue). Together with a biologist colleague, A. R. Martin, he developed micro-analytical methods for measuring the concentration of his experimental drugs in the blood of mice. Such studies of drug absorption in the bloodstream are standard practice today, but were virtually unknown fifty years ago.

Spinks contributed much important thinking and detailed work to the development of Paludrine, on such aspects as effective dosage, retention by the body and vital information as to which organs and tissues were most likely to be at risk from a build-up of the drug. A monograph on Spinks's life and work noted that he was able to suggest the optimum size and frequency of dosage to the clinicians conducting the first trials on cases of human malaria 'and to recommend a regime that distinguished between prophylactic and suppressive activity'. The administration of oral drugs in measured quantities to small animal species had hardly varied since the earliest days of experimental chemo-therapy, and the memoir recalls that one professional associate of Spinks's at ICI 'had only just abandoned his practice of grinding the test drugs with powdered biscuit and re-baking the mixture'.

Spinks and another of Rose's colleagues, the South African Jeff Thorp (who in 1986 shared Rose's office at Alderley Park), continued pioneering work in pharmocodymamics – the science of 'chasing up drugs in the tissue to monitor how they metabolize,' as Rose put it. Thorp was involved in the discovery and early stages of experiments on compounds to control cholesterol build-up in the body and in work on the insecticide 'Gammexane', ascorbic acid and steroid hormones. Alfred Spinks subsequently became research director of Pharmaceuticals, then deputy chairman of the division. In 1970, he succeeded John D. Rose on the main board of ICI responsible for research and development throughout the organization. He became an FRS in 1977 and died in 1982, remembered nationally as the author of the 'Spinks Report' on bio-engineering.

The First Usable Penicillin

While Rose and his fellow-workers at Blackley were absorbed in their anti-malarial research, another of the original team of chemists, Dr William Boon, was caught up in work of an equally far-reaching nature – the early development of penicillin. Shelves of books have been written about the discovery of penicillin by Alexander Fleming and the contributions of many other distinguished scientists including Sir Frederick G. Hopkins in Cambridge, Professor Howard Florey in Oxford, Ernst Chain and Dorothy Hodgkin. ICI's Dyestuffs Division played a small but vital role in the unfolding drama.

The sulphonamide drugs had proved effective against streptococcal bacteria and pneumonia, but were unable to combat the common range of bacteria called staphylococci, which cause a large number of different infections. Yet Fleming, in his original research in the 1920s, had written a report on the bacteria-inhibiting properties of penicillin which had been neglected ever since. When Chain, a Jewish chemist who had left Germany early in 1933, was working with Florey in Oxford he studied this report and, with Florey's support, embarked on a full investigation of how penicillin could be synthesized and purified.

Florey and his colleagues published a paper in *The Lancet* in August 1940 on the success of their treatment of staphylococci in mice, but there was little interest because it was felt that other projects, such as anti-malarials, were of greater importance for the war effort. Before this, Florey had tried to persuade Burroughs Wellcome to make enough penicillin for him to conduct proper clinical trials with it, but they were already fully extended in preparing blood plasma and vaccines for the armed forces. When the British Expeditionary Force withdrew from France at Dunkirk, and a German invasion of Britain appeared imminent, Florey and other scientists used to smear spores of their precious cultures on the inside linings of their coats in the hope that if Oxford fell to the enemy, at least one of them might survive to carry on the work elsewhere.

By January 1941, the Oxford School of Pathology had virtually turned into a factory for the production of penicillin. Florey, despairing of getting enough supplies from British manufacturers, turned to

America, where he met a more helpful response. But penicillin was still being produced by the fermentation method, and many companies were reluctant to embark on this – partly because of the experience of a firm called American Cynamid, whose new plant for pneumonia vaccines had been rendered obsolete after a few months by the invention of sulphapyridine, involving them in the loss of several million dollars. It was widely expected that penicillin, too, would soon be synthesized and manufactured on a large scale like the sulphonamides.

But before that was possible, its chemical structure had to be discovered. Dr Boon was involved in this investigation, and ICI undertook, in agreement with Florey, to make some penicillin for his clinical work. A team headed by Boon was set up at Trafford Park within the Dyestuffs Division in 1942 in order to produce the first medically usable quantities of penicillin. Shortly afterwards the Ministry of Supply became involved, wanting large-scale production because penicillin had by then become acknowledged as highly effective in treating wounds. The emphasis within ICI now switched to making penicillin by fermentation, and supplies were sent for structure analysis to Robert Robinson, who was rightly convinced that the antibiotic was a simple molecule and who was obsessed with the idea of producing it by deep culture. ICI managed to purify the culture, thus demonstrating that production was technically possible, and soon about 100 people around the world were working on the problem.

Early cultures of penicillin in milk bottles during wartime development by ICI's infant Pharmaceuticals Division.

Britain and America were officially working together on penicillin, and Dr Boon made two trips across the Atlantic in 1943 and 1944 with representatives of other interested pharmaceutical companies including Burroughs Wellcome and Glaxo. By this time a new method of manufacture, the so-called 'deep fermentation' process by growing the mould in tanks, was being actively pursued. This process, strongly favoured by Robinson, had been achieved in the laboratory but was proving very difficult to scale up for production.

The mystery of penicillin's chemical structure was not solved until 1945, when Dorothy Hodgkin – the subsequent Nobel prize-winner – proved by X-ray crystallographic studies that it contained the betalactam ring system. Total synthesis, though eventually achieved by American chemists in a very impure form, never proved an economic form of manufacture: even today, this remains true. The yields from fermentation have gone up enormously and even semi-synthetic penicillins such as 'Magnapen' depend on getting the basic penicillin made by fermentation.

Advances in Anaesthetics

As profits from the anti-malarial drugs began to rise sharply during the war, ICI set up a pharmaceuticals subsidiary, but it was still kept within Dyestuffs' orbit: there was an understandable reluctance in the parent division to hive off what looked like becoming a major money-spinner. Pharmaceuticals was set up as a company in 1942 (it became a full ICI division in 1957), but remained ill-defined and largely dependent on Dyestuffs in research and manufacturing for another thirteen years. The immediate postwar period, however, saw a change of direction: anti-malarials, successful though they were, would not be enough to sustain the growth of the new company. The overall market was too small, and there were too many companies in it. Garnet Davey explained: 'It was clear that we would have to go into what I would call the diseases of dysfunction, the ones that affected western civilization; heart diseases, arthritis, hypertension.' Heart disease was indeed one area where an ICI pharmaceutical researcher would make a major breakthrough comparable to that of Rose with Paludrine. But before that happened, the company became involved in an area more concerned with surgeons than physicians and here too, in the field of anaesthesia, one of its chemists was to make a discovery of vital importance to the future of ICI and of medicine itself.

The first half of the twentieth century had seen little advance in the science of anaesthetics, at least of the inhalant variety. What innovations there were had been made in the development of intravenous anaesthetics such as barbiturates and in muscle relaxants for use with anaesthetics. Inhalants – chiefly chloroform, nitrous oxide, cyclopropane and ether – had scarcely changed since the previous century and all possessed one or more serious disadvantage. Ether was highly explosive and had been the cause of many disastrous episodes in operating theatres, while chloroform was extremely poisonous, often resulting in liver damage that could be fatal. ICI had an early involvement in anaesthetics in 1940, when a London chemist noticed that youths working in an aeroplane factory had the habit of leaning over vats of trichloroethylene, used as an industrial solvent, in order to make themselves intoxicated. A surgeon named Christopher Hewer successfully used a sample of the solvent to anaesthetize a patient, and turned to ICI to obtain more. He learned that the company was already producing it in a very purified form for use in cleaning wounds and burns where grease was present. It later became a popular anaesthetic in childbirth.

Ten years later James Ferguson, at that time research director of the General Chemicals Division of ICI (he later became research director of the whole company) set out to review the company's range of fluorocarbons. These chemicals had been originally developed in America in the 1930s by General Motors and du Pont, as non-toxic, non-flammable, low boiling-point refrigerants for Frigidaire. Other work had subsequently been done on them in the States, where their ability to induce anaesthesia, though not safely, had been recognized, but Ferguson was unaware of this. ICI had become involved with them when seeking volatile compounds which were able to resist attack by uranium hexafluoride during the separation of uranium isotopes by diffusion – part of the secret work carried out for 'Tube Alloys' by ICI chemists unaware that they were doing preliminary research for a nuclear weapon.

In 1939, as a result of studying narcosis in experiments involving volatile organic compounds against grain weevils, Ferguson had advanced a revolutionary theory that connected narcosis to thermodynamic activity. He concluded that a similar relationship might work in anaesthesia and should be tried out with fluorinated compounds. The work was undertaken at Widnes laboratory and was assigned to a young chemist called Charles Suckling, who had joined ICI in 1942 at the age of twenty-two. He had started by making 'highly fluorinated compounds – I didn't know why, but it turned out that they were intended for gases to assist in the separation of uranium isotopes during the war. That was how I came into fluorine chemistry'. After the war Suckling continued to work on fluoro-organic compounds, usually as refrigerants but also in pest control. When he became involved in the anaesthetic work, he teamed up with the late James Raventos, an ICI pharmacologist working under Alfred Spinks at Dyestuffs. Their initial brief was itself an innovatory step at this stage: to define their target. It was not an easy task.

'The first question we had to ask in 1951 when we began thinking about searching for a new anaesthetic was just what a good anaesthetic ought to do,' recalled Suckling. 'We consulted anaesthetists and were told that a good anaesthetic should provide rapid and smooth induction not unpleasant to the patient, with no irritation of the respiratory tract; muscular relaxation and rapid and easy control of the depth of anaesthesia; a good margin of safety; an absence of sweating.' At that time many anaesthetists had a deep reluctance to depend on a single compound, preferring a mixture of drugs such as barbiturates to produce unconsciousness, nitrous oxide to maintain it and curare to aid relaxation. The resulting 'cocktail' could be made up precisely to the patient's individual requirements; and indeed, many anaesthetists still prefer this technique today.

All told, four people had to be satisfied by the ideal inhalant anaesthetic. The patient wanted to be rendered unconscious easily and pleasantly and to recover quickly, with no adverse after-effects. The surgeon required a non-explosive gas which in no way restricted surgical work. The anaesthetist needed a potent compound with a good safety margin, one which was excreted unchanged in chemical composition from the body, gave moment-by-moment control over the level of unconsciousness and produced no functional or organic damage. Last, but by no means least, the manufacturer wanted a chemical which could be simply and inexpensively made and was easy to purify, transport and store. The problem was to take from this formidable list of properties those which might be related to the physical and chemical properties of the fluorine-containing compounds under examination. As the number capable of being synthesized was very large, the chemists had to decide which criteria to adopt in order to define those which should be made first. What they finally selected were volatility, for simple vaporization which could be related to boiling point; non-flammability (this could be achieved by ensuring that few hydrogen atoms were present in the molecule); stability; and high potency – the latter so that the anaesthetic could be administered with large concentrations of oxygen.

In translating the requirement for potency into structural terms, Dr Suckling was guided by the gifted work and thinking previously done by Ferguson on the subject of narcosis. 'My contribution,' said Suckling modestly, 'was to spot what Ferguson's work was really saying – which was that almost any volatile, non-toxic compound would put you to sleep if administered at a particular concentration. But of course this didn't guarantee satisfactory anaesthesia.' In collaboration with Frank Bradbury, later founding Professor of Technological Economics at the University of Stirling, Suckling extended Ferguson's work with grain weevils. They found they could obtain more reproducible results with house flies. In the slippery glass flasks in which the tests were done

Dr Charles Suckling (centre) discovered halothane in 1955, the first great advance since the age of ether and chloroform. With him are Dr Michael Johnstone, who conducted the clinical trials, and fellow-researcher James Raventos.

it was hard to tell whether the weevils were anaesthetized or not. But with flies, when a light was shone on them to test their activity 'they either flew or they didn't', as Suckling put it succinctly.

Suckling used the relatively new techniques of gas chromatography, which gave the confidence of achieving a high standard of purity and at a later stage facilitated the scale-up of manufacturing techniques from laboratory to factory. 'I spotted that in the gas chromatograph I had two compounds which differed in their anaesthetic potencies: halothane and another one,' recalled Suckling. 'They had the same boiling point but differed in their potencies, and I could see that the one which contained the hydrogen was the more potent. The importance of this was that I was able to improve Ferguson's thermodynamic correlationship by applying a correction factor known as activity coefficient, and thus was able to tell Raventos exactly what concentration would be needed to anaesthetize mice.'

The compound later known as 'Fluothane' was in fact only the sixth compound that Suckling synthesized, and it was first prepared by him in January 1953. After extensive testing by Raventos and his colleagues, clinical trials started three years later, and the anaesthetist who carried them out was Dr Michael Johnstone at the Crumpsall Hospital in Manchester. Before accepting ICI's invitation to test the new drug, Dr Johnstone carefully examined Raventos's results and visited the

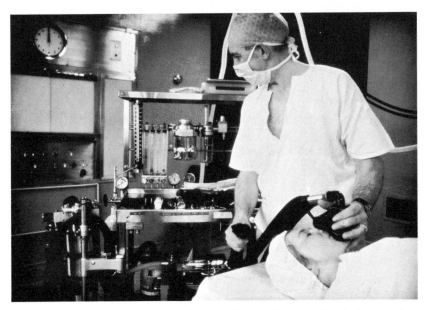

'Fluothane', as it is trademarked, is used extensively in hospital operations around the world.

laboratory himself to see different animals anaesthetized. He had to satisfy himself that the drug showed enough potential benefit to his patients to justify the inevitable risk associated with its use on an experimental basis. He decided that it did.

Dr Johnstone proceeded with great caution, but he soon recognized the enormous possibilities of 'Fluothane'. After a month's trial he reported to ICI that he was confident it had an important place in the operating theatre, noting that he was particularly impressed by the absence of shock syndrome. Patients' skin remained warm and pink while under the anaesthetic, which meant that their circulation was not affected; they came round quickly from unconsciousness and suffered much less post-operative discomfort, especially nausea, than was customary with most of the anaesthetics in use at that time.

While Johnstone was carrying out his clinical tests, the halothane compound was sent to the Medical Research Committee, which had been set up in 1955 to investigate new, non-explosive anaesthetics. But even after favourable reports from the committee, halothane met resistance from some members of the profession. Those who favoured the 'cocktail' method felt that a single drug was in some ways a retrogressive step. Also, because it was comparable to chloroform in its structure – both were chlorinated hydrocarbons, both non-explosive, both highly potent – there was a fear that some of the dangerous side-effects of chloroform, such as liver damage, might well be present in halothane.

Halothane also presented a challenge to the equipment makers. It called for a new generation of vapourizers more precise than the type hitherto used to administer the older anaesthetics, and also for new materials to be tested to ensure they would not be affected by prolonged exposure to the compounds; as aluminium was, for example. Manufacturers did respond very quickly to these and other problems, aided by the fact that ICI gave close attention to their technical problems. Dr Suckling recalled that as halothane was somewhat peripheral to General Chemicals' interest, he was given responsibility for most stages: 'I had to devise a manufacturing process, to find materials that would not be attacked by the compound. I had the experience of defining the target, choosing the compounds, collaborating with the pharmacologist, working out the process, providing the information necessary for its exploitation and use, following it right through, literally into the operating theatre.' He found it a 'tremendously influential experience, the general concept of design for scientists, one which I'm still pushing. We fail very often because companies do not recognize that the innovation has to satisfy requirements at every stage of its life. Take halothane. You've got to be able to manufacture it, store it. The anaesthetist will want to re-use it. You've got to find a closure for the bottle that will work . . . It was unusual then to follow something through in that way'.

In spite of some initial hesitations, anaesthetists soon came to acknowledge the advantages of halothane. By March 1958, two years after his initial tests, Dr Johnstone could record many thousands of cases successfully anaesthetized by halothane, which was manufactured under the proprietary name of 'Fluothane'. Johnstone believed that it 'might well be the safest and most effective agent available to anaesthetists . . . in all these thousands of cases there have been no deaths or post-operative illnesses in which halothane was directly implicated'. One of the most important factors, he added, was that much abdominal surgery could be performed 'while the patient breathes spontaneously'. Its demonstrable advantages even outweighed the fact that it was far more costly than chloroform: £10.5s (£10.25) per 250 centilitres against ten shillings (50 pence) a litre.

One of the most significant results of the halothane discovery was that it established a bridge between need and science, and showed how the body of scientific thought could be brought to bear upon a perceived target. It combined a desire to make use of existing fluorine knowledge and technology with a theoretical concept of narcosis, and was developed by a team that together contributed expertise in chemistry, physics, pharmacology and anaesthesiology. Halothane was, as Suckling put it thirty years later, 'just waiting to be discovered'. Despite the passage of time, 'Fluothane' remains one of the most widely used anaesthetics in the world today.

After his success with Fluothane, Suckling was somewhat cynically amused to be asked briskly by a visiting deputy chairman of ICI: 'Right, what are you going to invent next?' The research director hastily explained to the VIP that 'most people never find anything'. Suckling soon became involved in management himself, progressing eventually to research director of Mond Division, which by then had been formed to embrace the old Alkali and General Chemicals divisions. 'I worked very hard on the integral approach to product development and I introduced for the first time chemical engineers as full members of the research department.' After a period as deputy chairman of Mond, Suckling's last five years with the company were spent as general manager of research and development technology. By the time he retired in 1982 (having been made a Fellow of the Royal Society in 1978), the relationship between Dyestuffs and its lusty Pharmaceutical offspring had long since been satisfactorily resolved, but even while he was still at work on the halothane project, and other pharmaceutical research was progressing well, some confusion remained. In 1954 both Dyestuffs and Pharmaceuticals often found themselves wondering where responsibilities lay, and the technical managing director of Dyestuffs urged complete separation of the two divisions, saying: 'What is really needed is good and well informed leadership plus a close binding together of the three essential parts of the business, i.e. research, production and selling, with research in all its aspects the concern of one man.'

James Black and Beta-Blockers

At this stage Suckling referred to pharmaceuticals as 'a losing business . . . in the doldrums'. But change was not long in coming. In the early 1950s the pharmaceutical industry as a whole was experiencing one of the most rapid and fundamental upheavals of its existence. As synthetic products became more and more common, they were replacing the old-style medicines and bringing about a revolution in both pharmacy and medical practice. DDT was destroying mosquitoes and other disease-carrying insects while disease itself, as ICI's official history notes, 'was becoming preventable, curable, or controllable on a scale unimaginable fifteen years earlier, and the effects, particularly on the balance between population and resources, were rapid and immense'.

In its early days of pharmaceutical activity, ICI had made a deliberate decision not to take over existing businesses, after some unsuccessful approaches had all fallen through. The company's research director then, C. J. T. Cronshaw, believed in the company depending entirely on its own resources 'on the consideration that the best way thoroughly to master a new field of endeavour is to learn by one's own efforts all stages . . . We're not going to become another company selling Glauber salts – we're going to live and profit by our own discoveries'. Accordingly the new division did not take out licences to make other companies' products, nor did it buy information. But its early concentration on the chemotherapy of infectious diseases led it, in Frank Rose's opinion, to one lost opportunity: 'We lost out on the early days of anti-histamines. No one in the world had more experience on the basic structures; we could have spun off from the anti-malarial side. We were working more in the dark in the early days, but perhaps the targets were more numerous. Perhaps then it was easier to discover drugs because there were more gaps in medical practice.'

Finally, in 1957, ICI made the break and established all its medical business in a genuinely separate division at a handsome new site in Alderley Park in Cheshire. Twenty-one years after that first 'grant' of £15,000 a year for five years, the pharmaceutical side had indisputably come of age and was about to produce the discovery that would make it a major profit earner for the whole ICI group.

From the start in Alderley Park, one of the chief preoccupations was cardiovascular disease. At this date, in the late 1950s, James (now Sir James) Black was working as a physiologist and senior lecturer at the Veterinary School of the University of Glasgow. 'From time to time I had heard about this fairytale place ICI were building at Alderley Park.' Black had for some time been deeply interested in the treatment of angina pectoris, which was then usually treated by trying to increase the supply of oxygen to the heart by means of 'coronary vasodilator' drugs. He began to ponder an alternative method: might it be possible to reduce the demand of the heart for oxygen? The death of his father from a heart attack following a car crash made him focus on the role of stress, induced either emotionally or by exercise, in producing adrenaline and in precipitating an angina attack. His thoughts led to the hypothesis that it might be possible to develop a new approach, by blocking the action of adrenaline on the heart, thus reducing the supply of oxygen.

Garnet Davey, then research director of the newly emancipated Pharmaceutical Division, met Black in Glasgow and, learning of his interest, offered him a job. Black arrived at Alderley Park in July 1958 and immediately set to work on his ideas, filling Davey with enthusiasm as he described his concept of what became the world's first beta-blockers. Davey, a soft-spoken Welshman not given to hyperbole, describes Black as 'one of the two geniuses I have known in my life'. (The other was Sir Henry Dale, who was also involved in the sequence of knowledge leading to Black's discovery: he made the observation, described by Black as crucial, on reversing the pressure-raising effects of adrenaline.) 'Jimmy Black's idea was very imaginative,' said Davey, 'but more to the point, history was just at the right stage for it. There were some bits of essential knowledge about, but it required a genius to link them. Black linked them.'

The first of these 'bits of essential knowledge' was a discovery made by Ray Ahlquist in Des Moines, Iowa. In a paper published in 1948 he posited the idea of two distinct types of adrenotropic receptors, which he designated *alpha* and *beta*. A receptor is a point, usually on the surface of a cell, which 'receives' the 'message' of a chemical entering the body and which then triggers off the resulting chemical action or reaction. 'Ahlquist's theory,' explained Black, 'was that a cell responded to different substances because of the decoding machinery it had on its receptors. Ahlquist called them *alpha* and *beta*. They behaved as if they were different and he was the one who uniquely saw that.' Little attention was paid in 1948 – it was 'a paper before its time', said Black. He first came upon it reprinted in a 1954 edition of *Drill's Pharmacology*.

Meanwhile work carried out at the Eli Lilly laboratories in Indianapolis, quite independently of Ahlquist's research, discovered that a compound named dichloroisoprenaline, or DCI, negated the effects of adrenaline. Neil Moran of Emory University in Atlanta, Georgia, heard a paper on it at a scientific symposium in 1957 and asked for samples of the new drug to test its effects on the heart. He confirmed that it 'antagonized the changes in heart rate and muscle tension produced by adrenaline'.

By this time Black was well under way at Alderley Park with his programme to develop acceptable adrenoceptor-blocking drugs for treatment of heart disease. He seized on Moran's report and realized that it would be possible to synthesize an analogue of DCI which would be devoid of any intrinsic action of its own when bound to the receptors of the heart, which Moran had claimed belonged to Ahlquist's 'beta-adrenergic' type. As DCI itself *increased* the heart rate in one of his tests, he decided it was not suitable for clinical use, and searched for a compound without this effect.

In January 1960, John Stephenson, a medical chemist at Alderley Park, got the idea of replacing the two chlorine molecules in DCI by another phenyl ring, to make a naphthalene. He synthesized this new compound, which was named pronethalol. 'That was the first compound we made,' recalled Black. 'I wasn't trained as a chemist. I was just picking the thing up as I went along.' But he knew instinctively that what he was dealing with in pronethalol was a prototype. It was given the brand name 'Alderlin', derived from Alderley Park, and by June that same year Black and his colleagues were sure they had found what they were looking for. In 1962 clinical trials at St George's Hospital in London confirmed that it was indeed helpful in the treatment of angina, by blocking the cardiac effects of the sympathetic nervous system – the 'fight, fright and flight' reaction to stress which had been described by Walter Cannon in his book, *The Wisdom of the Body*, a formative source book to the young James Black. Even after this success, however, Black was not convinced that 'Alderlin' provided the ideal drug because there was a significant incidence of side-effects. Also, long-term toxicity tests on mice revealed that it could cause cancer of the thymus gland, although Black remains unconvinced that it is a proven carcinogen.

Work continued to find an improved version. 'I don't think there were any pressures to market pronethalol as a drug, rather than use it as a stepping-stone or probe, but if there were, Garnet kept them away from me,' Black recalled more than twenty years later. The 'stepping-stone' led to propranolol, devised and synthesized by Dr A. F. Crowther, which experiments showed to be about ten times as potent as its predecessor. Pronethalol eventually did come onto the market in the UK in November 1963 under a restricted licence, and clinical trials of propranolol started in early 1964. This satisfied all the required criteria and proved to be the first beta-adrenergic antagonist or 'beta-blocker'. It was launched as 'Inderal' (a near-anagram of 'Alderlin') in July 1965, only two years and eight months after it was first given to an animal; a remarkable achievement, and incidentally far quicker than would be possible today, when the average time to get a drug on the

Sir James Black, FRS, whose discovery of the first beta-blocker, trademarked Inderal, has enabled thousands of sufferers from heart disease and hypertension to live normal lives.

market from discovery is ten to fifteen years. Inderal proved a safe and effective treatment for angina pectoris, cardiac arrhythmias and hypertension, with hardly any serious side-effects.

Black left ICI in mid-1964, but the company continued work on beta-blockers without interruption. Rival companies produced various structural analogues of Inderal but few could claim any significant advantages over it with the exception of sotalol ('Sotacor'), which was synthesized by A. A. Larsen of Mead Johnson in 1960. Four years later, ICI medicinal chemists also synthesized sotalol and its acetamido derivative practolol, which was brand-named 'Eraldin' – another anagram of the original 'Alderin'. It was launched in 1970 for use in asthmatic patients, some of whom had been unable to use the early beta-blockers because they caused bronchospasm and wheezing. Unfortunately it had to be withdrawn in 1975 because of serious side-effects on a small number of patients who had taken it orally over a long period, some of whom, tragically, were blinded. Its use after that was restricted to specialized hospital units. Various alternative drugs were soon developed, including acebutolol ('Sectral'), metoprolol ('Betaloc' and 'Lopressor') and ICI's atenolol ('Tenormin'), which is now the world's biggest selling heart drug.

One very important use of beta-blockers – to relieve hypertension – was subsequently discovered by 'absolute luck', in Garnet Davey's words. A clinical pharmacologist named Brian Pritchard, then doing clinical trials with Inderal in the Department of Medicine in University College, London, noticed that patients with hypertension being treated for heart disease with the drug were all 'brought under control'. Hypertension is now the largest single use for Inderal and has enormously increased its market.

Robin Shanks, one of the discoverers of Eraldin in ICI, has written that Black's beta-blocker work 'clearly demonstrates that the successful discovery and commercial development of a new drug depends on the interaction of many factors including original ideas, foresight, intuition, careful scientific observation, integrated chemical and pharmacological effect and luck'. This is certainly true of the other case histories briefly outlined here, which although the most celebrated and (with the obvious exception of penicillin) among the highest earning of ICI's drug discoveries, are by no means the only important ones.

Garnet Davey, for instance, was involved in work on 'Nolvadex' (tamoxifen), the first anti-oestrogen to be used in cancer therapy. Work done in Israel had shown that a high oestrogen level was necessary for foetal implantation in rats, and Davey and a fellow ICI researcher named Arthur Walpole developed an anti-oestrogen compound that was completely successful in preventing conception in rats, but failed to work for human birth control. But during the clinical trials Davey and Walpole suggested that it be tried out as well for breast cancer, there being some evidence that this was stimulated by oestrogen and that therefore an anti-oestrogen should be beneficial. So it proved, and Davey estimates that roughly a third of breast cancer patients now benefit from this drug.

James Black, who was made an FRS in 1976 and knighted in 1981, was awarded the Nobel Prize for Medicine in 1988. He went on from ICI to make other important discoveries at Smith, Kline and French Laboratories and elsewhere, but he has an ambivalent feeling about the immense commercial success of the drugs for which he has been responsible. In 1986, when he was sixty-two and directing a small research unit at the Rayne Institute of King's College Hospital Medical School, he explained that he found it 'hard to live with' the celebrity of Inderal. 'The things I've been associated with happen to have made a lot of money, but commercial success has nothing to do with the quality of the science. It's the fact that so many people suffer from high blood pressure that has led to the attention. If high blood pressure had been as uncommon as multiple sclerosis, there wouldn't have been the same amount of notice taken of it.' In his soft Glasgow accent he added simply: 'I had fun doing it, it was tremendously exciting.'

During the 1960s the early policy in ICI of relying on the company's own activities in pharmaceuticals was reversed, and the division began to establish a network of wholly owned subsidiaries and to set up manufacturing plants in five European countries. In 1971 it acquired Atlas Chemical Industries, gaining direct access to the vast and lucrative American market, and began a programme of heavy investment in the United States. Stuart Pharmaceuticals Inc., one of its major acquisitions, developed and launched 'Hibitane', a chlorhexidine hand-scrub which became the leading skin antiseptic in the US, and also launched Nolvadex and Tenormin there. Hibitane and Nolvadex are also market leaders in Japan, where ICI has a joint venture company with Sumitomo Chemical Co.

The Pharmaceuticals Division, which will become the core of ICI's new biosciences company, Zeneca, now employs some 4,500 people in Britain and another 8,000 overseas. About 2,500 worldwide are engaged in research and development, evaluating between them some 10,000 new chemicals every year for the treatment of human and animal diseases. Only about twenty prove worthy of detailed study, and less than half that number will become 'candidate drugs' eligible for toxicity tests, prior to clinical toxicity trials. At later stages, even more compounds are eliminated: industry-wide, the final chance of commercial success is about one in 10,000.

The costs of all this are astronomical. In 1979, Garnet Davey estimated that it took around £100 million to develop a new drug: the figure today is likely to be much higher, probably in the region of £150 million, before any return is achieved. The research is highly organized and centrally planned from Britain, where research teams concentrate on different branches of medicine – cardiovascular diseases, the nervous system, pulmonary diseases, bacterial infections and so on, as well as genetic engineering, where many ICI scientists including Garnet Davey feel that future developments in cancer may lie. A major achievement already in this field has been the complete synthesis of a human leukocyte interferon gene, which has been used in a bacterial host to produce bacteriologically active interferon.

Frank Rose, the discoverer of Paludrine, used to muse whether 'organized research like this is as productive of new discoveries as the freedom we had years ago', and deplored the fact that everything had become so vastly expensive. 'There's a tendency for the accountants to move in and approve or disapprove of a project before you start.' Yet targets of one kind or another have always been there: what would the accountants have said in 1941, reviewing five years' budget for the infant pharmaceuticals business, if history and the needs of war had not taken a hand?

9

THE FARMER IN CONTROL

People have been trying to control pests and improve the yield of their crops since the cultivation of land began. Virgil in the second of his *Georgics* recommended dressing seed with ashes and other substances to preserve the crop from disease. Pliny's *Natural History* suggested some quite practical methods of pest control, such as sprinkling cabbage caterpillars with a compound of wormwood, along with more eccentric remedies like burying a toad in a jar in the middle of a field to prevent blight. In the eighteenth century, Jethro Tull and others recommended salt and lime as specifics against certain forms of infestation. The modern era of pest control began around 1860, when arsenical compounds were first used in the United States against the dreaded Colorado beetle, and in 1884 a French agricultural scientist discovered the fungicidal properties of copper sulphate.

But the great leaps forward in crop management, as in so many other areas of applied science, came with the Second World War and the spur it gave to improving domestic crop yields. The farmer of the 1990s can steer the course of nature in ways undreamed of in 1927 when ICI first set up its agricultural research centre at Jealott's Hill, near Bracknell in Berkshire. It was in the laboratories of Jealott's Hill that several of the most far-reaching discoveries were made, among them the hormone weedkillers and the powerful herbicide paraquat, which has been described by the man who first saw its potential as 'the most significant development in agriculture since the invention of the wheeled plough'.

Agricultural chemicals engaged the interest of ICI's management from the beginning, unlike its late-developing interest in pharmaceuticals. The field was a natural one for a company whose biggest capital asset at its inception was a nitrogen plant at Billingham intended to supply fertilizers to the farmers of Britain and the Empire. Demand for nitrogenous fertilizers rose during the 1920s, but it was clear that to make the most of Billingham's gigantic capacity, sales would need boosting by active marketing and promotion, an area which in those innocent days was commonly known in commercial firms as 'propaganda'.

136

Sir Alfred Mond, or Lord Melchett as he became in 1928, was one of the keenest advocates of propaganda for the firm's agricultural products, and he decided that the best method would be to set up an agricultural research station to back up the marketing drive with hard scientific knowledge. The station would have to be good enough to stand comparison with the best ones then operating in Britain – Rothamsted Experimental Station, for example, and the Royal Agricultural College at Cirencester, as well as with the growing number of influential research centres set up by private companies like that of William Cooper at Berkhamsted, started in 1902.

Mond and others on the ICI board realized, however, that it might be difficult to convince the academic and scientific world of the impartiality of company-sponsored research, especially since research and 'propaganda' were funded out of the same budget. Great effort, warned Mond in November 1926, would be necessary in organizing such a venture, 'which will not only be of great service to this country but to the whole of the Empire by developing and extending the area capable of producing valuable food crops. My ideal is to see, in this as in other chemical manufactures, our great organization controlling the production and sales of the whole chemical manufacture within the Empire. For this purpose we must take into our services the best brains available.'

One of the best brains belonged to Professor Sir Frederick Keeble, FRS, an old friend of Mond's, whom he persuaded to give up his post as Professor of Botany at Oxford and devote himself to research and propaganda in fertilizers at ICI. The vehicle chosen to establish a reaction station was Nitram Ltd, the selling agents for Brunner, Mond's subsidiary Synthetic Ammonia and Nitrates Ltd as well as for the non-ICI British Sulphate of Ammonia Federation. Nitram possessed an experienced team of qualified agricultural advisers who carried out field consultancy work and also produced brochures, sales leaflets and a journal entitled *Farm Notes on Profitable Farming*, which enjoyed a wide circulation.

In the summer of 1927, Nitram Ltd bought three adjacent farms near Bracknell: Jealott's Hill, Hawthorndale and Nuptown, to serve as ICI's centre for 'agricultural research and demonstration'. A laboratory was built at a cost of £15,000, together with other new buildings and improvements to existing ones. In all, the station had 160 acres of arable land, 350 acres of grass and 20 acres of grass and orchard. In 1929 ICI took over Nitram Ltd, Sir Frederick Keeble became the first director of the station and it was officially opened in June of that year, although work had already been progressing for a year in various outbuildings and old army huts.

The avowed aim of the research station was to popularize the use of nitrogen on grass by farmers in Britain and the Empire, and to encourage the adoption of an 'intensive system of grassland management', which the company claimed could substantially increase the numbers of livestock which could be supported by pastures. Soon after the opening, Keeble, evidently taking his cue from the imperial sentiments cherished by Mond, was urging his team at Jealott's Hill to regard themselves 'as an advisory service not only for the British Isles but also for the Empire. We regard the team we have built up at Jealott's Hill as an imperial general staff for agricultural research and we regard the advisory service in the same way as the nucleus of an imperial service'.

The worsening world economic situation and, in particular, the depressed agricultural market in Great Britain, formed a gloomy backdrop to the early years at Jealott's Hill. In 1931 Keeble's budget was halved and the research staff, like other senior staff throughout ICI, took a ten-per-cent salary cut which was not fully restored until April 1933. Keeble retired at the end of 1932, a disappointed man who had been unable to persuade the ICI board that in his view there should be 'a complete divorce of the chief advisory officers from direct selling work': the policy of mingling the budgets meant that if selling costs were being reduced, the amount spent on research was also cut down.

By this time Billingham was half closed down as the demand for nitrogen became far outstripped by supply. But work at Jealott's Hill continued, with increasing emphasis on crop protection. Its work in that area now began to conflict with that of a company called Cooper, McDougall and Robertson, an amalgamation of firms working in animal health and pest control. In 1937, accordingly, ICI and Coopers formed a joint company called Plant Protection Ltd, with offices in London and technical staff based at Yalding in Kent. ICI provided research facilities at Jealott's Hill; Coopers the commercial and distributive functions. It was never a particularly harmonious arrangement, but it worked well enough for twenty-one years until 1958, when ICI bought out the crop-protection interests of its partner and Plant Protection Ltd became a wholly owned ICI subsidiary.

Breakthroughs in Pesticides

Throughout 1938, as war became increasingly likely, plans gathered momentum for increasing Britain's self-sufficiency. Work at Jealott's Hill concentrated on intensive and extended grass production to give twice-yearly cropping in spring and autumn – what was known as 'early bite' and 'late bite'. Once war had actually broken out, the urgent need to 'Grow More Food', as the nation was exhorted, brought senior ICI agricultural staff into the corridors of power. Sir William Gavin, then the company's agricultural adviser, became chief agricultural adviser to the Ministry of Agriculture and ICI took part in a number of joint campaigns with the government, including one aimed at stepping up the production of silage. More significant, as far as future commercial prospects were concerned, were two wartime discoveries made at Jealott's Hill and nearby Hawthorndale, which were among the most important in ICI's history and indeed the whole history of crop protection. These were to come on to the market as 'Gammexane' and 'Methoxone'.

'Gammexane' is properly named gamma benzene hexachloride. It is a compound of benzene hexachloride (BHC), which was first recorded as being made by Michael Faraday in 1825 by bubbling chlorine through benzene in sunlight, resulting in what he described as a 'tenacious triple compound of chlorine, carbon and hydrogen'. BHC had been tested by ICI in the 1930s as a repellent to prevent clothes moths from laying their eggs. It proved unsuitable for this, but it was noticed that adult moths were killed by the exposure to the test substances, an effect for which any one in the batch might have been responsible. In 1942, a programme was begun to look for substitutes for derris powder, imports of derris being seriously affected by wartime conditions, in particular the Japanese occupation of Malaya.

Pesticide chemistry was still in its infancy at this time and, at Widnes, which had a large quantity of BHC in its store, the research staff tended to look on pesticide tests as a 'suitable destination for any intractable and evil-smelling residue for which no other use could be envisaged', as a history of Jealott's Hill put it. Widnes duly sent along its BHC for testing in the derris substitute programme and the research team soon became excited about its potential through an incident which happened one weekend. A sample of the product, newly arrived from Widnes, was sieved on a Saturday morning in a room where locusts were being kept in a cage. By Monday, they had all died, and the cages remained toxic to locusts for some time.

BHC was soon being tested in various formulations as both dusts and sprays on caterpillars, aphids, locusts and red spider mites which were living on potted plants in the laboratory: it proved fatal to most of the insects except for the red spiders. Plant Protection also tested it at Yalding and reported its performance as excellent on a number of field trials in Kent on raspberry beetles, caterpillars on raspberries and cultivated blackberries, flea beetles on swedes and turnips, and aphids on hops. It was subsequently learned that the compound's insecticidal properties had already been discovered in France, Spain and the USA, but nothing was known of this at the time ICI's work was proceeding independently.

For some time it was not realized that the true toxicity of the product lay in the gamma isomer; it was thought by the Jealott's Hill chemists that only alpha and beta isomers were present in the crude material. BHC was first code-named '666' within ICI, but as awareness

Not quite the pre-war pastoral it seems: these farmers in 1937 are killing weeds selectively by spraying with sulphuric acid. The 1940s brought ICI's discovery of hormone selective weedkillers.

grew of the role of the gamma isomer, it was renamed 'Gammexane'. Further work on it produced a high rate of success in killing a wide range of insect pests, particularly locusts, for which field trials were organized in Africa. In Britain, the most pressing problem besetting crops were wireworms in cereals and potatoes, which were proving particularly virulent in the large areas of grassland newly ploughed up for agricultural use in response to wartime needs. Flea beetles on brassicas were also troublesome, and for all these Gammexane proved effective.

The only drawback was that it produced a musty flavour in certain foods after crop treatment. Those working on the product then at ICI vividly recall the scenes which were a feature of daily life at Hawthorndale when a bell rang morning and afternoon and everyone assembled at the 'taint kitchen' to taste portions of food cooked and arranged on numbered plates. The menus featured mashed potatoes, swedes, carrots, onions, beets, fruit, chicken, eggs and even potato chips fried in fat from chickens which had been fed on grain treated with Gammexane. The worst effects were found to be on potatoes, which, even if grown on land treated with BHC for a preceding crop, were likely to be tainted for several years afterwards.

In the field of public health, Gammexane was unlucky in its timing. DDT was introduced to Britain by the Swiss firm of Geigy for the first time in the latter part of 1942, and its power against lice and mosquitoes immediately focused the government's attention on it. Jungle trials of DDT were under way before ICI had time to call attention to its own new product, and DDT gained a lead which proved virtually impossible to challenge. And where Gammexane might well have had a large sale in the veterinary trade as 'dips' against lice, ticks, blowflies, mites and so on, ICI was hamstrung by a previous agreement that reserved the 'dip' trade to Cooper, McDougall and Robertson. At a later stage a related product named Gammalin was widely used for the control of cocoa capsids in West Africa, while bodies such as the World Health Organization and the Anti-Locust Research Organization carried out studies using Gammexane against locusts, malaria and the tsetse fly.

The commercial development of Gammexane suffered not only from its timing but also from the fact that within ICI it was in effect 'nobody's child'. Responsibility for it was shared between General Chemicals, Agricultural, and the development and research departments in such an unstructured way that none of the four devoted full attention to it. One positive result of this, however, was the setting up of a Pest Control Panel so that future pesticides should not suffer from a lack of coordination within the company. Even with these drawbacks, Gammexane did prove a profitable product. It was also developed very speedily: first discovered in 1942, it was in widespread use within four years, and its development costs were ludicrously low by today's standards.

First Hormone Weedkiller

Almost parallel with Gammexane went the discovery of another agricultural chemical ultimately known as 'Methoxone' – the first of the so-called hormone weedkillers. This grew out of work done at Jealott's Hill in the 1930s on growth hormones or phytohormones, substances occurring naturally in plants which regulate their growth much as endocrine hormones do in animals. The existence of these chemicals had been discovered in Holland in 1926, and two related substances, alpha-naphthaylacetic acid (NAA) and beta-indoleacetic acid (IAA) were under particular study by ICI in 1936. Their chemists made the deduction that the organic part of the soil might contain growth hormone from decayed plants, and thus the soil itself might stimulate plant growth. Cuttings of various plants grown at Jealott's Hill, and later at the Royal Botanic Gardens at Kew, confirmed this theory. While these tests were being carried out, an ICI scientist named W. G. Templeman made a revolutionary observation: NAA did not just fail to stimulate plant growth; on the contrary, it depressed it. What was more, the depression was selective. Templeman's 1940 tests (now regarded as a classic of their kind) showed that a proportion of NAA in the soil killed yellow charlock without affecting oats grown simultaneously; further work proved conclusively that many of the most troublesome weeds growing in cereals or grass were killed off by NAA while most of the crops remained resistant to it.

There had been selective weedkillers before this date, but they owed their effect entirely to leaf structure and habit of growth. Cereals are 'waxy' and upright, while most of the weeds have hairy leaves which spread out horizontally. When the field is sprayed with a solution of the weedkiller, the spray tends to run off the upright waxy stalks of the grain and to remain on the leaves of the weeds, killing them. The effects of the hormone weedkiller are quite different, owing to basic differences in the nature of plants. Among the most active of the range of compounds tested was the sodium salt of 4-chloro-2-methyl-phenoxyacetic acid, known as MCPA. Another was 2,4-dichloro-phenoxyacetic acid (2,4-D).

In December 1942 the Ministry of Agriculture held a high-level meeting attended by a number of senior ICI executives including the chairman, the second Lord Melchett, W. G. Templeman and R. E. Slade, the company's research director. The chemical finally selected was MCPA, largely because ICI had good supplies of chlorocresol, which was one of its intermediate stages. It was decided to set up 300 experimental centres throughout Britain in the largest-scale trial of its kind attempted up to that time. Mobile teams toured the country in specially equipped lorries and tests were carried out on hundreds of different soils and crops, all in the utmost secrecy because of wartime security. This occasionally led to all sorts of excitement as the suspicions of country policemen were aroused by the sinister appearance of shrouded lorries, or when a sudden change in the wind blew the dust into someone's prized garden. But the enormous task was successfully accomplished and by 1946 MCPA was available to British farmers as a one-per-cent dust called Methoxone or 'cornland cleaner'.

Unfortunately the lucrative American market had been largely lost to ICI because of the wartime patent situation. Since work on weedkillers was entangled with highly secret chemical-warfare projects such as defoliation, the government had forbidden the filing of patents overseas and no normal commercial development had been possible. But in America the action of the 2,4-D compound had been described in a magazine article, patents applied for and work begun on it. By the end of the war the product was so widely and cheaply available in the US that Methoxone was in no position to compete.

The Americans had also successfully developed new types of spraying machinery which allowed the growth regulator type of herbicide to be applied in a very small volume of water, sometimes as little as four or five gallons an acre. After an intensive search for a British jet nozzle suitable for the purpose, this method was adopted in Britain, emerging as ICI's 'Agroxone' liquid. Together with an Agroxone triple strength solution, these introduced the widespread use of hormone weedkillers in Britain. The impact of these phenoxy acids, controlling a wide range of broad-leaved weeds in cereals, was enormous, but they still had one major drawback – they were ineffective against grasses.

As the 1950s progressed, crop-protection chemistry was carried out by ICI chemists at Blackley and Runcorn and the physical separation from the activities of the biologists and agriculturalists at Jealott's Hill became increasingly inconvenient. Synthetic programmes got 'out of synch' with the screening work in Berkshire, there were never enough opportunities for meetings and discussions and it became clear that a reorganization was needed. In 1954, Dr William Boon and his team of four organic chemists moved from crop-protection work at Blackley to join two colleagues in a formulation research section at Jealott's Hill, and they were in turn joined over the next two years by the first generation of organic chemists to be directly recruited there.

Methoxone was by now a big seller, and part of their work was to concentrate on building on the discovery of the selective hormonal weedkillers. In 1947, a field observation had recorded that a quaternary salt known as dodecyl-trimethyl ammonium bromide had a strong toxicity to plants. Eight years later, as part of the weedkiller programme, this chemical and a number of its close relatives were tested more stringently and it became evident that quaternary salts as a group were definitely herbicidal. Several of them were then chosen out of the specimen collection held at Dyestuffs Division in Blackley, and tested at Jealott's Hill. Two were outstanding in performance, killing all test plants at a very low application rate of 0.1 pound per acre. One of these was 2,2'-bipyridylium quaternary ammonium salt, now known as diquat. In a matter of weeks an even more active compound was synthesized and tested. This was 1,1'-dimethyl-4,4'bipyridylium dichloride, or paraquat.

The architect of the work on bipyridylium herbicides was Dr William Boon. Living in retirement in Sidmouth, on the Devon coast, he recalled in 1986 that the structure given to the diquat compound in the Blackley collection was 'completely wrong' and said that if the chemist who selected it had known the right one he would probably never have chosen it in the first place. Boon himself was quick to realize the supreme importance of the new compounds and it was undoubtedly his persistence and tenacity with the project that brought it to fruition against the scepticism of his senior colleagues. Today, paraquat is one of ICI's most important agricultural products, used by millions of farmers in 120 countries. At first, however, the properties of these compounds, diquat and paraquat, did not seem to be at all what was wanted. They certainly damaged green plant tissue very rapidly, but

Dr William Boon, responsible for discovering paraquat, seen here with Prince Philip, Duke of Edinburgh, on a visit to Jealott's Hill research station. Boon has called paraquat the most significant advance in agriculture since the invention of the wheeled plough.

they were almost immediately rendered inactive by the soil, ruling out their use as a soil treatment to prevent the growth of weeds. Nor were they particularly selective.

The subject was exhaustively debated and argued over at Jealott's Hill. It was Boon who realized that the criteria of selectivity and action through the soil were in fact irrelevant to a much more momentous purpose. He and his deputy were sitting one day in the study of a colleague, Stephen Crowdy (later Professor of Botany at Southampton University), talking about possible uses for the chemicals. Boon recalled: 'I said, we've got to think this round a different way. The fact that they aren't selective and don't stay in the soil isn't a disadvantage. It's the biggest advantage ever!' Boon had perceived that here was a product which, by a unique combination of instant action and rapid deactivation, had an entirely new potential for agriculture.

His managing director was not convinced, nor were his colleagues in sales and marketing, but after a lot of argument, the project was given the green light. Boon's dogged determination gave rise to an award known in ICI as 'the Boon award for perseverance', periodically given to research workers who stuck out against all opposition within their departments to get a project to development stage. Boon funded it himself from half the proceeds of a £1,000 prize, the Mullard Award, which he received from the Royal Society for his work.

Much of the early research on the bipyridyliums was aimed at discovering how the compounds actually worked, using improvised techniques in many cases. Forty-five years ago there were few of today's sophisticated methods of analysis, but even so, remarkable advances were made in finding out how the substances were taken up and moved within plants. It was also established that the conditions most effective for weed treatment with bipyridyls were high atmospheric humidity at a time when the soil is dry and cold. Low light or total darkness also proved beneficial.

Work on diquat concentrated first on potatoes, the tops or haulms of which have to be destroyed before harvesting. Up till then the usual method had been to desiccate them with sulphuric acid, sodium arsenite or sodium chlorate. All these are unpleasant and hazardous in use; in fact sodium arsenite was shortly afterwards removed from the market because of its extreme toxicity. Diquat proved a very effective substitute in trials in Britain and America, though there was a slight risk of adverse effect on the crop under the best conditions for application – high humidity and dry, cold soil. Farmers now get a regional advisory service from ICI on whether or not to spray diquat in certain weather conditions, a system which has worked successfully since 1968.

Diquat is effective within hours and has the advantage of being 'rainfast', unaffected by rainfall unlike most 'traditional' weedkillers. The residue it leaves in plant parts is low and harmless to animals, and it rapidly became popular for the pre-harvest desiccation of oilseed crops throughout the world, as well as for sunflowers, linseed, castor beans, poppies, cotton, sesame, radish and soya. While work continued on identifying the market for diquat, an ICI team travelled to the US to test it as a weedkiller on railroads and power lines, and for the defoliation of fire-breaks. They concluded that although it had a big future as a pre-harvest desiccant, especially for potatoes, it was not really acceptable for general control of vegetation. It was too poisonous to use on young cereals as a selective herbicide, yet not active enough for a general herbicide because its effect on grass was too transitory.

Something was needed with the attributes of diquat plus the ability to act on grass. At this point the amalgamation of the research facilities at Fernhurst, an estate in Sussex which Plant Protection had bought in 1945, with those of Jealott's Hill, provided the expertise and manpower needed for an intensive programme on diquat's close relative, paraquat.

In 1959, both chemicals were sent to Malaya for testing in the rubber crop where weeds, particularly buffalo grass, were traditionally treated with sodium arsenite. Growth started rapidly again after the use of diquat, but paraquat proved much more long-lasting. Both diquat and paraquat had the additional advantages in the Malayan climate of being more rainfast than sodium arsenite, and could be sprayed on to the bark of young rubber trees without damaging them. It was decided that paraquat should also be developed commercially.

A Swiss company had made the first batch of fifty pounds of 2:2' bipyridyl for conversion to diquat for the field trials, but this had cost £50,000 at a time when the crop-protection business was losing money for ICI (a situation that caused a major reorganization and a series of redundancies in 1959). ICI chemists then hit upon a method of making it which proved hopelessly uneconomic and, as Boon remembers, 'involved disposing of an awful lot of arsenic afterwards. It was mixed into concrete and dumped at sea'. The research director of ICI, Dr John Rose, told them that if they couldn't find a better method than that, they ought to forget the whole venture. Then, after a number of abortive attempts in Organics Division and in ICI Australia, two chemists, Frank Bradbury and Charles Suckling (the discoverer of halothane) succeeded in developing a process to make diquat at an economical price. Mond Division developed a process for the manufacture of paraquat. The plant was of such complexity that it assured ICI a virtual monopoly of manufacture of the product. In August 1962, paraquat was launched on to the market as 'Gramoxone'.

But its biggest potential had not yet been discovered; once again it was Boon's alert mind which seized on it. A grassland consultant from outside ICI made an observation which stuck in Boon's mind: 'When we plough up grassland, we bury so much of our fertility – we kill it.' Paraquat treatment, Boon realized, did exactly the opposite: it left the dead grasses on the surface instead of being ploughed under, and they acted as a mulch and a protecting agent against erosion in high, windswept places – the sort of pasture where conventional ploughing is most difficult.

The first sizeable experiments along these lines were carried out on the slopes of Aran in North Wales, where the ground was infested with *Nardus* and *Molinia*. A thoroughly unpromising site was chosen which, as Boon described it, 'for most of the year offered little more to the sheep living on it than exercise for the muscles of their legs and jaws'. A quarter of an acre was fenced off, sprayed with paraquat, limed, harrowed, and treated with fertilizer, then sown. Two matched groups of lambs were put out to pasture – one group on the re-seeded plot, the other on the rest of the mountainside. Over the test period of five weeks, the live weight gain of the lambs on the treated area was forty per cent greater than that of the others. The advantages, particularly to hill farmers, were obvious and enormous: little more than harrowing was needed after the old sward had been killed to prepare the ground for the new seed, and the disturbance of the soil, even with the light rotavation necessary to dispose of the dead plant tissue, was much less than with traditional methods.

After this work on grassland renovation got under way, paraquat research began to focus on arable crops. The first experiments involving Boon's ideas on what is now known as 'direct drilling' or chemical ploughing began in the autumn of 1961 at Jealott's Hill. A programme for winter wheat was designed to last for seven years and give three different treatments: ploughing and cultivating in the traditional way; spraying old sward with paraquat, followed by conventional ploughing and cultivating; and, finally, spraying the old sward with paraquat without any subsequent cultivation. In the third test, seed was drilled directly into the sprayed sward with a JEC Grasslands sod seeder, the only machine on the market at that time whose coulters were strong enough to penetrate undisturbed soil. Yields from the direct drilling experiment proved very encouraging, and other trials followed with wheat, barley and kale.

There were drawbacks to direct drilling, especially on heavy soils, and improved types of machinery had to be developed. Some early expectations went too far, predicting that the process would completely replace the plough, but it is no longer thought likely this will ever happen, despite growing awareness that traditional methods can sometimes prove harmful to the structure of the soil. Several million hectares of land each year are now drilled with the aid of paraquat. Boon has called it the most significant agricultural development since the invention of the wheeled plough.

ICI sent a team of research staff, forty or fifty strong, around the world to look at the possibilities opened up by paraquat 'chemical ploughing' – of establishing various crops without cultivation. The whole exercise cost about £1 million, but some of the more successful schemes are still big business for the company today. Brazil, for example, is now a major exporter of soya beans, which could not be grown there before paraquat because the soil was too easily eroded. In Western Australia, where farmers have to switch quickly from raising sheep on pasture to sowing the wheat crop, paraquat offers a special advantage because it enables a quicker turnover of crops than ploughing by mechanical means.

The last fifty years have seen a profound change in people's attitudes to pesticides: as Dr Boon said, with a touch of sadness, it has become 'a word with evil associations' in connection with dangers to the environment. Yet these have been of concern in the laboratory since the discoveries were made; certainly those of diquat and paraquat. Dr Boon formed an 'Ecology Section', probably the first of its kind, to look at the indirect effects of destroying certain aquatic weeds on which diquat was used in its early tests. By 1969, ICI brought all the facets of this work together into an Environmental Sciences Group at Jealott's Hill. One unforeseen commercial benefit of this came when, three years later, new and stringent regulations on pesticides were introduced by the US Environmental Protection Agency (EPA). ICI, then on the verge of entering the American market via a newly formed US subsidiary, was well placed to comply with the new requirements (which incidentally also had the effect of enormously increasing the development cost of new chemicals).

The speed and toxicity of paraquat as a weedkiller inevitably led to anxieties about its effect on humans. During all the years it has been on sale worldwide, there have been no fatalities or injuries recorded when it was being used properly. But as Dr Frank Rose remarked on pharmaceuticals in general, as soon as a new chemical comes along, someone sooner or later tries to commit suicide with it. Certainly paraquat is poisonous when swallowed, though no more so, Dr Boon stressed, than bleach or lavatory cleaners. Those accidents that have occurred, as opposed to deliberate attempts at suicide, have mostly happened when it has been decanted from its marked container into a branded drinks bottle. Gardening sheds are all too often places waiting for accidents to happen. On one such occasion, Boon recalled, a small amount of paraquat was kept in a fridge in a beer bottle.

Paraquat probably gained its sinister reputation when, during an inquest on a case of paraquat poisoning, the coroner asked if there was an antidote. The answer being no, Boon remembered, 'Every time it was mentioned in the press after that, it was the chemical which has no antidote. But 99 per cent of chemicals have no antidote at all – even aspirin and paracetamol. You can treat the poisoning, but not in a true antidote sense, where one chemical neutralizes another'.

Diquat is still used exclusively in Britain, mostly for desiccating potato haulms, and is sold, mixed with paraquat, as ICI's 'Weedol' for gardeners. William Boon's name is not on the paraquat patent, but discoveries owe their inception to many factors and his role was crucial in deciding, first, to test the quaternary salts, then to press ahead with their development and, above all, to persist with his conviction that the bipyridyls' very unselective nature and failure to linger in the soil was no drawback but provided an entirely new kind of agricultural tool. His citation as a Fellow of the Royal Society was a composite one for contributions to organic chemistry and to the development of bipyridylium herbicides.

Growing a New Protein

By the mid-1960s, the Agricultural Division was the most profitable in ICI. Its fertilizer achievements, as well as its work on herbicides and pesticides, had helped to develop a close and mutually beneficial relationship with the farming community. Achievement and innovation in heavy chemical engineering had formed a solid basis for success, and the company was among the foremost in the world in naphtha and natural-gas technology. It had introduced a satisfactory fertilizer in ammonium nitrate and solved the technical problems associated with nitrogen. There was a general feeling of being on a plateau, and a consciousness that something new was needed.

In 1967 Dr Peter King, a large and humorous man who later became General Secretary of the Society of Chemical Industry, was head of a research group in the Agricultural Division looking, as he put it, at 'what to do for an encore'. They wanted something 'very new and very big', and the date coincided with a wave of global anxiety about a threatened 'protein gap'. The world, so it was predicted by the World Health Organization and many other bodies, was going to run short of protein; in particular, the rich European countries which were not, for geographical reasons, among the chief producers of soya beans, the ultimate protein commodity. King and his team made a careful study of all the reports on this topic. The protein was not, in this case, for people to eat directly, but for animal feed, which ideally contains more protein than exists naturally in wheat or barley. Pigs and poultry need protein supplements, although the internal mechanism of ruminant animals like cattle enables them to produce most of the protein they need from grass. By this date, the pork and bacon industries in Europe were flourishing and, with the advent of the broiler chicken, poultry sales were rocketing. The EEC was spending around £50 million a year on fish meal as feed supplements, but there were strong indications that the world was becoming over-fished – the Peruvian anchovy was disappearing and herring fishing in the North Sea coming under severe restrictions.

King and his team decided to aim at making a truly new synthetic protein for animals – 'a scientifically produced animal nutrition product'. Their first intention was to synthesize protein by chemical means, but the chemistry involved was too complex and the plan was soon abandoned. Various fermentation processes were considered, and they decided to pick a substrate (a substance containing carbon that can be metabolized) 'on intellectual grounds'. The one they chose as a starting-point was a substance that had just appeared in abundant quantities under the North Sea – natural gas. Using this as a feedstock, bacteria or yeasts could in theory be grown in quantity, producing protein-rich microbial cells or single-cell protein (SCP).

The idea itself was not new. During the First World War the Germans had replaced much of the food they had previously imported by creating food yeasts, and in ICI in the 1940s there had been attempts at Jealott's Hill to produce protein economically from unicellular algae. These had not been successful, but since then there had been rapid advances in industrial bio-chemistry and British Petroleum as well as some Japanese companies were already experimenting with growing yeasts, using long-chain hydrocarbons from petroleum as the carbon source. These were, however, not likely to stay cheap and methane, the main constituent of natural gas, seemed a better long-term source.

In 1968 they started, as King recalled, 'searching the world for micro-organisms that would grow on methane', working with hundreds of experimental varieties from sources ranging from African deserts to swamps. None proved robust enough in culture; they were 'just delicate laboratory curiosities'. After spending a few hundred thousand pounds, they had nearly decided to call it a day.

However, one of the consultants on the project was Professor Roderick Quayle, then Professor of Microbiology at Sheffield University (later Vice-Chancellor of Bath University). He was working specifically on the 'metabolic pathways' used by methane bacteria to join carbon atoms together, an extraordinarily complex process for scientists to duplicate. Quayle discovered an entirely new pathway: that when bacteria lived on methane, what they first did was to metabolize all of it into methanol. It's a step that King said is 'still impossible in the laboratory except by smashing and reassembling the molecule – but the bugs were doing it'. However, there was a price to pay. Twelve per cent of the bugs' cell weight was represented by a single enzyme, methane nono-oxygenase, which carried out the conversion, and there were substantial energy losses along the way. The solution to the feebleness of the bacterial cultures was blindingly simple, said King: 'Feed the bugs on methanol, not methane, and you ought to be away.' It worked dramatically. The micro-organism eventually selected, *Methylophilus methylotrophus*, doubled in numbers in about half an hour and, in addition to methanol, needed only air, water and a few simple salts to grow. Work turned accordingly to using methanol instead of methane as the feedstock; it was safer and the division was a world leader in its chemical production.

Quayle, a quiet and modest man, refused to accept any money for his contribution, but he agreed to ICI providing his laboratory with some new equipment. Before long, with his aid, the scientists had cultures growing literally thick and fast – 'like great vats of mushroom soup', in King's colourful phrase. Because of their rapid growth, however, the organisms couldn't get enough oxygen. When a method was devised to give them more, they were killed by the carbon dioxide they exhaled – 'poisoned by their own bad breath', as King graphically described it. At this point the engineering resources of the division were brought into play and asked to solve the problem of making a vessel simultaneously providing pressure high enough to dissolve oxygen and low enough to let carbon dioxide escape. One mathematician pointed out that if you have a very tall column of liquid, you get this effect: the bottom has high pressure because of hydrostatics (such as a diver experiences at the bottom of the sea), while at the top, it is merely subject to atmospheric pressure. Out of this concept grew the pressure-cycle fermenter built at Billingham for the project. King described it as 'a sort of giant hydrogenatic lung, breathing in at the top and out at the bottom'.

Technically, it involved a fermenter loop thirty metres high or more, in which circulation was maintained through a cooler by injecting air into one side of it. At the base, hydrostatic pressure was enough to ensure the rate of oxygen absorption required by the cells, while carbon dioxide could evolve freely by the rapid circulation of the fermenter's contents through the lower pressure region at the top. If it worked it would lay the foundations for a further fifty-fold scale-up to commercial operation in a single-stream plant, which would be essential if the economies of scale were to be realized. There was much scepticism in the outside world and one distinguished MIT professor 'proved' that it was impossible, publishing the result in a learned journal.

From the early laboratory fermenters the process was gradually scaled up and, by early 1971, a continuous fermenter of one-litre capacity had been constructed, which could produce many tons a year. By September 1971, a pilot plant was working, plus a separator and a drying plant for 'harvesting' the protein. Extremely high standards of sterility were required in the plant because if any organism got in, it would grow and multiply so fast. 'We were aiming at standards a million times higher than in a transplant operating theatre.' The actual operation of the machinery was tremendously complicated; to keep it sterile, 350 valves all had to be opened and closed in a particular sequence. At first an entire team of PhDs was employed to carry it out, but that was hopelessly uneconomic, so they turned to computers and here, King recalled, ran into 'a new problem in physics'. They wanted two computers online simultaneously so that, if either failed, the other would take over with no delay whatsoever. 'We discovered that it is not possible for two computers to be absolutely simultaneous, even side by side and coupled by a relatively short piece of multiplex cable. The signal cannot go from one to the other quicker than the speed of light; one will always be behind the other. But since they were programmed to be simultaneous, they didn't know what to do. So we had to set one about four milliseconds behind the other. You could say they were identical twins, but one knew that it was born first!'

ICI's Central Toxicology Laboratory was in charge of the early testing of the microbial mass produced by the fermentation, and there were no major problems with pigs and broilers, laying hens and, later, veal calves. In all, the product was tested on about a quarter of a million animals. The experiments had two main objects: to show that there were no harmful effects of 'Pruteen', as ICI named its single-cell protein, either to the animals consuming it or to people eating them as meat, and to demonstrate that 'Pruteen' could be an economical addition to animal diet.

Then it all began to go wrong. The economics of 'Pruteen' were badly affected by two things. The first oil-price shock of 1973–4 indirectly pushed up the price of methanol. Also, Britain's entry into the

EEC raised domestic cereal prices in line with those prevailing in the rest of the Community, which meant decreased sale prices for 'Pruteen'. Between 1973 and 1974, something like £100 a ton was added to prospective manufacturing costs. Even so, the ICI board gave the green light in 1976 to an expenditure of £40 million on construction of a Pruteen plant on Teesside, the world's first commercial plant to manufacture protein from methanol. At its peak the plant could have produced 50,000 tonnes a year – but it never did. The second, overwhelming factor was the 'Green Revolution'. There was a grain surplus in India, soybean prices were falling, and the expected 'protein gap' never materialized. It was all rather sad, reflected King in his SCI office in 1986: 'The science was new and imaginative, the development worked, the technology was right, the plant ran – but the market vanished. What Pruteen tells us is that while all innovation is risky, and all research is a gamble, the attempt to make a single very large step is very, very risky – what we now recognize as "the Concorde syndrome".'

However, the work was by no means wasted. 'Pruteen' was found to be highly successful as a replacement for expensive skim-milk powder in the diets of calves and young pigs. The work on single-cell protein also led ICI into fermentation technology and biotechnology in general. The company's Biological Products Business at Billingham has been responsible for a number of significant product developments, most notably myco-Protein, a new human foodstuff similar to edible fungus, brought to market in partnership with Rank Hovis McDougall as 'Quorn'. Available both in its raw form of dried granules, resembling vegetarian mince, or as part of ready-prepared dishes, Quorn is seen as a potential global product for the new biosciences company, though it has initially been on sale only in southern England and the Benelux countries. High in fibre, low in calories and with no cholesterol risk, it has an obvious appeal to people looking for alternatives to meat and a number of lucrative added-value uses, particularly in the enormous markets for snacks and slimmers' foods.

Dr Peter Doyle, who succeeded Dr Charles Reece in 1989 as ICI's board director responsible for research, and who will join the board of the demerged biosciences company Zeneca, believes Quorn is a likely candidate to become one of the company's select band of discoveries that 'changed our lives', though few shoppers would make the connection, since the product is marketed by a different company, Marlow Foods. It is also a classic example of the quirky route that research often takes before it results in a marketable product.

'Pruteen was a technological triumph but perhaps the fundamental lesson the industrial researcher has to learn is that there is no straight line between excellent technology and profit,' observes Doyle. 'I don't think we realized the limitations of Pruteen for the human market, but it was clear that people at RHM saw in the fungal protein a much better product and that led us to our first joint venture (their product, our technology), and then ultimately, when it came to developing the product, to us buying out the rights to develop it.'

Ronnie Hampel, appointed chief operating officer in the leadership restructuring of autumn 1991, and chief executive designate of any demerged ICI heavy-chemicals side, goes further in his view of Quorn's potential. 'It's been much more successful than I thought in the UK,' he said in late 1991, 'and if it can be as successful as that in the UK it's a global product, and if it's a global product it's probably bigger than any current division of ICI.'

Another fascinating offshoot of Pruteen technology – which itself has attracted interest around the world, notably in 1981 from the then Soviet Union, the biggest manufacturer of foods from micro-organisms – is the non-oil based plastic initially known as polyhydroxy-butyrate (PHB), and now, in a reformulation with a co-polymer, as Biopol. Totally biodegradable and compatible with human tissue, it had to await the environmental revolution before its true potential was realized in the marketplace (see Chapter 10).

A Revolutionary Spray

Among all the innovations to come out of ICI's agrochemical labora-tories, the one that seemed to offer the most exciting possibilities in the mid-1980s – for dozens of fields in the wider world of industry – was the Electrodyn spray system, based on a revolutionary new way of using the energy contained in electrical fields. Electrodyn was the brainchild of one man, Dr Ron Coffee, although like most inventions it built on earlier work and, like Sir James Black's beta-blockers, was the result of an imaginative leap that put different pieces of knowledge together to make something that did not exist before.

Coffee, a dapper, effervescent man with a neat beard and voluble enthusiasm for his project, studied at London's Imperial College under one of the world's great contemporary inventors. This was Dennis Gabor, a Hungarian Jewish refugee from Hitler (and relative of the Hollywood Gabor sisters) whose inventions include holography (for which he received the Nobel Prize for Physics) and the flat cathode ray tube which was the basis of Sir Clive Sinclair's pocket television. Gabor was a brilliant physicist, 'a genius and the only man I ever knew who described himself as an inventor,' says Coffee. He instilled into his eager student the turn of mind that led naturally to invention and problem-solving; so much so that the young Coffee was even pleased when his car, an old prewar banger, broke down, because it gave him a problem to tackle.

By the early 1960s Coffee was working with another eminent

European physicist, the Corsican-born N. J. Felici, at the University of Grenoble. Felici, whom Coffee calls 'the father of applied electrostatics', was a special adviser on science to the French President and founded a company called the Société Anonyme de Machines Electrostatiques, which was the world's leading manufacturer of electrostatic machinery. Coffee's work with him concerned electric fields, an area which he says no one has ever fully understood. 'Most electrical energy is used in circuits; people fight shy of electrical fields because there seems to be no money in them. They are very mathematical, difficult even to talk about.' In past centuries their properties were employed for conjuring tricks by some, including an eighteenth-century French court entertainer and Benjamin Franklin. Lack of understanding has made them a capricious area of science, regarded almost as a 'black art' rather than a technology.

Felici was interested in the application of electrostatics to spraying techniques, and with Coffee he pioneered a crop-dusting machine, having reasoned that crop pesticides would distribute better if they could be electrically charged. The machine worked, but it was too big, too expensive and too heavy. What was needed, especially for Third World farmers, was something much cheaper and lighter, capable of being hand-held like the so-called knapsack sprays. Even so, Felici's machine, the size of a suitcase, was a considerable advance on its

Dr Ron Coffee, inventor of Electrodyn, which he believes could help turn Africa into a market garden and revolutionize many other industrial technologies with its use of electrical energy fields.

predecessors, which had filled a room, and he set up his own company to make them for industrial rather than agricultural use. The Felici machine, Coffee says now, was 'nowhere near enough of a breakthrough in generating high voltages. It took another ten or twenty years before we began to get solid-state, high-voltage devices, small, reliable and battery-driven'. By the time he himself had progressed to working on liquid electrostatic sprays, others had invented much cheaper, lighter, and highly reliable high-voltage generators.

Coffee went on to the University of the West Indies, Trinidad, a world-famous centre for studies in tropical agriculture, and kept up his interest in crop-spraying in such spare time as he had from lecturing in the faculty of engineering. His next academic post was in Hong Kong, where he became a senior lecturer in 1968. By this time he had carried out extensive studies on dust pesticides, 'trying to target the particles more precisely instead of covering everything like talcum powder'. By 1974 he had filed two patents on his inventions for ultra low-volume (ULV) spraying concerned with solid-state particles, and by now he needed help with further development costs.

On the last day of a leave in the UK, he walked into ICI's Plant Protection Division hoping to get some technical help as well as free chemicals on which to work when he returned to Hong Kong. The group manager he saw first immediately recognized the importance of the work Coffee was doing and drove him to see Dr Braunholtz, the research director at Jealott's Hill. Braunholtz did not hesitate either. He told Coffee ICI would like an exclusive option on the two patents and offered him £1,000 for a two-year option, 'which in 1974 seemed quite nice'. The following year Coffee was due for a twelve-months sabbatical leave and agreed to spend it with ICI, working on his invention. Braunholtz kept urging him to try to adapt it to liquids, which would have more commercial use. Coffee had never up till then done any work on the electrostatic charging of liquids; the technique, which he describes as 'very mysterious', is still not fully understood. But by the end of his sabbatical year, he had invented 'Electrodyn'.

The early version was known as 'Nimbus', and was promising enough for ICI to decide the whole concept was worth more development study. One of the main benefits of electrostatic spraying is that it requires only minute quantities of chemical, and Coffee had long thought that the amount of chemical applied to crops should be drastically reduced. 'Insecticides in some processes were being used with an overkill of 10,000. With modern, potent chemicals you need approximately one-thousandth of a millionth of a gram to kill a bug. But each droplet might contain 10,000 times the amount needed. It was a gross waste of chemical products and an obvious mismatch between the potency of modern agrochemicals and the crude equipment to apply them.' A pesticide droplet with an electrical charge in it, on the other hand, could be manipulated with far greater accuracy.

The traditional knapsack sprayer had one major disadvantage: it needed a large volume of water in which the chemical was mixed. Carrying the water was heavy work and reduced the time available for spraying. The operator also had to measure the dosage of the chemical correctly, mix it thoroughly, lift and walk with the backpack weighing around 20 kg, as well as cope with the problems of drift, clean the equipment thoroughly after use and dispose of surplus solution. The spray had to be maintained and worn parts replaced. Some of the main disadvantages had been reduced by the invention of the spinning disc type of applicator, which incorporated a disc powered by a torch battery. This rotated as the pesticide fell on it, and the chemical was then atomized as the disc spun at high speed. The technique was effective in reducing the volume of liquid but it did not solve the problem of drift, the battery life was short and the machines not entirely reliable.

Coffee knew that as water emerges from an ordinary spray nozzle, it does so in the form of droplets which vary in size, but there is an optimum size of droplet for any given biological effect; larger ones run off the plant and are wasted, smaller ones tend to drift. The best way to achieve a consistent optimum size would be to charge the droplets electrically. Once Coffee had succeeded in doing this, he discovered that they behaved in a particular way, moving in curved lines towards any earthed object, usually the crop to which they were applied, and then completely enveloping it. Stems, buds and leaves were covered with the liquid on both upper and lower surfaces, and the amount of liquid needed to achieve this was a minute fraction of that required by a conventional spray – as little as 0.5 to one litre a hectare.

This was a significant breakthrough, but now Coffee had to develop a vehicle for the safe and effective delivery of the pesticide. He invented a combined bottle and nozzle, patented and named as 'Bozzle', which together with the hand-held sprayer is known as the 'Electrodyn' spray. Inside the spray stick are four U-2 batteries and the high-voltage, solid-state generator. The size of the droplets is controlled by electro-dynamic action and can be as small as forty microns in diameter – about one-twentieth the size of a pinhead. Electric field propulsion forces them out at high speed and there is hardly any wastage or drift. The whole inexpensive apparatus weighs only 2.5 kg, and one 750 ml 'Bozzle' will typically treat up to 1.5 hectares, taking less than four hours to cover them, so that the operator can easily carry enough liquid for a full working day.

Electrodyn was patented in 1976 and went on sale in 1984. It won a leading environmental award and sold widely in a number of developing countries with support from the World Bank. The ergonomic and environmental advantages of the invention seemed enormous, and brought about significant improvements in crop yields – up to nearly sixty per cent in cotton-growing trials in Zambia. It was this market that Coffee saw as the natural first target for his invention, which was designed for smallholdings and for 'people whose lives literally depend on our chemicals'. He described it with some passion as 'the most important thing in human terms that I've ever done,' and envisioned it eventually turning Africa into 'the market garden for Europe'.

In 1986 Coffee declared confidently: 'We won't run out of ideas for it in twenty years. It's a whole emerging area of science technology which can be tapped into – a new way of converting energy. Everything you do in industry and engineering requires energy conversion, and if you can provide a new form of conversion it's like adding a new tool to a carpenter's bag, and a very key tool. This unusual thing is now ripe and ready for widespread use in the chemical industry.'

Despite its inventor's bright hopes, however, Electrodyn did not achieve those wider markets which its advanced technology had seemed to justify. In 1991, Coffee left ICI and moved to Oxford to continue development work on his brainchild. Dr Peter Doyle still thinks it is an exciting technology but believes that its applicability will be 'much more constrained than we thought initially'.

'I always saw the excitement of Electrodyn for controlled film coating – laying down a very even film through a linear nozzle – and we have one application that we are quietly working on in the context of aerosol development. But Electrodyn is perhaps the classic example of a technology in search of a marketplace.'

10

THE ENVIRONMENTAL
REVOLUTION

About the time Dr William Boon was developing his theories on bipyridylium herbicides, the American author Rachel Carson was writing a book that would lay a depth-charge under the public's attitudes to the chemical industry and its assumptions about technological progress. *Silent Spring*, published in 1962, shocked a generation with its revelations of the effects of DDT and the gradual poisoning by other chemicals of large areas of animal and bird life on the planet. Although Carson did not live long enough to see the full impact of her work, *Silent Spring* can lay claim to a niche on the small shelf of books that have changed the thinking of the century. Because of it, and the solutions it proposed, as a later writer on the environment dramatically expressed it, 'the world shifted course' (Bill McKibben: *The End of Nature*, Viking Penguin, 1990).

Carson may have fired the first shots in the environmental revolution that by the 1990s would be the single biggest challenge to the chemical industry (and many others), involving a fundamental reorientation of investment strategy, but it was not until the 1970s that scientific and public awareness began to coalesce and gather force. In 1971 an apparently minor decision by the Schweppes company not to accept the return of its soft-drink bottles sparked a demonstration by hundreds of British consumers who besieged the company's headquarters with a barrage of bottles. From this was formed the Friends of the Earth, Britain's first environmental pressure group. Greenpeace, which now regularly targets the chemical industry (and, in Britain, ICI in particular), originated in Canada in 1971.

Substitutes for CFCs

The early 1970s were also the years when scientists on both sides of the Atlantic started to investigate the long-term effects of chlorofluoro carbons on the world's upper atmosphere. CFCs, as they are now widely known, had been first developed in 1928 by a group of chemists at General Motors in the US led by Thomas Midgley (who was also responsible for adding lead to petrol to improve its performance). CFCs had the unique properties of being both chemically and thermally extremely stable, so they were safe for use in two huge markets – refrigeration (as coolants and foam-blowing agents for the polyurethane insulation), and aerosol propellants.

Their use in industry rapidly became indispensable – or so it was thought. In the US alone by 1990, $135 billion worth of equipment relied on the products. They could be used as solvents: 'Nearly all the printed circuit boards you see are washed with CFCs,' says John Beckitt, a leading member of the ICI team at Runcorn, now racing to develop safer alternatives. In medical applications, because of their low toxicity and chameleon ability to adapt, CFCs have been used as the propellant in asthma inhalant sprays to deliver the drugs directly into the lungs. They have been highly cost-effective in medicine because they remain inert in the body.

By 1974, nearly one million tonnes a year of CFCs were being produced. Then two American scientists, Sherwood Rowland and Mario Molina, spotted a possible link between CFCs and depletion of the ozone layer in the upper atmosphere. Precisely because the product was so stable, the chlorine in it could drift up to the stratosphere and hang there for anything between 50 and 400 years. By 1978 the US government was concerned enough about the risk of damage to the ozone layer to impose a ban on aerosols containing CFCs.

Development work on alternatives, by ICI and other chemical companies, had slowed down by the end of the 1970s when scientific opinion was divided on the risk factor. The discovery of a hole in the ozone layer over Antarctica, however, hugely accelerated the pressure to eliminate CFCs and threw all the chemical majors into an unprecedented race against time and each other. The Montreal Protocol of 1987 agreed to halve production by 1998, but the goalposts were moved dramatically in December 1991 by the UK government, in February 1992 by the US President, and later in 1992 by the European Commission in Brussels, which decided to phase out CFCs. Tighter deadlines were discussed by signatories to the Montreal Protocol at the end of 1992, resulting in global agreement on a phase-out by the end of 1995 – the end of 1994 in Europe.

ICI had anticipated such a move, having announced as early as 1988 its commitment to phasing out production of CFCs. The company has now advanced its target date to 1993 for stopping CFC 11 and 12, the two main potentially ozone-damaging products. 'We always recognized that regulation would probably be forced forward, which was why it was important to go as fast as we could,' says John Beckitt. Unlike other chemical companies which had identified substitute products, ICI decided not to develop the group of products known as HCFCs, in which some of the chlorine is replaced by less damaging

The KLEA 134a plant at Runcorn, Cheshire, a new business created by the environmental revolution to replace ozone-damaging CFCs in a huge range of industrial and domestic uses.

hydrogen, but which still retains the potential ability to affect the ozone layer. 'We took the view that these products would eventually be considered unacceptable and that society would drive for perfection,' explains Beckitt. (Limits on HCFCs were subsequently written into the Montreal Protocol in 1992.)

Instead, the ICI team went directly into work on HFCs, products with a zero potential for ozone depletion in which all the chlorine, not merely part of it, is replaced by hydrogen. Two products are under way, KLEA 134a, which was first developed at Runcorn in the laboratory as early as the 1970s, and KLEA 32. Both can be used in refrigeration and a wide range of other applications, and KLEA 32 has the advantage of a particularly low boiling point (minus 52°C compared to minus 27°C for KLEA 134a). The development of both was extremely fast: from a semi-technical plant at Widnes in 1987 to commercial production of KLEA 134a in a plant at Rocksavage, at Runcorn, in October 1990, beating du Pont's parallel work by three months. The Rocksavage plant was planned in 1989 and built in twelve months. A small plant for KLEA 32 began operating in 1992.

'We certainly have a lead with 134a and we've not been distracted by working on products like HCFCs,' says Beckitt. As well as du Pont, other companies in the US, Europe and Japan, are working on similar products and, by the second half of the 1990s, most of the bigger players are expected to be producing HFCs. The lion's share of the market, however, should go to the company that gets there first.

'It's a gargantuan task, substituting for CFCs, because the cost of converting equipment is several hundred billion dollars globally,' says Beckitt. It's not just a case of straight substitution either; for many applications a new lubricant has to be identified before 134a can successfully be used. (CFCs use mineral oil.) There are other technical differences requiring adaptation: for example, 134a used in a hosepipe in an auto air-conditioner diffuses out quicker than a CFC, so the charge is lost.

ICI has been liaising closely with its customers, testing their requirements against the new product and advising them to buy substitutes for CFCs where they can, even if made by another manufacturer. CFC production is now roughly half its 1986 level of 85,000 tonnes, and several key products such as polystyrene foam and flexible polyurethane foam are now being manufactured without CFCs, while propane is being substituted as a propellant for aerosols. A core of essential applications is left, however, where CFCs are still the only practicable products, but even these will be phased-out under the terms of the Montreal Protocol by the end of 1995.

Development costs for the CFC substitutes are huge – £100 million on R & D so far, and £30 million for the first plant at Runcorn. The US plant at St Gabriel, Louisiana, that was commissioned at the end of

1992 will cost $100 million, and sizeable budgets are in view for a plant ICI is building in Asia Pacific and a second is planned for the UK by the mid-1990s. In the second half of the 1990s, however, the new business should be a significant cash generator. As John Beckitt points out, ICI's production of CFCs was concentrated at Runcorn, 'but non-CFC production will be a global business'.

No large stocks of CFCs are left, and those existing will be destroyed when all applications have workable substitutes. ICI has developed a safe form of incineration to destroy the product, which, if visible (it is normally concealed in a pressure vessel), would look like a clear whitish liquid, slightly tinged with yellow. When they emerge into the atmosphere, most CFCs do so as a virtually odourless gas.

KLEA 134a, the first CFC substitute in production, holds a unique place in the historical spectrum of scientific discoveries by virtue of being a replacement product for an earlier scientific breakthrough. Never before has a successful product been forced out of existence by a global wave of public and political pressure, resulting in international regulation like the Montreal Protocol. 'What is unique about this,' says Beckitt, 'is the speed with which industry can tackle a global environmental problem which requires a totally new approach to speeding up technology development and applications development.'

Dr Peter Doyle, ICI's Director of Research, believes the HFCs certainly qualify as innovations to change life. 'It is a product with genuinely global impact, and it shows the importance of strategic science. Our 1980 R & D plans said the development of 134a would be dependent on the ozone controversy. It is also a very good example of consulting the customer. They rejected it earlier because of costs: the customers didn't know that the world was about to change, but the seeds of that change were already evident to people who were looking at science.'

Cultural Change

The speed of development when change came required a different cultural approach from that of the conventional research process where the chemist, the process engineer and the project engineer each contribute a part of the development chain, and where a new product is normally expected to take ten to fifteen years to bring to market from the research bench. When Beckitt took up his appointment in 1987, the Montreal Protocol was being drafted, and it was clear that the timescales then being discussed would shrink under further pressure.

The new culture was signalled by siting the office block for the process and project engineers next to Research and Technology at Runcorn, 'so that they were working cheek-by-jowl with the chemists'. Next, it was decided that one individual should pull all the strands together – under the old system, the process engineers would have had one functional manager, the project engineers another, and so on. The man selected for this task was Frank Maslen, who developed ICI's seminal Pruteen technology (see Chapter 9 for the Pruteen experiment), and who had the necessary range of skills, having managed projects and the process engineering and seen the development of a new technology through from the research stage.

Cultural change was reinforced by a 'mission statement', part of which reads: 'We welcome challenging and difficult targets because we are not afraid of uncertainty and the management of risk.' Beckitt believes this in itself marks a significant difference from the experience of many research teams in large organizations, where 'staff often do nothing for fear of doing the wrong thing'. Another key factor, he adds, 'is that we trust and believe in our people, and in the power of multidisciplinary teams to focus on and solve difficult problems, without always checking up on people and asking them questions.'

ICI is one of the few chemical majors able to bring together a number of key competences needed to develop a CFC substitute at high speed. It has the necessary catalytic fluorination technology and is the only CFC manufacturer in the world that develops and makes its own catalysts. It is also the only company that manufactures the new lubricants for CFC alternatives.

Chris Hampson, the soft-spoken Canadian who sits on ICI's board with responsibility for environmental matters in his portfolio, believes that the full impact of changing environmental values has yet to make itself felt across the span of ICI's chemical businesses. It may come, he suspects, even to affect basic products that now seem indispensable and incapable of substitution, such as chlorine (a key element in, for example, household salt manufacture and water purification as well as in the pariah CFCs). Greenpeace has called for an end to production of chlorine by 1993 – 'chlorine-free by '93'. Unrealistic though that always was, chlorine production, in 1992 running at 1.7 million tonnes a year from ICI, is likely eventually to become a much smaller industry, in Hampson's view.

'There's no doubt that a lot of end uses for chlorine will disappear, particularly those which result in the emission of chlorinated compounds. However, in many cases it is used to cause a reaction but doesn't end up in the final product. We need our managers to think more about these issues and to focus our process and product research on end uses where chlorine is an essential ingredient. So that we can use the product and still protect the environment, we need to discriminate between these continuing markets and those which will be reduced, and where we would be putting resources into a battle we cannot win.'

The environmental revolution in public opinion has changed the chemical industry and will continue to do so. It is irreversible under most future scenarios, except perhaps for some form of global industrial collapse. Hampson reflects in his high-ceilinged office at Millbank on the implications: 'I don't think there is any business we are in that won't be tremendously changed, both in the composition of the business – the products and services we offer – and the way in which we do things.' In the obvious area of ICI 'cleaning up its act' by reducing or eliminating pollutants to air, water or land, Hampson is confident that 'within five years or so' the company will be able to conquer most of the problems by 'doing things differently in manufacturing processes – though not without a certain amount of pain and expense of money and time'. Much less foreseeable, however, is the impact and extent of environmental pressures on the nature of the businesses themselves.

'We have quite a way to go in getting people to think more about how this will impact their businesses. Take the paints business, getting rid of organic solvents, introducing water-based paints, changing the nature of paints and the way in which they are applied. In agricultural chemicals, getting into new products which mimic things that happen in nature so that they are more environmentally friendly . . . I think increasingly you've got this life-cycle kind of analysis of the environment in which people look at how you produce, say, a dyestuff, how you ship it, what happens to the residue of unused dye, what happens to the effluent from the customer who uses the dye, what impact it has on the finished product. We haven't really got this kind of thing in hand yet.'

The environmental imperatives on ICI's businesses have been clearly spelled out in the last couple of years by Sir Denys Henderson, chairman since 1987. In a speech in November 1990 he said: 'What it amounts to is that society has added a new imperative to which every company must conform if it is to retain its licence to operate. For that reason, success in managing the environmental impact of what we do is an essential element in measuring the overall success of the corporation. It is therefore as important and indispensable an area in which to invest as, say, research and development, or training, or process technology. Each contributes to our competitiveness.'

Chris Hampson's appointment in 1987 as executive director with responsibility for the environment as well as health and safety was an early indication of Henderson's perception that a board-level strategy was necessary in this area. A first step was to ensure that all ICI's constituent businesses reported regularly on how they had improved their environmental performance, and this was made an obligatory part of the Autumn Budget Review process that each business undergoes annually. 'It is the first item on the agenda – even before profit and cash performance – and all our CEOs know it and prioritize their actions accordingly,' said Henderson in that keynote speech. (Soon afterwards,

ICI suggested that the performance targets which determine the pay of its senior managers would henceforth include environmental issues. Eventually all white-collar workers' pay is intended to reflect performance in this area.)

The next step was to establish a database from all the businesses internationally and from that to draw up what Henderson calls 'an adequate map of our current performance across the group', from which to set specific objectives for improvement and a timescale for meeting them.

As Henderson points out, even compliance with law and regulation now means moving forward, because legislation is changing so fast. Beyond compliance, however, ICI now has four principal objectives in environmental improvement:

- All new plants will be built to standards 'that will meet the regulations we can reasonably anticipate in the most environmentally demanding country in which we operate that process'.
- All wastes will be halved by 1995, with special attention being paid to hazardous waste.
- An even more rigorous programme of energy and resource conservation will be applied and is expected to yield substantial benefits by 1995. Both energy consumption and emissions of carbon-dioxide gas are about fifteen per cent lower than in the early 1970s, and in that time output has doubled.
- Waste-recycling programmes will be expanded, not only in-house, but in collaboration with ICI's customers (notably in a free recovery and recycling programme for industrial users of CFCs, and a recycling scheme in the UK for refrigerant recovered from domestic fridges).

To the question of cost in the worsening economic conditions of the early 1990s, Henderson replies simply: 'We cannot afford not to do it . . . Environmental performance is not a matter of choice. It is a precondition for remaining at the forefront of the chemical industry.' That said, however, he does frequently ruminate that, ultimately, costs have to be paid for. If some plants and processes are unable to justify the expenditure needed to improve current standards, 'they simply will not survive'.

'There will be some tough decisions to take because, ultimately, management has to earn an adequate return for our shareholders on total funds invested.' Yet Henderson is quick to point out that there are opportunities as well as potential threats in the new imperatives. 'The chemical industry has always lived by innovation . . . We see a number of areas where the solution to an environmental problem can open up business opportunities.' Some, like the race for CFC substitutes, have already been exploited, and there are others of great potential, such as water-based paint for cars. Manufacturers using it – Volvo is one example – can now reduce the use and emission of organic solvents by up to eighty per cent.

This 'Aquabase' technology has just been extended to the car re-finish industry for use in car bodywork repairs – a market as big as that for original manufacture.

Biopol – the Biodegradable Plastic

Perhaps most technically exciting – and a discovery which had to wait until environmental pressures propelled it into the limelight – is Biopol, the fully biodegradable plastic hailed by the American magazine *Popular Science* in 1990 as one of the one hundred greatest scientific achievements in environmental technology. Actually Biopol was a discovery of the 1970s, an offshoot of the costly Pruteen experiment (see Chapter 9) and then known prosaically as PHB, for polyhydroxybutyrate. Non-oil based, and made by natural organisms working on glucose, it was seen in those first years following the OPEC oil-price shocks as a potentially winning substitute for petroleum-based plastics, and a potential boon to developing countries with no oil but the ability to grow sugar.

But the price of oil stabilized, then fell, and more supplies came onstream. The world passed PHB by and, in 1985, Dr Eric Howells, a senior ICI research scientist at Millbank, used to carry a small chunk of it on his watch-chain as a laboratory curiosity.

The green revolution has opened up new horizons for the renamed plastic, now made to a different, co-polymer, formulation and easier to process. Its first commercial use was as shampoo bottles for the environmentally conscious German market, but ultimately its real value is likely to be realized in areas where fully degradable plastics can most benefit the environment, notably in feminine hygiene products, pantie-liners, disposable nappies, and the like. A biodegradable condom would be a dream product, says Peter Doyle, provided the material could take the necessary strain. Because Biopol's constituents are fully compatible with human tissue, it also has enormous potential for sutures and other internal medical uses. In Sweden there have been several remarkable 'Lazarus' experiments in which patients with limbs atrophied through severed nerves have been enabled to walk again by the use of Biopol to thread the nerve-endings together for natural healing.

Safe Treatment of Waste

Much of the research drive in the chemical industry's environmental technology now comes of necessity from its need to reduce or eliminate its own polluting agents. In 1990, ICI doubled the capacity of its Group Environmental Laboratory at Brixham, on the south Devon coast which, as early as the mid-1960s, had changed its role from that of testing paint to corporate research on the environment. With a staff of 87 and huge databases of environmental information, the Brixham laboratory is not only a technical resource for ICI but also contracts out its services to other organizations, including the public sector. Its principal activities are investigating the safe and effective treatment of all types of chemical waste; monitoring the effect of ICI operations on the local ecology; computer modelling to track effluent discharges and how they disperse; and detailed environmental assessments of ICI products. The £3 million extension in 1990 provided sixteen new laboratories, each of which can mimic almost any environmental situation.

In the late 1980s and early 1990s, a stream of new processes and recovery systems began to make an impact on the group's own businesses and beyond, creating fresh market opportunities for ICI along the way. A new process of ammonia synthesis, for example, developed to replace ICI's two ageing ammonia plants at Severnside, improves economy and saves resources by using less feed gas, land and steel for construction. It also cuts the waste products associated with the previous two-stage process of transforming methane and steam. The system is expected to be of interest to developing countries wanting

ICI's Group Environmental Laboratory at Brixham, Devon, which began corporate research on the environment.

smaller ammonia plants which will produce surplus carbon dioxide for urea-fertilizer manufacture, and in 1990 it won the Royal Society of Arts' Pollution Abatement Technology Award, sponsored by the Environment Foundation, the Department of the Environment and Shell UK.

The company is anxious to be seen to be 'cleaning up its act' in more public ways. At Christmas 1989, the familiar brown plumes of gas, a component of smog-inducing nitrogen oxides (Nox) that used to flow into the air above ICI's complex on Teesside disappeared for ever. Its removal was, admittedly, of more public-relations value than actual benefit to the environment: the gas stream contributed less than ten per cent of the total Nox emissions from the Teesside plant, but as a symbol it was a powerfully visible one. By 1995 the company will have spent about £80 million on anti-pollution schemes at its Teesside operations, including one to recycle waste sulphuric acid from plastics manufacture which has hitherto been dumped in the North Sea. Part of this has been spent on a complex at Billingham which will greatly clean up the production of methyl methacrylate (MMA) used in the production of Perspex and many other wares including polishes and paint.

In the past, most of the waste from MMA, a mixture of sulphuric acid and ammonium sulphate in water, was disposed of into the North Sea. A metric tonne of MMA produces three times its weight in waste. Now a £66 million acid-recovery system in the new Billingham plant reprocesses the waste and eliminates sea disposal, while the efficiency of the recycling will enable production of MMA to be doubled to around 200,000 metric tonnes a year.

Historically, Teesside was chosen by ICI in the 1920s for the ease of disposal it offered to get rid of chemical waste in the river and the estuary. Pollution in the Tees, for decades one of Britain's dirtiest waterways, was considerably reduced during the 1970s and 1980s, although environmental critics complain that ICI still has no integral installation to clean the water, such as those provided by some of the major Dutch and German chemical plants.

The need for industry to reduce pollution has produced a whole new environmental business in ICI Watercare, launched in 1990 with two main target markets: products for purifying drinking water and treating sewage; and the treatment of liquid wastes from industrial, particularly chemical, manufacturing processes. Systems are offered on a leasing as well as purchase basis, with the double benefit to customers of minimizing capital expenditure and keeping pace with evolving technology. The business, based initially in the Chlor-Chemicals Division in Runcorn, has a strategy for rapid growth built on international expansion.

John Coleman, environmental affairs manager at Millbank, believes that the main technological advances are now going to be driven by environmental concerns, as those of the 1970s and 1980s were driven by microelectronics. Over the next decade he sees change in three main areas: 'redesigning processes to eliminate waste, with huge technological leaps in that area; a major restructuring of the chemical industry with some products becoming totally unacceptable, and a huge market for clean-up and treatment of waste.'

Virtually all ICI's research spending now has environmental improvement as a principal objective, says Coleman. 'We wouldn't commission processes or products which didn't have a satisfactory environmental performance.' In 1992 ICI also published its first report on progress towards environmental objectives, giving data on waste and emissions wherever the company operates, and the number of prosecutions on environmental charges (36 in 1990, reducing to 26 in 1991). Many chemical companies claim that environmental statistics are too difficult to collect and interpret for public consumption, but Chris Hampson does not agree. 'If we are going to gain the public's trust, then we have to publish the results.'

11

2026: THE DAY AFTER TOMORROW

Professor Derek Birchall's prosaic, cluttered office at Runcorn, in the vast, anonymous complex that once housed ICI's Mond Division, is dominated by a large wall chart depicting the properties of the cuttle-fish bone. A drawer of his desk is filled with shells of all types and sizes. Together they form a key model for Birchall's researches into 'bio-mimicry', a new-born branch of bio-engineering which studies the processes of nature and seeks to replicate them through technology. It is a discipline with huge and exciting possibilities for the future.

'If you want to make things out of inorganic materials, like ceramics,' Birchall points out, 'you get a powder, mix it with water and put it in a furnace at 2,000°C. Nature makes shells at 20°C, and the structures are beautiful, they're perfect and they are exactly adapted to the mechanical demands made on them. We can't do that, we're not clever enough, but if we could design structures like that at only 20°C, it would transform technology. Bio-engineering is now a whole new science, learning how Nature does things.'

Birchall can justly claim to have stimulated a whole new area of scientific research. His macro-defect-free (MDF) cement, patented in 1981, a totally non-porous material as tough as cast iron, was based on observation of molluscs and cuttlefish bone. The spur for his search was the energy crisis of the early 1970s. The process of manufacturing metal is very energy-intensive; Birchall decided to look at what was economic in energy terms and readily available. 'Inorganic materials like sand and cement are very energy-cheap. The world makes about the same amount of cement a year as it does of steel, but it's pretty poor stuff if you compare its mechanical properties with those of metal, or with plastic. It's got all the strength of a ginger biscuit. So the question was, what would happen if you made it as strong as steel?'

Cement, as every builder and civil engineer knows, is strong under compression but fractures easily under tension or flexural stress. Reinforcing it with steel or asbestos adds tensile strength but reduces its ability to be moulded. Attempts to make a polymer from inorganic materials had been made in the 1950s and 1960s but had produced nothing beyond the silicones. Birchall and his team set out in 1978 to make a mouldable inorganic material by studying nature's own way with ocean creatures. A sea-shell, he pointed out, is like 'a ceramic made under genetic control', constructed from calcium carbonate crystals at ordinary temperatures and glued together with a tenuous layer of protein to give a strength higher than that of cement and tough enough to carve or machine into delicate shapes.

'We found the basic reason cement is weak is because it's full of holes, and that told us what we had to do – find out how the holes got there, and take them out. When we did that, we found cement got stronger and stronger, until we were making springs out of the thing.'

The product that emerged contained less than one per cent of air holes compared with 25–30 per cent in ordinary cement. The secret lay in binding the cement particles with a small amount of a water-soluble polymer and then rolling it through a mill, extruding and moulding it. An American technical newsletter in February 1985 described it as about one hundred times tougher than epoxy resins, with a strength comparable to that of cast iron and better than that of ceramics like alumina. The invention was described as 'a boon to industrial and undeveloped countries alike', and the newsletter predicted that production plants would spring up 'wherever cement raw materials are handy – and that's pretty near everywhere'.

It hasn't yet happened like that, and the famous cement spring is still just a scientific curiosity, albeit an impressive one. The reversal of the energy crisis, and the prospect again of cheap oil as a feedstock for plastics as well as an energy source took the heat out of the chase for non-oil-based materials and temporarily put such ICI inventions as MDF and PHB plastic (polyhydroxybutyrate, made by natural organisms) on to the back burner. With its good acoustic damping qualities, MDF is finding useful applications in equipment such as loudspeaker cabinets and hi-fi components but, as the American newsletter (*High-Tech Materials Alert*) commented: 'This extraordinary material is still far from what it could be – it's what Bakelite is to today's plastics.'

MDF is just one of the products of ICI's laboratories that may well have a part in transforming the world of the next twenty, thirty or forty years. The time lapse from invention to marketplace can take anything from ten to twelve years for advanced materials to twenty years for a revolutionary new drug or a product requiring similarly stringent trials, such as the anti-misting kerosene additive, Avgard, designed to prevent the lethal shroud of fuel droplets forming when a plane crash-lands. This is a by-product of the same technology that produced ICI's Dulux solid emulsion; it had already been seventeen years in development before its first abortive practical test in early 1986, and could take a further ten years before it is accepted for use by the world's airlines. In this sort of timescale, ICI's centenary year of 2026 is virtually the day after tomorrow. What sort of revolutions comparable to polymers and beta-blockers could be brewing now in the test-tubes?

Advanced Materials for Aerospace

In the realm of advanced materials, much is already under way. A whole new family of plastics, developed out of 'aromatic' chemistry with its high-density molecular structure (as opposed to the looser 'aliphatic' compositions) began to emerge in the 1960s, beginning with PES (polyethersulphone), far tougher than polythene in its resistance to heat: it won't decompose below about 400°C compared to polythene's 250°C. After a long battle over patents with US firms working on similar lines, ICI secured a world first and PES was launched as an engineering plastic for such uses as transformer windings, parts of electric motors and medical sterilization equipment. Then the search began for a less rubbery, more crystalline compound that would take high-precision moulding and could be used at high temperatures. PEEK (polyether ether ketone) came out in the early 1970s and found immediate application as a wire-coating material in the electronics industry.

An earlier discovery than PES, developed in the 1950s out of some du Pont technology inherited from wartime collaboration, was PET (polyethylene terephthalate), a polyester derivative from the same technology as Terylene. It started life in ICI as a base for photographic film but forty-odd years later, with a changed molecular structure, is widely used for plastic bottles (at one time an inter-divisional rival in ICI to the soda ash which goes to the glass industry). The liquid-crystal polymers that developed later out of PET have some remarkable optical and magnetic properties: some research chemists have talked in a visionary, science-fiction way about using the film like wallpaper to make a wall-to-wall TV screen. 'That's all rather far-fetched,' says Ron Feasey of ICI's Advanced Materials Group at Runcorn, 'but it's an indication that you now have polymer molecules with constructural properties which can form a solid object in its own right as well as having all these interesting electrical properties.'

The timetable varies from project to project but twenty years from discovery to full commercial exploitation is not unusual for new materials. 'We started research on PES around 1959–60,' says Feasey. 'I don't think anybody really felt confident that it was here to stay until fifteen or twenty years later.'

Since about 1980, the biggest ferment in synthetic materials has been in 'composites' – thermoplastics reinforced with fibre to form a light but stiff and immensely strong material that can make anything from high-performance tennis rackets to aerospace components. APCs – aromatic polymer composites – were originally another response to the energy crisis of the 1970s: to save fuel, engineers were looking for lighter-weight components for cars and aircraft. Also, ICI's plastics chemists were acutely aware that if their industry was to survive and prosper it would have to go for 'added value' and find ways of giving entirely new properties to existing plastics to extend their range of applications. 'There's a limit to what you can do with thermoplastics because of their basically floppy nature,' explained Feasey. 'You can have a polythene bucket, but you wouldn't want a polythene gas-holder. If we were going to develop our industry we had to find ways of making the material stiffer in order to make bigger things out of it.'

Polymers reinforced with glass fibre had been introduced – spectacularly in one case to build a 140-foot minesweeper. But ICI decided to go for the most demanding market, the aerospace industry. This offered more scope than the increasingly cost-conscious car industry; aerospace manufacturers would pay for the highest degree of strength combined with lightness and resistance to damage. ICI's most advanced plastic, PEEK, was chosen for combination with carbon fibre. At that time, around 1980, epoxy resins were the great hope of the US aircraft industry. Epoxy, however, has the disadvantage that it can suffer damage to its internal fibre layers without this being obvious on the outside. Samples of the PEEK composite, which offered improved damage tolerance, was easier to fabricate than epoxy and was thirty per cent lighter than aluminium, were evaluated favourably by the Boeing company and it was developed for aircraft use: the Westland helicopter company, for example, uses ICI's 'APC2s' for tail-plane components. In September 1984, the American journal *Chemical Week* reported that the National Aeronautics and Space Administration (NASA), in a $100 million development programme begun in 1976, was moving certain reinforced plastics into potentially large, primary applications such as aircraft fuselage, wings and cargo-bay components. Lighter materials in aircraft bodies could dramatically reduce a plane's fuel requirements, extend its range or permit an increase in payload. NASA's assistant director for aeronautics was quoted as saying composites 'could well become the principal material in aircraft'.

With this feeling in the air, it was not surprising that the ICI scientists working on APC were buoyed up by excitement and worked Saturday and Sunday night shifts as the project moved into high gear, even though at the time the Plastics Division was closing its technical centre at Welwyn Garden City and moving to the north-east to merge with Petrochemicals, with all the uncertainty that entailed about jobs. It was with some awe, Feasey recalled, that they realized they were on to something big enough to get involved with the US aerospace industry – 'it wasn't like selling bags of plastic chips to someone down the road to make washing-up bowls'. It took some

courage for the management of Plastics Division, fighting for its very
survival and having to cut costs in all directions, to proceed with the
high-risk APC research.

However, if the hoped-for markets opened up, Plastics would not
have the resources on its own to build plant, find the skilled technicians
and develop the sophisticated selling network required. The problem
was solved in 1983 by ICI's acquisition of the American Beatrice
group, which included the Fiberite company, suppliers of epoxy resins
to the US aerospace industry. ICI thus gained a foothold in the US
epoxy market while at the same time acquiring the resources to develop
its own alternative for the future. The long-term nature of any development associated with the aircraft industry meant that it would be well
into the 1990s before APC was a proven success. Then history inter-
vened: the collapse of Communism in Eastern Europe and the progressive winding-down of military arsenals on both sides of the superpower
divide brought the so-called 'peace dividend' – government money
that would no longer be invested in the defence and aerospace industries. It also brought much less demand for advanced materials such as
APC. As the US and most of the industrialized world tipped into
recession, civil aviation was also in decline. ICI's advanced materials
business began losing money, and the company has now virtually quit
the market, selling off its Beatrice interests connected with advanced
materials, though the company has, for the moment, retained the carbon fibre composite, Fiberite.

One of the significant changes made in ICI since the late 1980s has
been to cluster different kinds of advanced materials together under a
larger business grouping. While the composites once designated for the
aerospace industry have been diminishing – though PEEK is still growing in potential – other materials with adaptability to consumer markets remain strong. These include polyurethanes, which can be made
into scores of products such as shoe soles, car seats or insulation foam,
and acrylics, in which ICI and du Pont plan a product 'swap' – ICI's
European interests in nylon, a du Pont invention, for du Pont's acrylics
plants in the US. The deal, at the time of writing still grinding through
the regulating mills of Brussels and Washington, would make ICI the
world's largest acrylics manufacturer.

'Fewer but Better' Drugs

In pharmaceuticals research, the goal-posts have moved since the late
1980s. A new drug which then took perhaps ten years and £100 million in development costs before the company saw any return on capital can now take up to 15 years, depending on ever-more complex
regulatory requirements, and will cost around £150 million to bring to
market. Peter Doyle, ICI's research and technology director (who will

be a director of the new Zeneca biosciences company), thinks the trend now is for 'fewer but better' drugs to be developed.

In 1984, Dr William Duncan, then deputy chairman of ICI's Pharmaceuticals Division, called in a group of independent consultants to advise on its research programme. As a result, an internal 'strategy committee' was set up to identify areas of therapeutic treatment on which R & D should be concentrating over the remainder of the century. Cancer and cardiovascular disease were two key target areas chosen, both building on earlier ICI drug discoveries like Nolvadex and the beta-blockers Inderal and Tenormin.

In the cancer field, Nolvadex, launched in 1973, has proved its value for earlier use in the treatment of breast cancer and may, if current trials are successful, eventually be used for prevention. Zoladex, launched in the late 1980s for treatment of prostate cancer, was innovative in drawing on ICI's polymer expertise to create the tiny capsule, injected subcutaneously, from which the potent agent is released over a month.

Among heart drugs developed in the 1980s, the anti-hypertensive Zestril represents the fastest-growing part of the cardiovascular market, and research is under way to explore its application in other treatments – following heart attacks, for example. Diprivan, an intravenous anaesthetic that enables the depth of anaesthesia to be precisely controlled, was particularly fortunate in its timing, coinciding as it has with new techniques such as minimal access (keyhole) surgery and the trend towards shorter stays in hospital.

Zoladex, Zestril and Diprivan are confidently expected to more than compensate over the short term for the declining revenue as Tenormin goes out of patent in the US (in 1991 for angina use and 1993 for hypertension) and, together with Nolvadex and other new products, provide steady growth thereafter. The American market has accounted for nearly half the global sales of Tenormin, the world's tenth best-selling drug, but once a drug goes out of patent almost half the US sales are lost in the first year, although the decline then slows.

The question remains where the next big drug discovery will hit. David Barnes, chief executive designate of the new biosciences company, says there are some seventeen new products in the pipeline, and the next to be launched will be Meropenem, a hospital-only injectable antibiotic. This was discovered in the laboratories of Sumitomo, the Japanese company with which ICI has a joint venture in Japan, but the British company has worldwide rights to it outside Japan. Its major selling point is that it treats a very wide range of conditions from chest infections to sexually transmitted diseases, and it is free of the problems with kidney functions that have dogged a competitor product already on the market.

While new discoveries excite the public and a world-beating blockbuster like Glaxo's ulcer drug Zantac can build a huge cash mountain for its parent company, the profits to be made from durable staples are often overlooked but can be substantial. In ICI's case continually steady sellers include Sir James Black's Inderal and even such mundane products as Hibitane, a hospital antiseptic dating from the 1950s but whose range still stands as 'the benchmark for hospital antiseptics around the world', in Barnes's words. New markets continue to emerge for existing products, and demand increases in existing markets as habits and society change.

Into the Future

The naming of new products is generally a mundane process though occasionally it gains dictionary status like Perspex, Biro, Hoover and Thermos – all protected trademarks but often used indiscriminately to describe any hard, transparent plastic material, ballpoint pen, vacuum cleaner or flask for keeping food or liquid hot or cold. Sometimes, however, it can be a quirky business, even when done by computer. Derek Birchall recalled that when they were trying to find a trade-name in 1964 for Monnex, his new fire-fighting agent in the form of an alkaline metal powder, they wanted to commemorate Mond Division and fed various combinations into the computer. After much digesting of the various elements, what it came up with was 'Mondstink'.

'Saffil', Birchall's inorganic fibrous material that was designed to 'do most of the things asbestos does without being toxic', had an even more eccentric christening. He and his colleagues had been playing around with variations on words like 'safe', and 'filament' when, driving one wet, misty day to the Nobel Division at Ardeer, he leaned out of the car window to ask the way, and a woman with a soft Scottish lilt in her voice remarked, 'S'afful (it's awful) weather'. 'Saffil – that's a great name!' exclaimed one of Birchall's companions – and Saffil it became.

In 1984 Dr Eric Howells, then in charge of ICI's corporate research and technology, said that if he were asked to pick out the three most important ICI innovations from the public's point of view over the forty post war years, he would name, first, the beta-blocker group of drugs, then crop-protection products like paraquat and third, the family of thermoplastics and other advanced synthetic materials. In another thirty-three years, what might be the verdict of an ICI research director in 2026?

Professor Birchall attempted something of an exercise in futurology in a lecture in 1986. Looking first at materials like ceramics and composites, he suggested possibilities linked to his favourite theme of how nature constructs shells and bone. 'We shall learn how to self-assemble things; after all, biology self-assembles. You actually assemble yourself as you grow, and we will learn to do more things like that. On materials

Changing the world at the laboratory bench: Professor Derek Birchall, FRS, the inventor of 'Saffil' and macro-defect-free cement, so flexible that it can be bent into springs. 'One of my jobs,' he says, 'is to look at a vision of what the world will be and get ICI interested'.

science and medicine in between we shall get some new prosthetic devices that will be bio-compatible, part of us, which will replace both hard and soft tissue. We shall get new drugs from molecular biology. We shall manipulate genes, we shall learn to understand the process of ageing and what that means is that we shall have predictive medicine. At the moment medicine isn't predictive because you are sick when you go to the doctor. He doesn't tell you that you are going to be ill, he tells you that you *are* ill, but we are going to change that . . .

'We are going to have some very powerful theoretical techniques in [computer] modelling . . . we shall learn not to get sick. We shall have not just passive artificial organs but active ones . . . This area of computational experimentation and robotics and artificial intelligence will have an enormous effect which I don't think we have even started to think about, the material for which is the basis for the next technology expansion. There could not have been nuclear energy without the invention of new materials. There could not be electronics without the invention of new materials, and I regard materials science as basic to the next thrust forward . . . [it] is the science which does really change the whole of technology.'

Turning to society at large, Birchall predicts that the rate of change is going to be 'much, much faster than it has ever been, and the rate of technological change is going to be faster'. There are bound to be fewer people in manufacturing because of the change towards robotics and artificial control. 'The one thing that our ability to make new materials will do is give us greater ability to do things we cannot do now and go places where we cannot go now; the space shuttle is a very good example of that.'

Birchall's work in 1986 involved a mass of studies on reasons for ageing, much of it to do with oxidation of the iron that occurs naturally in the body, stored in proteins called transferin. 'We store a lot of it as rust . . . so that we are actually going rusty as we get older.' The ageing process will, Birchall is convinced, be a growth area for scientific development, and if it does not have the effect of turning people into wrinkle-free Dorian Grays, it will at least ensure that an increasingly aged population remains active much farther into old age than now. Inorganic chemistry, he says, is producing much fascinating information about elements like selenium. In itself, this is a highly toxic substance, but without a trace of it the body runs a high risk of cardiac disease. Selenium, whose main biological use at present, he adds in a typical Birchall aside, seems to be as a cure for dandruff, is also 'one of the defence systems that we have against oxidation'. There is a lot of evidence, he says, that many diseases of the arteries and bones associated with ageing are related to oxidation biochemistry, 'and that is one area of organic chemistry that is going to grow'.

On synthetic materials, Birchall believes that we are now in an era comparable to the 1780s when the dramatic shift from cast iron to steel brought about the industrial revolution. 'Basically we couldn't have developed if we had not changed from cast iron to steel. We are in that situation again – but one that I think is going to take us into the next generation of ceramics.' This, as he admits, is 'one of the big hype subjects': in 1980 the world market for advanced ceramics such as alumina carbides and nitrides and silicon boron amounted to £4 billion a year. In AD 2000, 'the predictions are that the advanced ceramics business will be in the order of £10 billion a year.' But that won't happen, he warns, unless the inorganic chemist tackles the problems of unreliability. 'The failure rate for an advanced ceramic is fifty per cent at least and nobody is going to fly an aeroplane with a ceramic engine with that sort of probability of failure. New process technology has got to be invented to do away with that unreliability.' Then there is the problem of brittleness. Ceramics have to be made as tough as polymers or metal, 'and I think that is what is going to happen. I predict for the future that we shall have ceramics which will look like steel compared to cast iron'.

The first wave of the chemical industry, Birchall observed, 'generated bulk chemicals by the thousands of tonnes with great efficiency, and . . . enabled subsidiary industries like cotton and wool to grow and make the chemicals for them. The second wave, which I think we are already well into, is not like that: the second wave is where we make chemicals deliberately for specific effects. Electronics is a super example of that, where you make silicon metal not because it is a metal but because you can get its electrical properties by having high purity . . . I think science in the second wave is pushing us into biology and also into materials.'

While some of ICI's targeted growth areas for the 1990s failed to sustain their promise, notably speciality organic chemicals for the electronics industry (the so-called 'E' Group, however, did develop a distinctive new business in colour imaging), others that hardly existed in the mid-1980s have blossomed. The most sensational – because of its capacity to identify criminals – is 'genetic fingerprinting', a technique discovered out of blue-sky research at Leicester University by Professor Alec Jeffreys and patented by the Lister Institute of Preventive Medicine in Stanmore, Middlesex. As it did with Terylene, the first polyester fibre, in the 1940s, ICI took on the commercial development and marketing, forming a new division for the purpose in 1987, Cellmark Diagnostics.

Professor Alec Jeffreys of Leicester University who discovered the DNA sequences of 'genetic fingerprinting,' now widely used in criminal forensic work, paternity checks and plant breeding, where gene-mapping in seeds could help to 'design' disease-resistant crops. Here he holds up a complicated case for examination at Cellmark Diagnostics, a company ICI created to develop and market the technique commercially.

Jeffreys' discovery is one of the most important in genetic science since Crick and Watson unravelled the DNA mystery in 1953, and probably the single most important development in forensic science since fingerprinting itself. It enables identification of that 'stutter' sequence of DNA which is unique to each individual (except for identical twins), and for the first time makes evidence against a criminal irrefutable in law. Within two years, application of the technique by British police forces brought convictions against forty rapists and two murderers. Colin Pitchfork, a double rapist and killer, was caught after Leicestershire police mounted the first mass genetic-screening. The technique is more widely used to prove or disprove family relationships, for example in paternity suits and immigration claims.

A wholly unexpected yet highly valuable use of the technology to ICI itself – and now to its new biosciences company – lies in gene-mapping for the seeds business. Hitherto, a plant breeder trying to develop a particular strain had to grow a number of specimens in order to select from them; now, the relevant data can be identified at the seed stage. Genetic mapping hugely advances the possibilities of building resistance to disease into plants and 'designing' improved strains of fruit and vegetables, such as the 'non-squashy tomato' which ICI expects to market by 1995.

This development is likely to be one of the first big commercial payoffs from the seeds-investment programme, begun in the mid-1980s and always expected to be a long-haul business. The tomato ripens slowly and resists premature decay; its juice is thick, not watery, and it has a better and more consistent colour than conventional varieties. US ketchup manufacturers who participated in trials with the new strain reported that their productivity improved by forty per cent.

ICI now wants to 'participate in the added value', as David Barnes puts it, and is negotiating with manufacturers for a percentage 'royalty' on their savings or profits. 'In the past ICI sold hundreds of tons of polymer dirt cheap and left it to the manufacturer of plastic buckets to make the profit. We don't want to make that mistake in seeds. We want to participate in the productivity benefits down the line.'

The genetic tool-kit discovered by Alec Jeffreys is a brilliant example of bio-technology enabling new businesses to be created within the chemical industry: a principle on which rest many of the hopes for ICI's biosciences offspring. Ironically for the market-driven philosophy which has increasingly dominated ICI and other chemical companies, it arose out of pure blue-sky research. As *The Financial Times* observed of ICI's development of Tempro removable paint, a water-based product that came out of an exercise in lateral thinking: 'It is a case of technology accidentally creating customers rather than market demand leading to new products.' That will happen many more times on the road to 2026.

Some of the life-changing discoveries chronicled in this book remain leading products for the company – as well as Hibitane and Inderal, Fluothane anaesthetic is still a staple pharmaceutical, used extensively in hospital operations around the world. ICI Pharmaceuticals, now Zeneca, can boast ten products on the World Health Organization's list of essential drugs for developing countries, six of them discovered in ICI laboratories.

Perspex retains its pre-eminence in its field, astonishingly in view of the advances in plastics technology since 1932. (In 1960, an internal study showed Perspex and polythene as by far the biggest earners for the company up to that date.) But low-density polythene, on which ICI built its plastics business, has now made way in importance for developments like plastic film and advanced polymers for tough, reinforced, space-age materials.

Terylene, which led to the creation of ICI's fibres business and to the company's status as one of the world's major fibres manufacturers, is now focused on speciality uses rather than mass-production of textile fibres, which has been licensed to others around the world; polyester technology has made ICI the market leader in Europe for the manufacture of plastic bottles, and polyester film is a feature of every computer and every tape-recorder.

Paraquat continues to be a huge earner worldwide. The reactive dyes pioneered in the 1950s have helped push ICI into the top-six colours manufacturers in the world. In 1984 Pruteen fermentation technology spawned a new Biological Products Business at Billingham with marketing targets in food, agriculture, chemical and process technology. Polyurethanes, developed as a rigid foam for insulation and refrigeration in the mid-1950s, is now an international speciality business operated from Europe and the United States and producing hundreds of applications from shoe-soles to adhesives.

The future of innovation within the ICI companies is bound to be influenced by changes that took place over the 1980s. There is now much less emphasis on corporate laboratory activities and more on research within individual businesses, though Dr Peter Doyle, director of research, has expanded the company-wide network of science strategy groups set up by his predecessor, Sir Charles Reece. There are four of these, each made up of a dozen senior research managers and representing four 'prime technologies' – biosciences and bio-technology; materials; chemical synthesis and catalysts; and process technology. Five more strategy groups handle 'support technologies' – toxicology; formulation capability; analysis and instrumentation; information technology; and physics. The emphasis on technologies in the scientific infrastructure is reflected in ICI's use now of 'R & T' (research and technology) in place of 'R & D' (research and development).

The growth of information technology over the last five or six years

Sir John Harvey-Jones, charismatic Chairman of ICI from 1982 to 1987. He changed the company's philosophy towards 'inventing into the marketplace', and made it the first in Britain to break the £1 billion profit barrier. 'The great satisfaction of an industrial career is creating something which wasn't there before.'

has been phenomenal and is now 'absolutely critical to effective research', in Doyle's words. 'The ability to use information technology to generate, manage and analyse data, to extract information from it, but above all to carry out modelling, to put mathematical terms to possible experimental processes and test these out . . . that has developed at an astonishing rate and all businesses use it.'

ICI's ambition, said Doyle in 1991, was always to be ' a company that recognizes and nurtures growth points in science'. High science, after all, was at the heart of everything it produced, though few consumers would appreciate, for instance, the clever chemistry that enabled the brush strokes on gloss paint to disappear and the edges to meld smoothly.

Doyle divides research into 'applied' and 'strategic': the latter has a longer time-frame but both have foreseeable applications. Blue-sky research, which formerly took ten per cent of the R & D budget, now is virtually a thing of the past. Doyle calls it 'fundamental' research and thinks it belongs in the universities. But he is concerned to ensure a 'proper proportion' of strategic, long-term research and that economic pressures do not tilt the balance too sharply towards applied, short-term goals.

The great debate among scientists between 'market pull' and 'science push' will doubtless never reach a conclusion, although ICI's maverick Professor Derek Birchall has always argued eloquently in favour of the latter. 'The exciting thing about scientific experiments is that they can alter future possibilities,' he said in a lecture in the mid-1980s. 'It is often the case that, because of an experiment, "the future is not what it was" . . . The huge market for polyethylene came about because it was discovered, and was not created because it was needed.'

Such 'step-change' inventions as polyethylene are less likely in a market-oriented industry. It is hard to conceive of another great romance of science such as Fawcett and Gibson finding a strange 'waxy solid' in their test-tube, or Whinfield and Dickson creating Terylene in their backstreet laboratory. 'The amateur inventor is dead,' said Dr Charles Reece in 1985. 'Success now is about people being product champions, and organizations allowing product champions to survive.' In this book, Dr William Boon is a rare example of the inventor or key discoverer acting as product champion, though even in the 1960s he could not have taken paraquat through to full development on his own.

Yet if proof were needed that the springs of innovation still flourish strongly in a market-driven company, it is not hard to find. A quarter of the products sold by ICI today were not on the market only five years ago.

12

<hr>

UNDER SIEGE

Denys Henderson, who became ICI's eleventh chairman in 1987, is a compactly built Aberdonian, a solicitor by training, with a brisk, friendly manner that, beneath the geniality, suggests a disciplined pugnacity and a shortish fuse. Those who had underrated him in the wake of the charismatic Harvey-Jones were forced to revise their view in the testing year from May 1991 to May 1992 when ICI faced the possibility of a hostile takeover bid from the cash-rich Hanson conglomerate. Henderson's aggressive defence and nimble corporate footwork cut away the ground beneath whatever intentions Hanson may have had – they were never spelled out in the long war of nerves – by a combination of pre-emptive restructuring and cost-cutting in ICI and a ruthless exposure of Hanson Group's own vulnerable spots.

Lord Hanson might have judged his adversary better had he been familiar with Henderson's favourite reading and formative literary influence, the little-known trilogy by Lewis Grassic Gibbon called *A Scots Quair* that tells a saga of grinding struggle in rural Scotland in the depressed 1920s. The books, which Henderson has re-read with emotion many times since discovering them at Aberdeen University, celebrate among other qualities the tenacity and perseverance of the northeastern Scots, among whom he grew up.

The lightning reaction of an organization that many viewed as sluggish and bureaucratic was not the only surprise in Henderson's locker. At the end of July 1992, two months after Hanson had sold his shareholding and while most of industry and the City was quietly winding down for the summer-holiday lull, Henderson announced that the board was considering the revolutionary plan to split ICI into two separately quoted companies: one based on the bulk-chemical, commodities side from which the group had originally sprung, and the other, by demerger, spinning off the high-flying pharmaceuticals division, already virtually autonomous within ICI, plus agrochemicals, seeds and speciality chemicals.

Nothing in the company's six-and-a-half decades had been so radical: the proposal, which would not be put to shareholders until after

Sir Denys Henderson, Chairman of ICI since 1987. A shrewd Aberdonian who trained as a lawyer, he has steered the company through an unprecedented period of change, seen off a potential takeover threat and led the historic decision to demerge ICI's businesses.

the Annual Results in February 1993, would enable each half of the business to capitalize on its strengths and minimize weaknesses, and it received a generally favourable reaction from the financial press. The heavy-chemicals company, including paints and explosives – two areas in which ICI is the world leader – would retain the name ICI and come under the direction of Ronnie Hampel as chief executive officer, while the drugs, seeds, specialities and agrochemicals side, initially re-christened ICI Biosciences, would be led by David Barnes, a high-flyer who had been tipped as a future chairman of ICI. Henderson would remain as chairman of both companies and Millbank, at any rate for two years, as the corporate headquarters of both.

In November 1992, however, it was revealed that, for a number of commercial and legal reasons, the biosciences company would not carry the famous ICI initials as part of its name but would take the completely new title of Zeneca, with the ancient alchemical symbol of a crossed Z. This well-kept secret truly marked a watershed in nearly seventy years of corporate history. Which way – and how prosperously – would the two rivers run now?

Bulk chemicals, which might be thought the Cinderella of the two with its less glamorous products and chronic cyclical pressures, could in fact yield very solid long-term growth. It has, on occasions when the supply-and-demand balance is tight, shown higher profit margins, al-beit on lower sales, than the added-value businesses, and commodity chemicals like acrylics are sound cash generators. The division of the corporate businesses would also put two dominating global earners into the 'new ICI' portfolio – paints and explosives.

Nor did anyone overlook the benefit – demonstrated a few years earlier by BAT 'unbundling' itself under threat of takeover from Sir James Goldsmith – that splitting the group would make it far less attractive to an asset-stripping predator. Indeed, the plan would set free ICI's pharmaceuticals business to enhance its post-demerger rank-ing in the world league by acquisition or merger. When pushed, senior ICI management will now concede that an opportunity was probably missed in the mid-1980s to gain critical mass by acquiring the Beecham company before it was merged with America's Smith-Kline. Nothing of suitable size and price has since come on the market.

Years of Radical Change

Henderson's demerger bombshell, engineered in high secrecy at the end of 1991 and for months known only to a tiny group within the top management of ICI, confirmed in dramatic style something that had long been obvious within the company, though not as much to the outside world as Henderson might have liked – that the group had undergone more radical change since 1987 than over any comparable span in its history. As well as adapting to a stupendous series of global economic storms (chronicled later in this chapter), it had gone through an immense amount of restructuring and redirection of its international markets, with substantial acquisitions and divestments; pioneered swaps with America's du Pont and Germany's BASF over acrylics; got out of 'heartland' commodities like soda ash and salt; weathered the onslaught of the environmental revolution and its pressure groups (and developed the first marketable CFC replacement in rapid time), and tackled the rising challenge of the Far Eastern chemical industries with a big manufacturing build-up in Asia Pacific, including China. 'I don't think any British company anywhere has had that amount of change in that time,' says Henderson.

Henderson, born in 1932, arrived at the chairman's office up a typical ICI career ladder, starting almost at the same time as his predecessor, though they sprang from very different backgrounds. Harvey-Jones, a former submarine officer, joined ICI in 1956 as a work-study official, celebrating his release from the constraints of naval convention by growing his hair long and affecting loud-coloured ties. Henderson, having qualified as a solicitor, joined in 1957 as a lawyer in the company secretary's office. Conservatively barbered and tied, he progressed through the agricultural, explosives and paints divisions, becoming chairman of the latter and a member of ICI's main board in 1980. His legal and commercial skills set up ICI's acquisition team in the mid-1980s when the company began to reposition itself globally with inroads into the US chemical industry.

Henderson's succession was predicted, though in the ICI tradition he was one of three prominent candidates, all of whose names, as it happened, began with the letter H. In the last year of Harvey-Jones's chairmanship the two worked amicably together, dividing the executive and non-executive workload and, at Christmas 1986, sent out a joint Christmas card depicting the pair in jolly cartoon form.

Harvey-Jones had certainly swung the company in a different direction, and imbued it with a new ethos, that of 'inventing into the marketplace', as he liked to put it. The need for innovation to grow new businesses was, however, under ever more demanding pressure for the company to perform a starring role in the stock market and satisfy the pension fund managers and other vast institutional investors. That was not a problem which, before the 1980s, had much bothered his predecessors.

Reflecting late in his chairmanship, Harvey-Jones said: 'The nature of a company is rather like that of a human body; cells die the whole time and have to be replaced by new cells. One recognizes that the very successful businesses in the company will peak, and you have to have others coming up the whole time to replace them. If we don't follow that approach, the company cannot survive in the long haul.'

Clearly, the kind of planning required to produce a succession of rising short-term profits could not sit easily with research programmes that might take – and had taken in the past – twenty years to show any return on capital. Yet without such programmes, ICI would today be without its hugely profitable pharmaceuticals business. 'Pharms', as it is known in the company, started in 1937 and did not make any money until 1962.

Finding New Markets

Henderson inherited in 1987 a very different company from that which Harvey-Jones took over from Sir Maurice Hodgson in 1982, although Hodgson did much, largely uncredited, work in preparing the ground for the Harvey-Jones reforms. Hodgson set four principal targets: to reduce numbers employed (a trend already noticeable from the 1960s); to improve energy use in the wake of the OPEC oil shocks; to improve the capital productivity of new plant; and to reduce working capital. Building on that, Harvey-Jones, the former work-study officer, stripped out some layers of management and set the divisions free to operate as hard-edged businesses. The strategy helped to bring ICI from its traumatic losses of 1980–1 to a sensational £1 billion profit in 1984–5. The group's cost base had been dramatically reduced in time to benefit from a buoyant world economy, weak pound and strong growth in the chemical industry.

Harvey-Jones also changed the company in a more fundamental way. In the past, ICI had based its divisions on technology and grown its new businesses around the edges of that technology. Pharmaceuticals and agrochemicals, for example, both derived from the technology of the prewar Dyestuffs Division. Harvey-Jones identified the need to seek markets first and deliberately target them by 'taking bits and pieces from all sorts of different technologies and putting them together . . . a very long-haul job'. In 1986, he ruminated that seeds, into which ICI was pouring millions in resources, would be 'a twenty-year haul, but we're intellectually sure that by the year 2000 or 2010 the seeds business will have taken over many of the things at present supplied by fertilizers and agrochemicals '.

Seeds are a classic example of what Harvey-Jones meant by the company taking bits of different technologies and combining them towards a market goal. The main skill bases involved were genetic engineering and plant biochemistry, fields in which ICI had been working respectively for about fifteen and fifty years. Putting them together could change the genetic properties of plants: breeding plants with a highly selective resistance to disease and pests, for example, or plants which produce their own insect repellent, or vegetables and fruit which delay their own processes of decay. The obvious base from which to exploit such a combination commercially was seeds, and when a suitable acquisition in the US came along in the shape of Garst Seeds, the technologies were grafted to it.

ICI in the Harvey-Jones era underwent another fundamental shift in its approach to innovation: maximizing the number of markets that could be served by one invention, even if each market was relatively small in itself. The outstanding example was polyurethanes, one big invention that eventually spawned 2,000 different products, each representing a speciality market such as the best grade for shoe soles.

'I'm a man who believes in letting a thousand flowers bloom', Harvey-Jones once said. 'ICI in the past always wanted to invent big things like polythene and polyester and took the view that there was no point in doing anything unless it was going to be a £10 million or £20 million business. We can't afford that. There's nothing the matter with having twenty £1 million businesses providing you don't load them with massive overheads.'

A New Global Strategy

All these changes within ICI paled, however, before the creation of its new global strategy. For most of its history, ICI had been steered by territorial imperatives: formed as a defensive operation against IG Farben in Europe and du Pont and Allied in America, it spent the years up to the Second World War in a cosy cartel that gave it free rein in the old Empire. But from 1951, when a US judge ruled under anti-trust legislation that ICI and du Pont could no longer continue their convenient division of markets, it was clear that ICI had to make its own way in the US, the world's biggest customer base for chemicals – though it would be another twenty years before it embarked on the acquisition trail there with Atlas Chemicals.

In conjunction with Chris Hampson, then general manager, Henderson as planning director in the late 1970s drew up a double-barrelled strategy in world markets: to get bigger overseas by acquisition and to aim at being in the top two or three in all chosen businesses. The first secured the second through a string of judicious US purchases: Glidden took ICI to No. 1 in paints; Stauffer took it to No. 2 in agrochemicals; Atlas Explosives to No. 1 in that area.

Beyond all this was the growing conviction that heavy chemicals, the foundation stone of ICI in 1926, could turn into a millstone for the future. The business was always highly cyclical and, in time, the newly industrializing countries of Asia Pacific would become a much cheaper manufacturing base. As early as the mid-1980s, petrochemicals and plastics (P & P) had become a serious loss-maker. The move to higher added-value chemicals – what Hampson dubbed 'the tilt to effects' – was accelerated.

In September 1986, towards the end of Harvey-Jones's chairman-ship, ICI announced a radical restructuring of the company, merging four of the mainstream chemical businesses into a Europe-wide group with net fixed assets of more than £1.25 billion and turnover of around £3.5 billion. The historic Mond Division, which had traditionally re-garded itself as the leading edge of ICI, disappeared into the new Chemicals and Polymers Group based at Mond's old headquarters in Runcorn, along with the agricultural, fibres and petrochemicals and plastics (P & P) divisions. From 1 January 1987, ICI was virtually divided into two distinct arms: the old bulk chemicals and the speciality growth sectors on which many of the company's future hopes were pinned. It called up echoes of IG Farben's strategy long ago, and though no one suspected it then, it foreshadowed the potential of separating the two sides into new companies in 1993.

By 1987, too, the group was tilted on a new, international axis, mainly looking to the world's biggest chemical markets in North America. 'When I went to the US in 1973 (after the Atlas purchase) to work in our agrochemicals business there ICI had sales of $200m and about 1,000 people,' recalls Ronnie Hampel. 'Now we have sales there of over $5000m ($5bn) and 18,000 people.' The transforma-tion was worked 60 per cent organically and 40 per cent by acquisi-tions, led by the $750 million purchase of Beatrice Chemicals in 1984. That company provided a foothold for advanced materials, a bright hope of the mid-1980s, in the vital North American aerospace market, but the defence cutbacks at the end of the Cold War, coupled with recession in civil aviation, caused a fundamental revision of strat-egy, and by 1992 ICI was phasing out its advanced materials sector – a trend subsequently confirmed by other companies involved in that business.

Garst Seeds followed in 1985 and purchase of the Glidden Company for $580 million in 1986 made ICI the world's biggest paint supplier. In 1987, the acquisition of the Stauffer group for $1.7 billion, Hender-son's first major decision as chairman, opened the vast North American agrochemicals market to ICI and recouped the bulk of its price from sales of businesses which were not considered strategically relevant.

Denys Henderson, whose knighthood came in 1989 (all but one ICI chairmen have received one), now surveyed a company which earned nearly a third of its revenues in the Americas, a quarter in Continental Europe, a quarter in Britain and seventeen per cent in the Far East, including Australia. At the start of the 1980s, forty-two per cent of ICI's sales had been in Britain, but the group's traditional manufactur-ing customers, in such industries as shipbuilding, cars and textiles, were decimated during the decade. Workforce numbers had also dramat-ically shifted to reflect the new global patterns, with only two fifths of the staff based in Britain at the start of the 1990s. By then, too, sales in the UK had fallen still further and those in mainland Europe and Asia Pacific increased.

If Henderson, however, had hoped for a calm period of consolidation, it was not to be. Before he had been six months in the chair, ICI was being buffeted by an unprecedented sequence of external crises, beginning with the stockmarket crash of October, 1987. That was followed by the onset of the deepest recession since the 1930s, beginning in 1990; by Iraq's invasion of Kuwait in August 1990 and the subsequent oil price hike; by full-blown war in the Gulf; by chaos in Eastern Europe; by the impact of the 'peace dividend' on the defence and aerospace industries; by the contortions of Britain's entry and exit from the European Exchange Rate Mechanism (ERM) – entered at too high a rate, Henderson always believed; by the increasing competitive threat from Asia Pacific, especially in bulk chemical production, and finally, by the unwelcome attentions of the Hanson Group in what was widely assumed to be the curtain-raiser to a hostile bid for ICI.

'A Flash of Insight'

In late 1989, Henderson was hit, as he recalls, by a sudden 'flash of insight' while on a visit to Phoenix, Arizona. At around 7 a.m. Phoenix time, Alan Clements, then ICI's finance director, rang him with the year's third-quarter results. They were about £100 million less than expected – 'and what really caused us concern was that the shortfall was in things like speciality chemicals and advanced materials. I thought: my God, our claims for being more robust are not as sustainable as we thought'.

The unease persisted into 1990, despite a decision to get out of fertilizers, an historic ICI business, and a further pull-back on capital expenditure. By summer, Henderson was also getting 'a nasty feeling in the pit of my stomach about the direction of the world economy'. The Beatrice acquisition, which had never lived up to expectations, was dismembered and the advanced materials side sold off, keeping only the speciality chemicals.

In September 1990, with Iraq's invasion of Kuwait looking likely, at the very least, to provoke a global oil crisis, and with recession deepening on both sides of the Atlantic, Henderson set up two task forces, one under Ronnie Hampel to look at organizational structure, the other under Tom Hutchison to assess long-term strategy on markets and businesses and to identify survivors and losers. The brief was to decide where ICI should be going in the future and how best to structure the company to get there. The work was done against a backdrop of what Hampel calls 'pretty harsh criteria' assuming lower growth in the 1990s, higher capital demands and more pressing requirements for R & D and environmental resources.

'It was a process of intellectual fumbling around,' says David Barnes, the ICI director responsible for North America, who sat on Hutchison's committee. 'As we got deeper into the exercise, it became clear that we had far too many businesses to sustain them all.' Environmental costs (underestimated by the whole chemical industry, in Henderson's view), were an important element in determining which businesses had a strong enough cash-flow to survive and hence in the eventual shape of ICI's demerger blueprint.

Hutchison's group had the harder task. As Hampel says, 'you've got to know what businesses you are in before you start talking about how you are going to manage it.' Was the 1980s strategy still valid? Yes, was the conclusion, but the businesses needed to be even more focused, and several rigorous stages of sifting down were gone through. During this process a 'fault line' or 'cleavage' as Barnes calls it began to reveal itself down ICI's myriad activities, though no one was yet seriously considering demerger.

Hampel's task force, studying organizational structure, consisted of two other directors and two general managers, one of whom sat on both task-force groups. Hampel talked to around seventy people inside ICI – all the board directors, including the non-executives, the general managers and the chief executives, and 'about a dozen outside companies'. He and Hutchison kept in close contact and meetings were held at Millbank. The task forces worked at great speed, completing their brief in two months flat. Hampel is a man who gets things done fast by a ruthless application of logic; when he was handling acquisitions, he says, his technique was 'to put the lawyers and finance people into a room and not let them out for anything. If you let them out of the room they will go off and do something else'.

After the year-end results in February 1991, Henderson announced the fruits of the exercise. There would be seven core businesses – pharmaceuticals, agrochemicals and seeds, specialities including Quorn and Biopol, paints, materials, explosives and industrial chemicals, embracing Tioxide. The overarching goal was to be globally strong in all the company's markets, and anything that did not meet that requirement was dispensable. The latter included fertilizers at Billingham and even such an historic staple of ICI as soda ash. ICI's oil interests had been divested – its 25-per-cent stake in Enterprise Oil sold at the peak of the market – and what Henderson calls the 'de-imperialization of ICI' had begun to take effect in Canada, when the group bought out its minority interest in Canadian Industries Ltd (CIL). Geographic markets would be even more closely targeted on Europe including the UK, the Americas and Asia Pacific. Other territories in the old protected imperial markets would receive less resources. Divestments, factory closures and retrenchments throughout the world would reduce ICI's workforce by about 11,000 (the losses would reach 20,000 by 1993).

Henderson remarked at the Annual Results in 1991 that the restructuring was a 'once in a decade' event, adding – ironically, as it turned out – 'an organization is a hardy plant but one shouldn't pick it up by the roots too often.' The assembled industrial correspondents and analysts – and perhaps even Henderson himself – would have been astonished to think that in just over a year, the ICI chairman would be announcing proposals for a complete demerger of the company.

Hanson Drops a Bombshell

That intervening year was to ensure there was little prospect of ICI's roots being left in peace. On 14 May 1991, nine weeks after the restructuring announcement, Hanson Group through its merchant bank Smith New Court bought a £240 million, 2.8-per-cent stake in ICI, enough to trigger alarm about the intentions of Britain's most famous takeover barons, Lords Hanson and White. On the surface, it seemed bizarre for Hanson, whose group's rapid earnings growth had been built on low-tech acquisitions like London Brick, Ever-Ready Batteries and Imperial Group, seriously to contemplate taking over a science-based, research-intensive multinational with the biggest R & D budget in British manufacturing. If he were to spin off the juicy pharmaceuticals operation, what could he do with the heavy chemicals? Hanson's financial controls, too, were known to be so stringent that all capital expenditures of more than £1,000 (a pretty basic computer, say) had to be authorized personally by Hanson or White – a ludicrous proposition applied to ICI.

But no one at Millbank was under any delusions of safety: Hanson had nurtured ambitions over ICI for years and was seriously testing the waters. (He once told Henderson in friendly fashion that both companies had international positions and his group 'would quite like to get alongside you', to which the Aberdonian retorted that there was no compatibility whatever between bricks and pharmaceuticals.)

So Millbank went on red alert, its 'war cabinet' of senior management, including Henderson, deputy chairman Frank Whiteley, Ronnie Hampel and finance director Colin Short, meeting daily at 8 a.m. before most of the staff arrived for work. Since becoming chairman in 1987, Henderson had kept by his desk a thick grey-covered ring-binder file with plans for defence against a predator. Now it was dusted off. At the first meeting of the 'war cabinet', Henderson told his colleagues: 'We will make four assumptions. One, that he will bid. Two, that if it is referred to Brussels we will not be let off the hook. Three, that you should not assume the institutional investors would not be interested. And four, that we will win.'

A battery of City and PR advisers was rolled up to match the big guns of the Hanson camp, which included former prime minister

Margaret Thatcher's one-time PR guru, Sir Tim Bell. During that first month of attrition Henderson tried once to slip away, for his customary late-spring week of golf on the south Devon coast, but after two days of trying to keep his mind on his game he gave up in exasperation and returned to mastermind the far bigger match being waged between Millbank and Hanson's head office by Hyde Park Corner.

An Aggressive Defence

On the principle that the best defence is offence, and despite the fact that no bid intention had been – or ever was – signalled, ICI proceeded to take Hanson's credentials apart with devastating effect. Undoubtedly the most effective exposure, though ICI always claimed it came independently through press scrutiny of Hanson's accounts, was to reveal that £7 million of shareholders' money had been written off in a failed bloodstock investment. Lord White's passion for racehorses was too well known for commentators to fail to make a connection, though this was strongly denied by the Hanson group. Lord Hanson was stung by the assault, by the way ICI had rapidly mustered support among MPs, trade unions and press opinion, and by the way in which the City suddenly began to question the quality of earnings in its former favourite growth stock. Hanson bawled out his top PR adviser, Sir Tim Bell, in a letter that unaccountably got leaked to *The Observer*. The invincible pair began to look vulnerable.

Internally, Henderson told his chief executives in the seven core businesses that they could help by delivering their budgets and by proceeding with restructuring plans even more vigorously. 'And thirdly,' he said, 'you can make it absolutely clear to your people that we will cope with this situation at Millbank, and they must get on with running their businesses to the best of their ability.'

As the defence plan took shape in those early-morning meetings, ICI's top management were looking very critically and in great detail at both its own company and Hanson. One strong theme that had emerged from the task-force exercise, contrary to much of the public talk about group-wide synergy and the need to keep ICI integrated, was that the synergy was actually developing down two different tracks; that, buried in ICI's sprawling global mass of companies were two potentially robust business entities, split down David Barnes's 'fault line'. But the full implications were not realized until a young high-flyer at merchant bankers S. G. Warburg spelled out the persuasive commercial arguments for a demerger.

ICI meanwhile hammered out its principal message to its 350,000 shareholders, to the City and to would-be predators: this was a global, highly complex and integrated set of businesses in the throes of restructuring itself into seven globally competitive divisions. It was a big player of national and international importance in an industry that required long-term investment in R & D. The clear implication was that this was a league beyond the powers of Hanson management, however skilfully that management made its own assets sweat.

From Henderson's point of view, the timing of the Hanson affair was intensely irritating – not that any timing would have been acceptable. ICI's carefully laid plans to restructure, divest and cut costs suddenly looked like a reaction to the Hanson threat, and every ICI plant closure or sale was scrutinized by the press in that context. It also ate into top-management time and, most crucially, unsettled employees who were already anxious about the future and the deepening recession.

Some of ICI's competitors were not above dropping heavy hints to customers that the group's future was in doubt, or to suggest that merchant banks had approached them trying to pre-sell parts of ICI. In recruitment, too, there were disturbing hints that bright young scientists were being affected in their career decisions, adding to the already growing difficulties of persuading an environmentally conscious generation to work in the chemical industry.

Speaking late in 1991, when the Hanson threat had receded, Henderson firmly denied that any divestments had been treated as a 'fire sale' or major decisions accelerated. A few cost-cutting measures had been brought forward, but the main strategic planks remained as they had been in the 1990 platform. Reflectively, Henderson added that one of the media comments had been that ICI would never be the same again. 'I think that's probably true, but equally true for Hanson,' he opined.

Throughout 1991, which was widely expected to be an election year, the implications of ICI changing hands became a subtext to the political cliffhanger over the election date. Intense lobbying took place on both sides, dismayed scientists wrote to *The Times*, unions organized protest marches in towns that would see massive job losses if the company were dismembered, and opposition leader Neil Kinnock stated flatly to a business magazine in late summer that a Labour government would certainly intervene and not leave a bid to the EC authorities (*Director*, September 1991).

It was assumed that Lord Hanson, a huge corporate donor to Conservative Party funds, would not want to embarrass the new Major administration in the run-up to an election, but Henderson and his war cabinet remained wary, convinced that any slippage in ICI's performance could provoke a pounce.

Whether Hanson in the end was deterred by the strength of Labour's showing in the opinion polls as the election options narrowed is something known only to him and his closest advisers. But as polling day approached on 9 April 1992, no one would have given either

Major or Hanson much of a chance to achieve their respective dreams. On 10 April Major confounded the pollsters with a twenty-one-seat majority, but Hanson never made his move, and on 8 May 1992, with the stock market at a post-election peak, he quietly sold his stake in ICI for a reputed £42 million profit. The global vision of 'Imperial Hanson Industries', as *The Financial Times* had once sketched the might-have-been scenario, vanished like Prospero's cloud-capped towers and gorgeous palaces, leaving not a wrack behind.

The Demerger Proposal

Or did it? At the end of 1991, while Hanson was still a looming threat, Henderson telephoned Sir David Scholey, chairman of ICI's chief merchant bank advisers, S. G. Warburg, and asked for someone on his staff – 'a lateral thinker' – to take a fresh look at the restructuring strategy from a City and stock-market perspective, and at the whole chemical industry as it might develop ten years on. Scholey gave the task to a formidably bright thirty-six-year-old called John Mayo and, after six intensive weeks of poring over existing ICI documents and discussions within the group, Mayo reduced a dozen possible plans to one – demerging ICI into two. He spent six hours one Friday in Henderson's office, from 9 a.m. to 3 p.m., going through a thick file of projections with the chairman. Driving home that evening, Henderson thought about his coming retirement in 1995 and all the efforts that the management team had already put in. 'My God,' he thought, 'do I really want all this hassle?'

The plan had a successful role model in Courtaulds' demerger in March 1990, in which textiles, the 'old' Courtaulds, was separated from the newer chemicals side, to general stock-market admiration. When it was announced, Henderson phoned Courtaulds' chairman, Sir Christopher Hogg, an old friend, and asked him to lunch. The discussion that followed, talking among other things of a 'release of energy' into the two new companies, stayed in Henderson's mind and was to be a conditioning factor in his response to Mayo's proposal. Perhaps even more significantly, there was the example of BAT, under threat from Sir James Goldsmith in 1990, which moved with unexpected aggression and speed to 'unbundle' itself of such non-core activities as insurance, thus pre-empting Goldsmith's likely strategy in appealing to shareholders. Hanson's view of ICI was known to be similar to Goldsmith's of BAT: that an over-cautious, complacent management was failing to unlock shareholder value from the parts of the whole.

In March 1992, a small team at the highest level of ICI – Henderson, deputy chairman Frank Whiteley, Hampel, Barnes, finance director Colin Short, the general manager for planning and the group company secretary – began developing the Mayo proposal, which was code-named Project Dawn. The team was nicknamed the Dawn Patrol, although its work was more a case of burning the midnight oil than early-morning cabals. Later, for security reasons, the Mayo plan was renamed Project Mortar and the team became the Mortar Board. The main core of half-a-dozen senior executives was bolstered by around thirty support staff, a group which gradually swelled until the number of ICI staff in the know on the eve of the July announcement reached nearly 200. It was astonishing that the secret held.

A month after the Mortar Board began its work, four weeks during which Mayo had been sent to talk to all other ICI directors individually, including the non-executives, to put his case for demerger, Henderson called a Chairman's Strategy Conference, an occasion when ICI directors meet to discuss strategy but not to take final decisions. By this time, having been persuaded of the 'sheer business logic' of the plan, Henderson decided he should give a strong lead to the board and, at the end of a day of intensive discussion, he made an uncharacteristically

David Barnes, chief executive-designate of the new Zeneca company, comprising ICI's pharmaceuticals 'jewel in the crown' and other rapidly growing biotechnology businesses.

Ronnie Hampel, chief executive-designate of 'new' ICI, the heavy chemicals end of the business which also embraces paints and explosives, two areas in which ICI holds a world lead.

long speech, saying that he was not asking for a vote, but for a verdict on whether demerger was the right direction for ICI to explore further.

The answer from the board was 'yes', though a lot more work needed to be done. A second Chairman's Conference was held in June at the headquarters of ICI Pharmaceuticals at Alderley Park, Cheshire, going in depth into the prospects for that business as the core of the new biosciences company, and it was the positive outcome of this meeting that put the demerger process into high gear. Formal approval by the directors was given at a board meeting on July 29, when it was decided that Henderson would act as joint chairman of both companies for the remainder of his term of office – until 1995 – and that they should continue to be headquartered at Millbank for the time being.

Planning the 'Hive-Down'

During the four months of secret meetings and intensive study by task forces and project teams set up by the Dawn Patrol/Mortar Board, an enormous range of issues was covered in planning the 'hive-down' of 400 companies in 150 countries around the world. Everything was reviewed in detail, from employees' pensions and profit-sharing schemes to consulting lawyers on minimizing tax liabilities, deciding on R & D synergies and a myriad other aspects. Also under review, though this was kept confidential until a late stage in the hive-down, was the question of an entirely new name for the biosciences company that would sever the formal connection with ICI. The group's working title, at first the humorous 'Phab Labs', was 'ICI Biosciences', or 'ICI Bio' for short, and this was how commentators assumed the new company would be floated. However, ICI's own research suggested that a new name would establish the company's independent credentials and prevent confusion between the two. Courtaulds' demerger had been initially successful using the parent name on both companies, but its board had later regretted not going boldly for different titles. In ICI's case there were also some legal and cost implications urging a change.

Though ICI as an historic and world-famous corporate brand might be thought to have had powerful advantages for the new group, in both pharmaceuticals and agrochemicals it is individual brands that register most strongly in the marketplace – the heart drugs Inderal and Tenormin, for example, or the weedkiller paraquat. Nevertheless, David Barnes, the new company's CEO-designate, knew it would be 'an emotional decision' and much effort and consultation would go into the final selection.

Alongside all this hard planning, a certain amount of smokescreen activity went on to maintain the fiction that ICI business was being conducted as usual, and that nothing extraordinary was going on.

'It was a bit like planning D-Day,' recalls Barnes. Meetings were called to discuss business that would now never happen and strategy that would not be relevant after July. One contingency plan was drawn up for a press release in case of a leak; another in case of a really well-informed leak. A key fiction was the cover story for summoning all ICI's European chief executives to London for a briefing on July 29, the eve of the public announcement. To mention a major strategic discussion on the open communication system would trigger alarm bells, so executives were told that the senior management was concerned about the quality of the latest trading figures and required a full briefing before the interim results were declared.

The summons was mandatory, which required executives to break their holiday plans if necessary, the only exception being if they were already on another continent, in which case they should send a deputy. They were told to meet at ICI's conference centre near Heathrow and take the first available plane home afterwards: this was in order to be able to brief their staff simultaneously with Henderson's announcement in London. One German manager was actually *en route* to his holiday on the *autobahn* when his secretary called him on his car phone. He debated with himself for a few moments, then turned the car around.

Most of those summoned to London assumed it was in connection with a bid of some kind. When they learned the truth, the reaction was first surprise, then enthusiasm. 'There was hardly any adverse comment,' says Barnes. 'The general attitude was, it makes sense, and we never thought you'd have the guts to do it.'

Henderson took off for a South of France holiday in August and, musing in his deckchair, with time to think long about the business, he realized that it was important to stress the future growth strategy for each company beyond demerger. He worked this out in a neat acronym which pleased him: 'We have to be "Pregnant" – Profitable, Rewarding to shareholders and employees, an Exciting company and a Growing company.'

For the remainder of 1992, the machinery went into overdrive to complete the 'hive-down' by the end of December, so that the new, renamed company could be registered on 1 January 1993, and the group assets allocated between the two. Paper piled up on David Barnes's desk as the so-called long-form reports, to be condensed into a possible prospectus for Zeneca, came in from all parts of the business. They covered everything from industrial sites to employees' wage negotiations and environmental problems, all needing to be sourced and verified by independent accountants.

Then there was the sensitive matter of selecting the new company name. ICI called in a specialist consultancy, Interbrand, to handle the change, and from 1,000 possible names they had worked down to a list of 35 by mid-October. Within a month, a short list was presented for the final selection: Barnes was determined that every ICI director would have a chance to comment and suggest. It was important to have a decision in good time to register the new company on January 1: if the choice were delayed, the cost involved in repackaging some 14,000 product lines would be considerable, and the marketing impact much diminished. 'I will predict this with certainty,' Barnes said in early October. 'Everyone will hate the name when they hear it. Six months later it will have an image of its own.'

The Dynamics of Separation

By the end of 1992, the still-speculative prospectus for each new company looked promising enough, even in a depressed economic climate. 'New' ICI offered a solid, if partly cyclical, group of businesses with leading global positions in paints, explosives and titanium dioxide and international strengths in hugely versatile materials such as polyurethanes, acrylics and polyester film. It also commanded global strengths in polyester intermediates, surfactants and catalysts, and a coming business of huge potential was the programme of CFC substitutes being developed at Runcorn (see Chapter 10). Most of these businesses would benefit from synergies in chemical engineering, polymer science, colloid science and process technology, among others.

Zeneca had as its crown-jewel ICI's internationally respected ethical drugs business, the fourth most profitable in the world though much lower down the league in terms of sales. Although Tenormin, its globally dominant heart prescription drug, was already out of patent in the US, new drugs such as Zestril, Diprivan and Zoladex would compensate for that decline up to 1994, after which other products in the pipeline would accelerate growth once more. Some old staples of ICI Pharms would also go on making money hand over fist, among them Hibitane, still after forty-odd years the best-selling hospital antiseptic and a benchmark for similar products around the world.

Beyond pharmaceuticals it embraced speciality chemicals, including a cluster of small but brilliant bio-technology-based businesses such as Biopol, Quorn and Cellmark Diagnostics. The group also encompassed the world's No. 2 agrochemical business and the fascinating genetic developments going on in seeds (see Chapter 11), to which the gene-mapping technology of Cellmark Diagnostics opened great new windows.

'Seeds are still an investment in the future rather than a profit-earner of today,' says David Barnes, 'but we are hitting all the technical milestones well ahead of our original timescale, and in 1994–5 we will begin to get the first commercial payoffs.'

All these businesses also had a synergy of R & D: an historical factor in ICI's own development. Early stars of the pharmaceuticals business in the 1930s grew out of dyestuffs technology, notably the sulphonamides and the anti-malarial mepacrine, which literally turned people yellow. Likewise, certain modern drugs and agrochemicals share the same intermediates.

Economic conditions clouded any certainties on the date of the flotation, but most expected it to be in spring or early summer of 1993. Despite his gloomy assessment of the British economy – which had proved correct since the late 1980s – Henderson remained convinced that the grouping of core businesses in the new companies would enable each to respond more flexibly both to economic circumstances and to the great changes he expected to come within the global chemical industry as the new century approached.

Towards the end of 1992 he expressed the confident hope that if demerger went ahead, the market would capitalize the separated companies to 'make one and one more than two'. Both businesses would be well up the Fortune 500 league, he pointed out, and the dynamics of separation would work to ensure that growth continued.

'People are going to be forced to concentrate on areas where they have real strengths and skills, where they have real global muscle, and where they will have a competitive edge. Being seventh, eighth or ninth in the world just won't be good enough.'

Sir John Harvey-Jones, who went on from the ICI chairmanship to popular success as a writer, lecturer and television company doctor in the *Troubleshooter* series, once summed up the satisfaction of an industrial career as 'not just inventing some new product; it is creating something which wasn't there before'.

That could epitomize not only the life-changing innovations and discoveries from ICI laboratories chronicled in this book but also the company's bold decision to rebirth itself as two new industrial giants. Sir Denys Henderson and his colleagues, advancing into uncharted territory in 1993, see what they are trying to do as every bit as pioneering as the work of the founding fathers, Alfred Nobel and Ludwig Mond, who were fascinated in equal parts by scientific possibilities and business opportunities, and who never, in their own time, resisted the shock of the new.

APPENDICES

THE 'AQUITANIA AGREEMENT' 1926

Proposed amalgamation of

Brunner, Mond & Co. Limited.
Nobel Industries Ltd.
United Alkali Co. Ltd.
British Dyestuffs Corporation Ltd.

It is suggested that this amalgamation should take the following course:

A Company to be called 'Imperial Chemical Industries' with a sufficient capital for the immediate and anticipated requirements of the scheme would be formed.

This Company would be in the first instance a Holding Company and would acquire by exchange as many as possible of the shares of all classes of the merging Companies.

The shares of ICI would be limited to two classes:

(a) Preference shares carrying 6%
(b) Ordinary shares.

The existing Preference shares in the merging Companies would be exchanged for preferential shares in ICI, the existing rate of dividend carried by such shares, the security behind them, and their current market value being taken into consideration.

The following rates of exchange are suggested:

Brunner, Mond 7½%
    Preference shares: 3 ICI shares for 2 B.M. shares.
Nobel Industries 6%
    Preference Shares: 11 ICI shares for 10 Nobel shares.
United Alkali 7%
    Preference Shares: 7 ICI shares for 6 U.A. shares.

The relative value of the ordinary shares in the respective Companies (in the case of Nobels this includes Deferred shares) would be determined by the relative earning capacity of the Companies.

For the purpose of such determination the earnings of 1924, 1925 and 1926 would be taken into consideration, together with such adjustments as may be necessary for potential increase particularly in regard to Billingham, and for abnormal conditions affecting either of the years in question, e.g. the Coal Strike.

This earning capacity would be capitalized on a basis to be agreed and which would determine the number of shares in ICI to be exchanged for the ordinary and preference shares of the respective Companies.

It should not be necessary to issue any shares for cash.

The interests of the Debenture Holders and of minority shareholders in the merging companies or any of their subsidiaries remains unaltered.

The Board of Imperial Chemical Industries might in the first instance consist of twelve members, and the following are suggested:

Chairman:	Sir Alfred Mond
President and Deputy Chairman:	Sir Harry McGowan
Independent Directors:	Lord Reading
	Lord Ashfield
Representing Brunners:	Sir John Brunner
	Henry Mond
	G. P. Pollitt
Representing Nobels:	H. J. Mitchell
	Sir J. Stamp
	B. E. Todhunter
Representing British Dyes:	J. G. Nicholson
Representing U.A. Co:	Sir Max Muspratt

The functions of the Board at this stage would be the control of the major lines of policy and finance and they would lay down for each of the merging companies limits with regard to Capital expenditure and similar matters within which they would operate.

This may be regarded as the first stage of the merger organization, and up to this point the Central staff could probably be limited to:

A Secretariat
An Accounting Department
A Share Transfer Department

The next step would be to ascertain in what Departments administration can advantageously be centralized, to what extent, and how soon, this can be done.

This will probably require a good deal of investigation and will most likely have to proceed in easy stages.

Concurrently the question of manufacturing concentration has to be considered with the possibilities of eliminating redundant or inefficient plant, the reduction of stocks and other economies which should flow from a merger.

Before any effect can be given to centralizing administrative departments suitable premises in London will be required and these must be able to accommodate a large number of people. The number of employees on the central administrative staff of Nobels alone is approximately 450 and if it is proved ultimately advisable to deal with centralization for the merger on the same lines this number might be doubled.

The administration of certain departments, e.g. Technical, Research, Development, Legal, etc. could probably be centralized rapidly but the Heads of such Departments should be situated in London and directly responsible to the main Board.

The centralized control of other departments such as Buying, Sales, Costing and Publicity would follow as and when investigation showed it advisable to do so.

The status of the subsidiary Boards and the expense of their administration of the subsidiaries would gradually decrease in proportion as common Departments were absorbed by the Central administration until their functions are finally reduced to production on the lines laid down for them by the Main Board.

The cost of the Central administrative departments would be distributed over the subsidiaries and refunded by them to the Main Company.

Note
To carry out the assessment of earning capacity it is suggested that the following Committees should be formed:

(a) To investigate Brunner, Mond and Nobels [*sic*] figures:
    3 representatives of Brunner, Mond
    3 representatives of Nobels.
(b) To investigate United Alkali figures:
    3 representatives of Nobels.
    3 representatives of United Alkali.
(c) To investigate British Dyes figures:
    3 representatives of Brunner, Mond.
    3 representatives of British Dyes.

Such Committees should take action at once and be prepared to report in four weeks.

APPENDIX I TO M.A.U.D. REPORT

Nuclear Energy as an Explosive

Note by Messrs I.C.I.

(1) Work on the exploitation of nuclear energy to provide an explosive in the form of a bomb which can be dropped from the air has now reached the stage when the problems connected with large-scale production can be defined. It is the opinion of Imperial Chemical Industries Ltd that these problems can be overcome and that a manufacturing plant can be erected.

Note. In the following, the symbol U is used for the ordinary isotope mixture of uranium and the symbol ^{235}U is used for the separated reactive isotope.

(2) The use of nuclear energy to provide an explosive involves the following processes:

(a) Production of UF_6.
(b) Separation of the reactive isotope.
(c) Production of massive uranium metal (235) from $^{235}UF_6$.

The production of a 1 kg per day of ^{235}U involves the manufacture of 450–650 kg/day of UF_6, and it is considered that this quantity of UF_6 can be made on a commercial scale. The process which is recommended is the one which has been used for the preparation of 3 kilos of UF_6 for M.A.P. and involves the direct reaction between fluorine and metallic uranium. A plant to manufacture 450 kilos per day of UF_6 would cost approximately £100,000. The whole plant could be completed in approximately eighteen months if certain investigations are started at once.

The separation of the reactive isotope in a diffusion plant of the type suggested by Professor Simon appears to us to be practicable on the scale of up to 1 kg ^{235}U per day. The total capital expenditure for a plant of this size is estimated to be about £5,000,000.

If every possible effort is made we believe that a separation unit could be ready for testing by March 1st, 1942, and the detailed design of the actual units for the plant should then be ready between June and September 1942. During this time plans could be prepared for the full-scale plant and preliminary work could be started on the site.

After August 1st, 1942, we consider that manufacture of separation units could start and in six months (i.e. by February 1st, 1943) a steady output of these units would be going to the factory site. These would be installed and production of $^{235}UF_6$ could be started in the autumn of 1943 and the first bomb would be produced by the end of 1943. Within a year the plant would be producing 30 kg per month (1 kg (^{235}U) per day), if this output were required.

This estimate is not based upon any firm figures for speed of production given by Messrs Metropolitan-Vickers, but it is given after a thorough discussion with Dr Guy on the assumption that the highest priority is given to the production of the units in the engineering shops where they would be made.

The $^{235}UF_6$ separated in such a plant can be converted to metallic uranium (235).

(3) The essential raw material for the process is uranium, of which the known supplies are very limited geographically. The two most important sources of the ore are in the Belgian Congo and Canada. The ore is now mined for its radium content and the output of uranium before the war was approximately 300 tons/year.

There is a stock in Canada of probably 500 tons of uranium. In this country there is sufficient for research and development of the process of making metallic uranium.

For the manufacture of UF_6 we recommend that the metallic uranium should be made by reducing the oxide with calcium hydride. The fluorine could be recovered from treated UF_6 and used again to react with more uranium.

(4) The diffusion process for the separation of the reactive isotope has now reached a stage of development at which we recommend that a production committee should take charge of the problem. This committee would see that all the problems to be solved for the construction of a full-scale plant were investigated so that the results would be ready as they were required. It would also examine and report on the cost of smaller plants if, for technical or other reasons, it was considered desirable to produce less than 1 kilo per day. The committee would recommend a suitable site for the plant.

I.C.I. is prepared to take executive charge of this work on behalf of the M.A.P. The arrangement would be similar to that already made in other cases with this Ministry.

Cost of Uranium Bombs

Capital cost of the Isotope Separation Plant to make 360 kilos per year	£5,000,000
Working cost for 1 year	£1,500,000
Cost of uranium and other materials	£2,000,000
Cost of case and charging 36 bombs at £300	£10,000
	£8,510,000

If the total cost is charged to the 36 bombs cost
  per bomb is   each   £236,000
  (One bomb is equivalent to 1,800 tons T.N.T.)

Cost of T.N.T. Bomb
Capital cost of T.N.T. plant to make 65,000 tons
  per year   £5,050,000
Cost of manufacture at £90 per ton   £5,850,000
Cost of case and charging of 65,000 bombs each
  containing 1 ton T.N.T. at £50 per bomb   £3,250,000
                                                           £14,150,000

If the total cost is charged to the 65,000 bombs
  the cost per bomb is   each   £218
and the total cost of 1,800 tons T.N.T. in bombs
  would be   £392,000

APPENDIX VI TO M.A.U.D. REPORT

Nuclear Energy as a Source of Power

Note by Messrs. I.C.I.

(1) The use of nuclear energy for power production is being studied in many countries. If this problem is solved it will lead to new sources of power which will affect the distribution of industry over the world, because this source of energy will be so easily transportable compared with coal, oil or electricity.

It is essential that Great Britain should take an active part in this research work so that the British Empire cannot be excluded by default from future developments.

This source of power may have important applications to military purposes.

(2) The Government Maud Committee and the I.C.I. Research Department believe that Dr Halban's scheme is feasible and that the reaction will go and can be controlled.

It has not yet been done because large enough quantities of heavy water have not been available.

(3) To start nuclear power production it is necessary to have about 10–20 tons of heavy water and it may be necessary to make metallic uranium of high purity in amounts of 1–20 tons.

(4) With the knowledge at present available to I.C.I., a plant to produce 1 ton/month of heavy water would have a capital cost of approximately £3.5–£5 million and running costs of £400,000 per year. Such a plant could not advisably be erected now in this country.

Sufficient heavy water might alternatively be brought from the U.S.A., or I.C.I. may be in a position to obtain from Du Ponts technical information which would enable a heavy water plant to be erected and run at a lower cost.

It is considered that the preparation of the necessary amount of pure metallic uranium is technically possible and we have reasons to believe that we are as far advanced in knowledge of its production on a large scale as any other country. The cost of uranium might be about £2,000 per ton.

(5) In this aspect of the problem the essential raw material is uranium, of which the known supplies are very limited geographically. The two most important sources of the ore are in the Belgian Congo and in

Canada. The ore is now mined for its radium content and the output of uranium before the war was approximately 300 tons per year.

There is a stock in Canada of probably 500 tons of uranium. In this country there is sufficient for research and development of the process of making metallic uranium.

(6) I.C.I. Research Department believe that I.C.I. is one of the few companies in the world capable of undertaking this research and commercial development. Dr Halban is prepared to enter into negotiations with I.C.I. to carry on this work with him subject to his existing agreement with His Majesty's Government (Ministry of Aircraft Production).

APPENDIX VII TO M.A.U.D. REPORT

Note by Imperial Chemical Industries Limited
(1) There must always be a very close relation between the exploitation of nuclear energy for military explosive purposes and for power production in peace and war. The development of one will have a considerable effect on the development of the other.

The use of nuclear energy for power production may affect the distribution of industry over the whole world because the source of energy will be so much more easily transportable than coal, oil or electrical energy from water power. It is quite possible that ships may be propelled by nuclear energy before the end of the war.

The importance of the whole subject makes it essential that the present ideas and research work should be developed by a firm in the United Kingdom for the British Empire, whatever may be done in other parts of the world.

(*Note.* In the following, the symbol U is used for the ordinary isotope mixture of uranium and the symbol ^{235}U is used for the separated reactive isotope.)

(2) *The use of nuclear energy to provide an explosive* involves the following processes:

(a) Production of UF_6.
(b) Separation of the reactive isotope.
(c) Production of massive uranium metal (235) from $^{235}UF_6$.

The production of 1kg/day of ^{235}U involves the manufacture of 450–650 kg/day of UF_6, and it is considered that this quantity of UF_6 can be made on a commercial scale. The process which is recommended is the one which has been used for the preparation of 3 kg of UF_6 for M.A.P. and involves the direct reaction between fluorine and metallic uranium. A plant to manufacture 450 kg/day of UF_6 would cost approximately £100,000. The whole plant could be completed in approximately 18 months if certain investigations are started at once.

The separation of the reactive isotope in a diffusion plant of the type suggested by Professor Simon appears to us to be practicable on a scale up to 1 kg ^{235}U per day. The $^{235}UF_6$ separated can be converted to metallic uranium (235).

(3) The diffusion process for the separation of the reactive isotope has not reached a stage of development at which we can recommend the formation of a production committee to take charge of the

problem. This committee would see that all the problems to be solved for the construction of a full scale plant were investigated so that the results would be ready as they were required. It would also examine and report on the cost of smaller plants if for technical or other reasons it was considered necessary to limit production to less than 1 kilo per day. The committee would recommend a suitable site for the plant.

In this case I.C.I. would be prepared to take executive charge of this work on behalf of the M.A.P. The arrangement would be similar to that already made in other cases with this Ministry.

(4) *The use of nuclear energy as a source of power*, following the work of Dr Halban, could be developed commercially in several ways. The most hopeful of these involve the production of metallic uranium of high purity in amounts of 1–20 tons and the production of heavy water on a scale of approximately 1 ton per month.

With the knowledge at present available to I.C.I., a plant to produce 1 ton/month of heavy water would have a capital cost of approximately £3.5–5 million and running costs of £400,000 per year. Such a plant could not advisably be erected now in this country.

It is considered that the preparation of the necessary amount of pure metallic uranium is technically possible and we have reasons to believe that we are as far advanced in knowledge of its production on a large scale as any other country. Our collaboration with Professor Haworth is developing rapidly.

(5) If it be decided that the large scale development should take place in the United States or Canada, we believe that I.C.I. in collaboration with nuclear physicists in this country should continue to work on the problem so as to be ready to exploit any successes in the national interest.

I.C.I. would hope to be able to influence Du Ponts to support Dr Halban's work in the U.S.A. in such a way that the future interests of the British Empire in this new source of power are safeguarded.

(6) In both aspects of the problem the essential raw material is uranium, of which the known supplies are very limited geographically. The two most important sources of the ore are in the Belgian Congo and in Canada. The ore is now mined for its radium content and the output of uranium before the war was approximabely 300 tons/year.

There is a stock in Canada of probably 500 tons of uranium. In this country there is sufficient for research and development of the process of making metallic uranium.

30th June 1941

PATENTS

ICI has always been conscious of the need to protect its innovations by seeking patents. As well as the fundamental advances described in this book, the course of a research programme gives rise to many patentable inventions relating to improvements in the way in which products are made, used or constituted. Since 1926, ICI has applied for patents on over 33,000 inventions resulting in over 150,000 patents in countries all over the world. At present the group has about 50,000 patents internationally: 27,000 will belong to the new Zeneca Company and 23,000 to ICI.

Among the UK and European patents relating to significant products described in this book are the following, with their trademarks and patent numbers:

polyethylene	'Alkathene'	471590
acrylic sheet	'Perspex'	395687
		427494
process for sulphonamides		552887
chlorguanide, an antimalarial	'Paludrine'	577843
chlorhexidine, an antiseptic	'Hibitane'	705838
polyurethane developments		580524
		790420
		848671
		874430
		1184893
reactive dyes	'Procion'	797946
		798121
plastic film production		741963
halothane, an anaesthetic	'Fluothane'	767779
diquat, a herbicide	'Reglone'	785732
paraquat, a herbicide	'Gramoxone'	813531
pronethalol, a B-blocker	'Alderlin'	909357
propranolol, a B-blocker	'Inderal'	994918
tamoxifen, a cancer treatment	'Nolvadex'	1013907
atenolol, a B-blocker	'Tenormin'	1285038
single cell protein	'Pruteen'	1353008
		1370892
electrostatic spraying	'Electrodyn'	1569707
solid emulsion paint		2151248

flexible cement		EP 21682
polyester fibre	'Terylene'	578079
bulked polyester fibre	'Crimplene'	881729
		921583
PEEK		EP 1879
inorganic fibre	'Saffil'	1360197
fire extinguisher	'Monnex'	1118215
		1168092
Benzifuranone	'Dispersol'	1568231
disperse dies		EP 33583
(Queen's Award winner)		EP 146269
PHB biodegradable	'Biopol'	EP 52459
plastic		
*edible protein	'Quorn'	1346061
from micro-organisms		1353008
propofol, intravenous	'Dipravan'	1472793
anaesthetic		
goserelin, treatment		
of prostate cancer	'Zoladex'	1524747
		EP 58481
CFC replacement	'Klea'	1578933
		EP 449617
hexaconazole, a	'Anvil'	EP 15756
fungicide	'Planets'	
fluazifop-p-butyl,	'Fusilade 2000'	EP 3890
a herbicide		
lambda-cyhalothrin,	'Karate'	2000764
an insecticide	'Icon'	
water borne car		EP 38127
basecoat paints		

* Exclusive licence from Rank Hovis McDougall

INDEX

215